A SELECTION FROM

𝔗𝔥𝔢 𝔖𝔭𝔦𝔯𝔦𝔱𝔲𝔞𝔩 𝔏𝔢𝔱𝔱𝔢𝔯𝔰

OF

S. FRANCIS DE SALES

BISHOP AND PRINCE OF GENEVA

𝔗𝔯𝔞𝔫𝔰𝔩𝔞𝔱𝔢𝔡

BY THE AUTHOR OF "LIFE OF S. FRANCIS DE SALES,"
"LIFE OF FÉNELON," ETC. ETC.

CONTENTS.

LETTER	PAGE
I. To a Novice. On the Right Use of Feelings	1
II. To a Bishop Elect	7
III. To the Abbesse du Puits d'Orbe. On Suffering	9
IV. To the Same. On Devotion	14
V. To Mme. de Chantal. On the Duties of a Widow	18
VI. To the Archbishop of Bourges. On Preaching	19
VII. To President Frémiot. On Preparation for Death	38
VIII. To the Abbesse du Puits d'Orbe. In Sickness	41
IX. To the Same. On Meditation and Prayer	43
X. To Mme. Brulart. On True Devotion	44
XI. To Mme. de Chantal. On Intellectual Temptation and Liberty of Spirit	50
XII. To the Same. On Temptations of the Will	57
XIII. To the Same. On Patience under Temptation	62
XIV. To a Lady. On Conformity to God's Will	63
XV. To Mme. Brulart. On Submission to her Husband	68
XVI. To the Same. On the Sanctification of Married Life	70
XVII. To the Abbesse du Puits d'Orbe. On Little Troubles	72
XVIII. To Mme. de Chantal. On Abjection	73
XIX. To a Young Lady. Concerning her Vocation	79
XX. To Mme. Brulart	80
XXI. To Mme. de Chantal	81
XXII. To one of the Bishop's Married Sisters	83

CONTENTS

LETTER		PAGE
XXIII.	To a Curé. On Abiding in his Work	85
XXIV.	To a Lady at Court	86
XXV.	To Mme. de Chantal. On the Death of Jeanne de Sales	88
XXVI.	To the Same. On Spiritual Hunger	92
XXVII.	To the Same	93
XXVIII.	To a Lady. On Interior Peace	95
XXIX.	To Mme. Brulart	96
XXX.	To a Lady in Sickness	97
XXXI.	To Mme. de Chantal	98
XXXII.	To Mme. de Miendry. Against a Troubled Mind	100
XXXIII.	To a Married Lady. On Quietness of Mind	101
XXXIV.	To a Lady, in Sickness	103
XXXV.	To his Sister, Mme. de Cornillon. On the Death of their youngest Sister, Jeanne de Sales	104
XXXVI.	To a Lady. On the Distractions of a Busy Life	105
XXXVII.	To Mme. de Chantal. On the Presence of God	107
XXVIII.	To Mme. de Chantal. On his Mother's Death	109
XXXIX.	To a Lady, involved in Legal Affairs	112
XL.	To a Gentleman, going to the Court	113
XLI.	To a Married Lady	118
XLII.	To a Married Lady	119
XLIII.	To Mme. de Chantal, when absent on Family Business	120
XLIV.	To a Lady. On withheld Communion	121
XLV.	To Mme. de Chantal. On Spiritual Dryness	122
XLVI.	To a Young Lady, who wished to join the Order of the Visitation	124

CONTENTS

LETTER		PAGE
XLVII.	To a Lady under Trial	125
XLVIII.	To a Lady living in the World	126
XLIX.	To a Lady. On the Death of her Child	128
L.	To a Lady	130
LI.	To M. de Rochefort. On the Death of his Son	131
LII.	To Mme. de Chantal. On Simplicity	132
LIII.	To the Same	133
LIV.	To the Same	135
LV.	To a Religious. On Self-love	136
LVI.	To a Religious—the Bishop's Niece	138
LVII.	To the Mère de Chastel	139
LVIII.	To a Religious of the Visitation	141
LIX.	To one of the Bishop's Spiritual Children	142
LX.	To a Married Niece	142
LXI.	To a Religious of the Visitation	145
LXII.	To the Mère Favre, Superior of the Visitation at Lyons	146
LXIII.	To a Lady who feared Death	147
LXIV.	To a Lady	150
LXV.	To a Lady	152
LXVI.	To Mme. de Chantal. On the Death of M. de Sainte Catherine	153
LXVII.	To a Superior of the Visitation. On Spiritual Dryness	154
LXVIII.	To a Superior	156
LXIX.	To a Lady, who had praised the Bishop extravagantly	158
LXX.	To a Lady. On Prayer	159
LXXI.	To a Lady	160
LXXII.	To a Gentleman. On the right use of Holy Scripture	162

CONTENTS

LETTER		PAGE
LXXIII.	To Mme. de Chantal. On Self-renunciation	163
LXXIV.	To a Lady, who had lost her only Son	165
LXXV.	To a Young Lady	166
LXXVI.	To a Religious	167
LXXVII.	To the Abbesse Angélique Arnaud, of Port Royal	169
LXXVIII.	To a Superior of the Visitation. On her Duties	170
LXXIX.	To a Lady. On the Death of her new-born Child	172
LXXX.	To Mme. de Chantal	173
LXXXI.	To a Superior of the Visitation	175
LXXXII.	To a Religious of the Visitation	176
LXXXIII.	To a Superior of the Visitation. On Unwise Abstinence	177
LXXXIV.	To a Religious	178
LXXXV.	To the Abbesse Angélique, of Port Royal	179
LXXXVI.	To Mdlle. de Frouville	181
LXXXVII.	To a Lady, expecting her Confinement	183
LXXXVIII.	To a Young Lady in Illness	186
LXXXIX.	To a Superior of the Visitation	187
XC.	To the Portress of a Convent of the Visitation	188
XCI.	To a Lady. On Confession	189
XCII.	To a Lady	191
XCIII.	To a Novice. On her Profession	192
XCIV.	To a Lady	193
XCV.	To the Abbé . . . . On Friendship. (With his own Portrait)	195
XCVI.	To Mme. de Chantal	196
XCVII.	To the Same	197
XCVIII.	To a Superior of the Visitation. On supposed Visions and Revelations	199

CONTENTS

LETTER		PAGE
XCIX.	On the same Subject	201
C.	To a Superior of the Visitation	203
CI.	To the Same	204
CII.	To a newly appointed Superior	206
CIII.	To a Superior of the Visitation	209
CIV.	To the Same	210
CV.	To a Religious of the Visitation. On the Earthly and Spiritual Mind	212
CVI.	To a Religious of the Visitation	215
CVII.	To a Religious	217
CVIII.	To a Widowed Religious, who was expecting to hear of the Death of her Child	218
CIX.	To a Religious	219
CX.	To a Religious	221
CXI.	To a Religious	221
CXII.	To a Religious	223
CXIII.	To a Religious	224
CXIV.	To the Abbesse Angélique Arnaud, of Port Royal	225
CXV.	To the Superior of a Carmelite Convent	228
CXVI.	To a Religious	230
CXVII.	To a Religious	231
CXVIII.	To a Religious	231
CXIX.	To a Young Lady	232
CXX.	To a Young Lady	235
CXXI.	To a Widow. Concerning her Child's Education	236
CXXII.	To one of the Bishop's Married Sisters	237
CXXIII.	To the Same	239
CXXIV.	To a Cousin	241
CXXV.	To a Lady	242

CONTENTS

LETTER		PAGE
CXXVI.	To a Lady. On the Death of her Sister	244
CXXVII.	To a Widowed Lady	245
CXXVIII.	To a Friend	246
CXXIX.	To a Married Lady	246
CXXX.	To a Married Lady	248
CXXXI.	To a Lady under Depression	249
CXXXII.	To a Lady. On Spiritual Coldness	250
CXXXIII.	To a Lady. On the Restraint of Natural Quickness	251
CXXXIV.	To a Lady. Concerning her Child's frequent Communion	254
CXXXV.	To a Lady	257
CXXXVI.	To a Young Nobleman	259
CXXXVII.	To a Lady, recently come under his Direction	261
CXXXVIII.	To a Lady, expecting her Confinement	266
CXXXIX.	To a Lady	267
CXL.	To a Lady	268
CXLI.	To a Young Lady	270
CXLII.	To a Lady of high Rank, who was entering upon Legal Proceedings	273
CXLIII.	To a Young Lady. On Meekness	278
CXLIV.	To a Lady	279
CXLV.	To the Same	281
CXLVI.	To a Lady, expecting her Confinement	282
CXLVII.	To a Young Lady. On the right use of high Aspirations	284
CXLVIII.	To a Lady	289
CXLIX.	To a Young Lady. On her Entrance into the Fashionable World	290
CL.	To a Young Lady, living in the World	291
CLI.	To a Married Lady	293

CONTENTS

LETTER		PAGE
CLII.	To a Lady	294
CLIII.	To a Gentleman. On Depression of Spirits	295
CLIV.	To a Lady, who was calumniated; and concerning an Annual Review of Conscience	299
CLV.	To a Widow. On her Husband's Death	302
CLVI.	To a Lady. On the Death of her Sister	304
CLVII.	To a Friend, who had lost his Brother	305
CLVIII.	To Mme. de Chantal	306
CLIX.	To a Friend. On the New Year. (Probably President Favre)	311

SPIRITUAL LETTERS

OF

S. FRANCIS DE SALES.

I.

To a Novice.

ANNECY, *Jan.* 16, 1603.

MY DEAR DAUGHTER IN JESUS CHRIST,

MAY God be your rest and your consolation. I have received your two letters, and in answer I beg that you will use no ceremony with me; so far as it is God's Will, I bear you all the affection that you desire. I have a true love for your soul, because I believe it to be His Will; and a tender love, because you are yet weak and young. Use full freedom and confidence in writing to me, and ask whatever you think to be for your good. Let this be said once for all.

You ask how far you may encourage excited feelings, saying that without such you grow cold and languid, while at the same time you are suspicious of them. Another time, give me some instance of the precise matter—*i.e.* tell me what particular sentiments you have mistrusted, and I shall know better how to judge. Meantime I would say in reply, feelings and sentiments may come from

[1] In the Edition Blaise.

friend or foe—in other words, from the Holy Spirit or the evil one. The signs which prove whence they spring are too many to enter upon generally, but some few will suffice.

I. If we do not stop short in feelings, but use them as a recreation, after which we return with fresh vigour to our duties and the work God has given us, it is a good sign, for He sometimes sends such feelings with that intent; He condescends to our infirmities; He sees that our spiritual taste languishes; and He gives us, so to say, a spiritual sauce, not as our real food, but to excite an appetite for solid meat. But the evil one would make us stop short in mere feelings, and so by degrees destroy our spiritual digestion.

II. Good feelings do not arouse any proud thoughts, but rather strengthen us to reject such as the devil may suggest: they keep our better nature subject and humble, remembering that Caleb and Joshua would not have brought grapes from the Promised Land to stimulate the Israelites' courage, if they had not known how that courage was flagging. So, when we have good feelings, we may own our weakness, and humble ourselves lovingly before the Bridegroom of our souls, instead of imagining that they are given us as a reward.

III. Again, good feelings do not leave us weakened, but rather the stronger; not sad, but glad; whereas such feelings as are hurtful leave us disturbed and unhappy, although they may have begun by being pleasant. Past good emotions set us forward in good ways, as they were intended to do, but such as have not a holy source leave us empty and desolate when they are gone. Good sentiments draw us to love Him Who inspires them, rather than the feelings themselves; whereas we love such as are hurtful solely for the enjoyment found therein. And we are not eager to seek or grasp what is purely good, but rather take it all calmly; while excited feelings, which spring from an evil source, make us restless and eager. Some such tests as these will enable you to gauge your feelings; those which come from God are not to be rejected, but rather received in God's Name, with these two conditions, that you are ready to be guided by the advice of your superiors, should they judge your feelings not to be profitable or to God's Glory; and that you be willing to live without such solace when God may think you fit and capable for so doing. Accept them meanwhile as wine given by the physician to strengthen your spiritual digestion, notwithstanding the fever of your imperfections; as S. Paul counselled his disciple to drink some wine because of his bodily weakness, even so I counsel you with respect to your spiritual weakness.

This answer will be clear, I hope; I would add, do not hesitate to receive whatever God may send you, on the right hand or the left, with that preparation and resignation which I have already taught you. Were you the most perfect person in the world, you should not refuse anything God sends, but as it is, you may believe that He gives you such feelings to strengthen your imperfection.

I see you say that your feelings are earthly; even so they need not be rejected if they lead to

God, only you must be on your guard, and not be taken unawares by any such.

Now I must tell you that I think you are too much disturbed by an eager search after perfection, and that it is this which makes you fearful about these feelings and consolations. And I would recall to you what we read in the Book of Kings, *i.e.* that God is not in the great and strong wind, or the scorching fires of agitated feeling, but in the soft, almost imperceptible, breeze of calmness and gentleness. Let yourself be led by Him, do not think so much of yourself. My rule for you would be to make a general resolution to serve God in the best way you can, and then not to waste time in subtle dissection as to what is precisely that best way. This is an impertinence peculiar to your keen, elastic mind, and it would fain overpower your will, and hamper it with deceitful wiles.

You know that, speaking generally, God would have us serve Him by loving Him above all, and our neighbour as ourselves; and for yourself specially He would have you keep your Rule. This is enough—it must be done in simple faith, without any subtle refinements for the present, as we must do all things in this world, where perfection is not to be found, waiting for the day when it may be done after a heavenly and eternal fashion. But eagerness and agitation are of no good. Your wish to do right is good, but let it be free from excitement. I would forbid any such excitement, as the source of all imperfection.

Therefore do not be eager to find out whether

you are in the path of perfection or not, and that for two reasons. First, because, if we were quite perfect, we should not know or believe it, but regard ourselves as most imperfect;—there is no need to examine as to whether we are imperfect; how can we doubt it? Nor should we be astonished or disheartened at our own imperfection, but rather humbled, for thus we shall learn to correct our faults and improve gradually—which is one main use of imperfections; nor are they to be dealt with as sins. Again, all such eager research, if made with anxiety and perplexity, is pure waste of time;— just as though soldiers, while awaiting a battle, were to weary themselves with sham fights among each other; or musicians were to practise till they are too hoarse to sing: a perpetual self-inspection wearies the mind, and renders it incapable of action when really necessary. This is the first rule I would give you.

The second is in our Saviour's words, "If thine eye be single, thy whole body shall be full of light."[1] Simplify your judgment, do not indulge in so many questionings and replies, but go on quietly and in confidence. Let there be nought to you in this world save God and yourself;—all else should not be able to touch you, except as He may command. I intreat you not to look so much hither and thither; keep your eye fixed on God and yourself—and you will never see aught save goodness in Him, unworthiness in yourself;—but you will also see His goodness mindful of your unworthiness, and your worthless self the object of

[1] Matt. vi. 22.

His Goodness and Mercy. Therefore keep your eyes firmly, resolutely fixed thereon, and let the rest go by with a passing glance. Moreover, do not dwell overmuch on what others do, or how they advance; look upon them with a single, kindly, loving eye; do not expect perfection in them any more than in yourself, and do not be surprised at the various forms of imperfection which you meet; imperfections are not more imperfect because they are unwonted. Imitate the bee, which gathers honey from all manner of flowers.

My third rule is, that you strive to be as a little child, who, while its mother holds it, goes on fearlessly, and is not disturbed because it stumbles and trips in its weakness. So long as God holds you up by the will and determination to serve Him with which He inspires you, go on boldly and do not be frightened at your little checks and falls, so long as you can throw yourself into His Arms in trusting love. Go there with an open, joyful heart as often as possible;—if not always joyful, at least go with a brave and faithful heart.

Do not shun the society of your Sisters, even if it is not quite to your taste; rather shun your own taste, if it be not quite in accordance with their ways. Cultivate the holy grace of bearing one another's burdens, so, S. Paul says, we fulfil the law of Christ.

Say often with the Psalmist, "I am Thine, Lord, save me;" and with Magdalen, "Rabboni, which is to say, Master." And then leave the rest to Him. He will work in you, without your aid, and yet at the same time by you and for you, to the sanctification of His Name, to Which be all honour and glory.

Your affectionate servant in Jesus, etc.

II.

To a Priest about to be consecrated Bishop.

ANNECY, *June* 3, 1603.

. . . . You are attaining the summit of ecclesiastical life, and I would say to you, as it was said to the shepherd who was chosen to be King of Israel: "Mutaberis in virum alterum." You must be altogether a new man, both externally and inwardly, and to attain this great and solemn change you must stir up your whole mind. . . . . Thanks be to God Who has given you the desire so to do; I trust that He will also give you the power, and so perfect His work in you.

In order to effect this change, you must seek the assistance both of the living and the dead; of the living, for you should seek out one or two very spiritually-minded men, by whose intercourse you may profit. Such confidence is a great relief to the mind. . . . .

Then as to the dead, you must have a little library of two kinds of spiritual books; one kind suitable to you as an ecclesiastic, the other specially so as a Bishop. Make use of Grenada's works, almost as a second office book; they will frame your mind to a true loving devotion. To read profitably you must not be voracious, but weigh and ponder, applying what you read bit by bit to your own soul, with much meditation and prayer. [Here follow the names of various other spiritual authors of that day—Stella, Arias, Avila, etc., and specially the Fathers SS. Augustine, Jerome, Gregory, and Bernard.]

I would further say that it is of infinite importance that you receive consecration with the greatest reverence and devotion, and with a full apprehension of the dignity of the ministry. The beginning is most important in all things, and we may well say, "Primum in unoquoque genere est mensura cæterorum."[1]

I would also urge upon you great confidence and love for your Guardian Angel, the patron of your Diocese. .... Make a resolution to be diligent in preaching to your people. The Council of Trent, as well as all the Fathers, considers preaching to be a foremost office of Bishops. Do not aim at being considered a great preacher; do it simply as God's Will and your duty—a Bishop's fatherly sermon is worth more than the most elaborately got-up discourses of other men. He does not need much; his sermons should be about practical matters, not studied or curious; his words simple and unaffected; his action natural and fatherly, not studied; and then let his words be few, they will be enough. .... I pray you, commend me to God; I will do the like for you, and will ever be yours, etc.

---

[1] "The first step is the measure of all that follows."

III.

To Madame Rose Bourgeois, Abbesse du Puits d'Orbe.

April 18, 1604

. . . . YOUR father has told me how much you are suffering. . . . . The Lord be praised! This is the most sure and royal road to Heaven; and from what I hear, you are likely to travel along it for some time; your father tells me that you are still in the doctor's and surgeon's hands. I feel exceedingly for your sufferings, and commend them often to our Lord, that He may make them useful to you, and that at the last it may be said of you as of Job, "In all these things he sinned not."[1] Courage, my good sister, my dear daughter; look at your Bridegroom, our King, crowned with thorns and stretched upon the Cross, so that we "may tell all His bones."[2] Bethink you that the bride's crown may not be softer than that of her Bridegroom? "As the *rose*[3] among thorns, so is my love among the daughters."[4] 'Tis but the natural place of the flower, no less so of the bride. Accept your cross, embrace it a thousand times daily for love of Him Who sends it you. It is a costly present, the gift of Love. Often set the Crucified Saviour before your eyes, measure your sufferings with His; and yours will seem greatly the less. How great will

---
[1] Job i. 22.   [2] Ps. xxii. 17.
[3] The Bishop puts "Rose," which was the Abbess's Christian name, instead of "Lily," as in the text.
[4] Cant. ii. 2.

be your eternal happiness, if you bear these little pains He sends you patiently!

You are not mistaken in believing that I am near you in these trials; I am near in heart and affection, "I pour out your complaints before Him, and show Him your trouble,"[1] and it is a great comfort to me. But, my dear daughter, be brave, have confidence: "If thou wouldest believe, thou shouldest see the glory of God."[2] What do you take the bed of suffering to be but a school of humility, where we learn our weakness and misery, how vain, sensitive, and feeble we are? You have learnt the manifold imperfections of your soul on that bed; ... it is one great use of affliction that it teaches us to look into the depth of our nothingness and bad dispositions. But, my dear child, we must not be downcast thereby, we must rather cleanse and purify our minds the more, and make better use of confession than heretofore. These anxieties which have assailed you do not surprise me; but do not be disturbed, or let yourself be carried away by the tide. Let the enemy rave at the door, let him knock and batter, and do his worst; we know that he cannot enter the soul save by the door of one's own consent: keep that well shut, and there need be nothing to fear.

You ask me to say some words to you concerning the peace of the soul and humility; I gladly would, but I hardly know what I can say in so brief a space. You may well couple the two together;— the first cannot exist without the last. Nothing can really disturb us save self-love and self-esteem.

---

[1] Ps. cxlii. 2.   [2] John xi. 40.

If we have no tenderness of heart, no taste or sentiment for prayer, no inward sweetness in meditation, we begin directly to be downcast :—if we find it difficult to do right, if hindrances come between us and our good intentions, we grow anxious and eager to thrust them aside. Why is all this? Because we like consolation, ease, comfort. We would fain pray in *eau de naffe*,[1] and exercise holiness by eating sugar, not considering how our Dear Lord fell on His Face in agony, while His sweat was, as it were, great drops of blood, through the intense conflict between His inclinations as Man and His resolution as God. And while self-love is one cause of our troubles, self-esteem is another. Why are we so astonished, disturbed, impatient when we commit some fault? Doubtless because we thought that we were good, stedfast, firm ; and finding that it is quite otherwise, we are vexed and put out ; whereas, if we realised what we are, so far from marvelling because we fall, we should rather marvel how we ever stand upright ! But we like nothing save what is pleasant, and we do not like to be brought face to face with our own weakness and worthlessness.

There are three things, my daughter, which, if we do, we shall be at peace : Let us strive earnestly to seek God's Honour and Glory in all things ; let us do what little we can to that end under the guidance of our spiritual Father ; and then let us leave the rest to God. He who makes God the object of all his intentions, and does what he can, has no reason to torment himself, or to be disturbed or

---

[1] *Eau de naffe* is a scent made from orange flowers.

fearful. God is not terrible to those who love Him. He is satisfied with a little, for He knows so well that we have not much to give. Remember, too, that our Lord is called the Prince of Peace in Holy Scripture, and that wheresoever He is Lord alone, He keeps all things in peace. True, before peace, He sometimes requires war; dividing the heart and soul from affections to which they cling; such as excessive self-love, self-confidence, complacency, and the like. And when He tears us from these cherished passions, He seems to be scarifying the very heart, and we can hardly help resisting a process which is so painful. But even such resistance is not devoid of peace, if, however overwhelmed, we still strive to unite our will to that of our Lord, nailing it to His Cross, and working steadily on in our appointed course—even as He resigned His Will to His Father's. Surely it well befits the Prince of Peace to be at peace amidst war, and to possess sweetness amid all bitterness. Learn, then, that while we think we have lost our peace amid troubles, it is not really so if we are renouncing ourselves, and clinging to God's good pleasure, obeying Him in our daily duties. Learn, too, that we must suffer pain while God tears off the "old man," in order to put on the "new man, which after God is created in righteousness and true holiness."[1] Nor need we be disturbed, or imagine ourselves displeasing to God, therefore. Be sure that all restless, excited thoughts do not come from God, the Prince of Peace, but are temptations of the enemy, to be rejected and banished.

[1] Eph. iv. 24.

Strive everywhere and in all things to be at peace. If trouble comes from within or without, receive it peacefully. If joy comes, receive it peacefully, without excitement. If we must needs fly from evil, let us do it calmly, without agitation, or we may stumble and fall in our haste. Let us do good peacefully, or our hurry will lead us into sundry faults. Even repentance is a work that should be carried on peacefully.

Read the 15th, 16th, and 18th chapters of "The Spiritual Combat," which will fill up this outline.

Humility prevents our being worried by our own or other people's imperfections; why should we wonder to find in others what abound in ourselves? Humility makes our heart tender towards both the perfect and imperfect; through reverence for the one, and compassion for the other. It makes us receive trials patiently, knowing that they are deserved; and blessings thankfully, knowing that they are undeserved. As to externals, I should advise you daily to make some act of humility, either in word or deed. Of course I mean words which really come from the heart, such as humbling yourself before an inferior; or in act, undertaking some lowly office in the house, or for others. Do not be distressed because you cannot meditate while confined to bed, for to bear the rod of the Lord is not less profitable than meditation, inasmuch as it is better to be on the Cross with our Saviour than merely to gaze upon Him. But I am sure that as you lie upon your bed you offer your heart to God a thousand times during the day, and that is enough. Be very obedient to your doctors;

when they forbid anything, whether it be fasting, mental prayer, saying offices, all perhaps except ejaculatory prayer, I beg that, by the respect and love you bear me, you will obey implicitly; it is God's Will for you. When you are cured and strong again, you will resume your path, and with God's Blessing make great progress; our journey takes us beyond this world's bounds and limits.

.... It is time for me to go to mass, where I shall offer our Dear Lord for you and your house, asking the Holy Spirit to inspire your every act and thought to His Glory and your own salvation. I pray that He may preserve you from useless anxieties and depression, and that He may rest in your heart, so that your heart may rest in Him.

Amen.

IV.

To the same.

My Dear Daughter, *May 3, 1604.*

You fill the double position of a Religious and an Abbess; you are bound to serve God in both, and all your aims, practices, and affections ought to tend so to do. Remember that there is no one so happy as a devout Religious; no one so unhappy as a Religious who has no true devotion.

Devotion is neither more nor less than a prompt, fervent, loving service of God; and the difference between an ordinarily good man and one that is devout lies herein, *i.e.* that the first observes God's commands without any special fervour or promptitude; whereas the latter not only keeps them, but does it willingly, earnestly, and resolutely. Now a true Religious should be devout, and strive to attain great promptitude and fervour. To this end it is necessary to keep the conscience clear from sin. Sin is a heavy burden, and he who carries it cannot go fast onwards. Therefore be frequent in confession, and never allow sin to harbour in your soul. Then, too, we must rid ourselves of whatever may hinder our course, through the affections; withdrawing them not only from evil objects, but from that which is not actually good. Moreover, such fervour must be asked of God, and with this aim you should be diligent in prayer and meditation, never letting any day go by without spending a short hour therein.

As to prayer, as a first rule I would say, Never neglect the appointed offices of the Church : it is better to leave any other prayers unsaid rather than these. After the office, give the preference to meditation : it is the most useful and acceptable to God. And thirdly, accustom yourself to use ejaculatory prayer, which consists of loving aspirations seeking God's Help. This will be greatly promoted by keeping that point of your meditation which you relished most present to your imagination through the day; and it is also useful often to touch the Cross, or any other object of devotion which you wear, in honour of Him represented thereby; and when the clock strikes to say some heartfelt words, as " Hail! Jesus ;" " Now is the time to awake out of sleep ;" " Mine hour is come " or the like. Do not, if possible, pass any day without some spiritual reading which may nourish a devout mind within you.

Make a habit of placing yourself in the Presence of God before going to bed, thanking Him for having preserved you, and making your examination of conscience, as you have learnt to do. Do the same in the morning, preparing yourself to serve God through the day, offering yourself to His Love. I should recommend that your meditation be made in the morning, and that you read the point on which you propose to meditate overnight.

In order to attain a holy promptitude in well-doing, do not let any day go by without some special act done with this intention : such a habit helps forward devotion not a little. And you will never omit your regular Communions and confessions, kindling in your heart a holy reverence and spiritual joy at receiving your Beloved Saviour, and making a fresh resolution to serve Him fervently, which must be followed up well and stedfastly.

On the days of Communion, maintain as devout a mind as you can, longing after Him Who dwells within you ; gaze upon Him perpetually with your inward soul, where He reigns as on a throne, and offer all your senses and faculties to Him. This should be specially done after Communion, in a short meditation.

Beware of being melancholy or ungenial to those who live with you, lest they should attribute it to your devotion, and consequently think lightly of that ; rather seek to afford as much satisfaction and comfort as possible to all around, so as to make them esteem and honour your devotion, and imitate it. Cultivate a gentle, cheerful, humble spirit, which is the aptest to devotion; as also evenness of mind, not being eager for this or that. Go calmly along your way, with full confidence in God's Mercy, Which will lead you safely to the Heavenly Home, and the while beware of giving way to vexations or irritation.

As Abbess—that is to say, Mother of a Religious House—you are bound to seek the good of all your Religious, specially in the perfecting of their souls, and therefore you must give heed to reform both their conduct and the whole House.

To do this well, you must be gentle, gracious, cheerful, not beginning by finding fault with things tolerated hitherto, but letting your own life and conversation be an example to all. . . . . Do not be over-eager; let all you do be done gently and cheerfully, less by force of authority than by example. . . . .

To all these duties God calls you. Listen and obey. You cannot take too much trouble or patience in pursuit of so great an aim. Happy you, if at the end you can venture to say in our Dear Lord's words, "I have finished the work which Thou gavest me to do."[1] Desire this, seek for it, think of it, pray for it, and God, Who gives you the will to serve Him, will also give you strength to do it.

[1] John xvii. 4.

V.
To Madame de Chantal.

MADAME, ANNECY, *May* 3, 1604.

In compliance with my promise of writing to you as often as I can, I write now. The farther we are separated externally, the more I feel bound to you inwardly; nor will I cease to pray our Dear Lord that He will perfect in you His holy work, *i.e.* the longing and desire to attain unto Christian perfection, a desire which you ought to cherish fondly in your heart, as the work of the Holy Spirit, and a ray of His heavenly Light..... This desire is one of the pillars of your temple; the other is your love for your widowhood, a holy and needful love, without which your position would be unreal and false. S. Paul bids us "honour widows that are widows indeed;" but such as do not love their widowhood are not true widows; it is not of them that God declares Himself the Defender and Protector. Thank God for having given you an earnest love for your condition: cultivate it diligently, and you will find ever-increasing comfort. At least once every month examine yourself as to whether these two pillars are firm..... Beware of scruples. Keep yourself in God's Presence, and avoid all hurry and disquiet: nothing is a greater hindrance in the way of perfection. Cast yourself, not vehemently but gently, into the Saviour's Wounds. Have an exceeding confidence in His Mercy and Goodness, and be sure that He will not forsake you; but nevertheless cling closely to His

Holy Cross. Next to the Love of our Lord, I would commend to you that of His Bride, the Church. Thank God continually that you are a member thereof. . . . Have a tender compassion for the pastors and preachers of the Church, and pray for them that God would enable them to win many souls and save their own ; and herein do not forget me. Write to me as often as you can, and with the fullest confidence—my great desire for your good and your progress will be furthered by knowing often how you fare. Commend me to our Lord. I need it above all men. I pray Him to fill you abundantly with His Holy Love, and all who belong to you. Believe me always your most true servant in Jesus Christ, etc.

VI.
To the Archbishop of Bourges.
On Preaching.

MONSEIGNEUR, *Oct.* 5, 1604.

Nothing is impossible to love ; and it is love which makes me—a poor, incapable preacher myself—undertake to tell you what I think about really good preaching. I am not sure whether it is your love for me which thus calls forth water out of stone ; or whether it is mine for you which causes a rose to blossom amid thorns. Forgive me this conceit: the figures of water and of roses are not appropriate to any Catholic doctrine, however poorly expressed. May God bless my undertaking.

I propose to consider preaching under four

heads, *i.e.* I. The preacher; II. The end or aim of preaching; III. The matter preached; IV. The manner of preaching it.

I. No one should preach who is not qualified to do so by, 1st. A rightful mission; 2nd. Good doctrine; 3rd. A good life.

1. As to mission, I will only observe that Bishops have more than an ordinary mission; they are the fountain-head, whereas other preachers are but as the streams which flow thereout; and the trust of preaching is solemnly committed to them at their consecration,[1] at which time they receive a special grace, which should bear fruit. S. Paul exclaims, "Woe is unto me, if I preach not the gospel;"[2] and the Council of Trent speaks of preaching as foremost among episcopal duties. This thought should encourage us, inasmuch as God is our special Helper, and the preaching of Bishops has a value greater than that of other men. However abundant the rivulets may be, men like to drink of the fountain-head.

2. As to doctrine, it must be pure, but it need not be learned. S. Francis, though a great and admirable preacher, was not learned; Cardinal Borromeo was very far from being a deep theologian, yet he worked wonders; and there are numberless similar instances. Erasmus (who was

---

[1] In the Roman Pontifical, the consecrating Bishop presents the Bible to the Bishop who is being consecrated, saying, "Accipe Evangelium, et vade, predica populo tibi commisso." And in the English Consecration Office, in like manner, the Bible is given into his hands, with the words, "Give heed unto reading, exhortation, and doctrine," etc.

[2] 1 Cor. ix. 16.

eminent in letters) says, that the best way of learning is to teach; by preaching a man becomes a good preacher. I will only add this, That preacher knows enough, who does not try to appear to know more than he really does: If we are unable to speak fittingly of the Mystery of the Holy Trinity, it is better not to attempt it: If we are not sufficiently learned to explain S. John's " In the beginning was the Word," let us leave it alone; there are many other practical points to be treated, and we need not attempt everything.

3. As to a good life, it is as much a necessity to a good Bishop as to a good preacher. "A Bishop must be blameless," S. Paul says.[1] But both Bishop and preacher must aim at something more than avoiding mortal sin: they must shun venial sin, and even many acts which are not positively sin at all. S. Bernard says, " Nugæ secularium sunt blasphemiæ clericorum."[2] A layman may lawfully indulge in games, field sports, and social recreations, which give rise to serious scandal in a Bishop, or other ecclesiastic. If men can say of the preacher, that he has plenty of time for amusement and is fond of it, it will avail little to teach and preach mortification and self-denial. . . . I do not mean but that some decorous recreation is allowable, but it should be used with the greatest circumspection; field sports are altogether forbidden, as also all superfluous expenditure in festivities, dress, or books; in Bishops I hold such to be seriously sin-

---

[1] 1 Tim. iii. 2.
[2] "What are mere trifles in the laity are blasphemy in ecclesiastics."

ful. S. Bernard says, " Clamant pauperes post nos, Nostrum est quod expenditis, nobis crudeliter eripitur quidquid inaniter expenditur."[1] How can we rebuke the world for its superfluities if we indulge in the like? S. Paul says that a Bishop must be "given to hospitality,"[2] but that does not consist in giving entertainments, rather in gladly receiving at his table all to whom such reception is due; and the Council of Trent orders that the Bishop's table be frugal. ("Oportet mensam episcoporum esse frugalem.") There are exceptional occasions, which discretion and charity will discover.

It is well never to preach without having first celebrated, or at all events having the wish so to do. S. Chrysostom says that the lips which have received the Blessed Sacrament are specially powerful against the devil. One seems to have more right then to use S. Paul's words, " Christ speaking in me;"[3] one has much greater boldness, fervour and light: "As long as I am in the world, I am the Light of the world," our Saviour says.[4] Most assuredly, He Who is Light itself gives us light when He dwelleth in us; and it was after the breaking of bread that the disciples at Emmaus had their eyes opened and knew Him.

At all events one should have been to confession, remembering David's words, "Unto the ungodly said God, Why dost thou preach My laws, and takest My covenant into thy mouth?"[5] and S.

---

[1] "The poor cry out, That which you spend is ours, you cruelly deprive us of all you expend uselessly."
[2] 1 Tim. iii. 2.   [3] 2 Cor. xiii. 3.   [4] John ix. 5.
[5] Ps. l. 16.

Paul, "I keep under my body, and bring it into subjection; lest that by any means, when I have preached to others, I myself should be a castaway."[1]

II. The end or aim of preaching, and the means by which the preacher should seek that end. He must instruct and move his hearers—teach them concerning virtue, to love and practise it; concerning vice, to hate and shun it: giving light to the understanding, and vigour to the will. Thus, on the day of Pentecost, God sent tongues of fire upon the Apostles, that henceforward Apostolic lips might bear forth the message of light and warmth. Then again the preacher should please his hearers by the holiness of his doctrine, and by pious and suitable affections winning the soul to Heaven, but not by another kind of attraction, which merely tickles the ears—a worldly elegance, or mere secular eloquence, curious expressions, fanciful words and narrations. All such I utterly reject for the preacher. Let him leave these to secular orators who do not preach Jesus Christ crucified,—"Non sectamur lenocinia rhetorum, sed veritates piscatorum." S. Paul condemns "itching ears," and consequently those preachers who pander to their gratification. When a sermon is over I would not have the hearers go away saying, Oh, what a great orator! What a memory, what learning, what eloquence! I would rather hear them say, How great a blessing! how necessary true repentance is! how Great, how Good God is! Still more would I accept their amendment of life as a tribute.

[1] 1 Cor. ix. 27.

to the preacher. " Ut vitam habeant, et abundantius habeant."

III. As to the matter preached. S. Paul sums it up briefly. " Preach the Word."[1] For this Holy Scripture affords abundant material. Are we not to use the writings of the Saints and doctors of the Church? you ask. Indeed, yes. But what are their writings save the exposition and setting forth of Holy Scripture? It is as the breaking of a loaf into pieces for distribution ; as the cracking the shell of the nut to obtain fruit. They are the channels through which it has pleased God to give us the true meaning of His Word. So of the Lives of Saints : what are these save practical illustrations of the Gospel? The difference between the Word and the Saints' lives is like to that between music in score, and the same music sung by living voices.

Then as to the introduction of profane—*i.e.* secular history. Such may be good, but it should be sparingly used, like mushrooms in cookery, and carefully handled. S. Jerome says that such illustrations should be treated as the Israelites treated those captives whom they wished to marry, cutting their hair and paring their nails — *i.e.* stripping them of their heathen character, and subjecting them to the Gospel and to Christian truth, "separare pretiosum a vili." Thus we should separate Cæsar's valour from his ambition ; Alexander's greatness from his pride ; Lucretia's chastity from her self-murder. But if you come to the poets' mythological fables, I say, let us have none of those, unless indeed they be used with the utmost circumspec-

[1] 2 Tim. iv. 2.

tion, and as antidotes. Some poetry is useful, and the Fathers occasionally used it. Even S. Bernard did so, and S. Paul himself quoted Aratus and Menander. But as to mythology, I do not find it in the Fathers' sermons, except in one of S. Ambrose, where he alludes to Ulysses and the sirens. And so I say, let us have none of this, or so little as to come to the same thing. We must not try to put Dagon into the Ark of the Covenant.

Natural history is very different. God made the world, and every part thereof speaks of His praise and glory. It is a book full of His Word, but in a language which not every one can understand. Those who have learnt to read it in meditation, may well use it. This is what S. Anthony did, who had no other library. And S. Paul says, "The invisible things of God from the creation of the world are clearly seen, being understood by the things that are made."[1] And David, "The heavens declare the glory of God."[2] In truth, nature is a book full of similes, "a minori ad majus." The Fathers use it liberally, and so does Holy Scripture: "Go to the ant, thou sluggard;"[3] "As a hen gathereth her chickens;"[4] "Like as the hart desireth the water brooks;"[5] "The daughter of My people is become cruel, like the ostriches in the desert;"[6] "Consider the lilies, how they grow;"[7] and numberless other instances.

Clear interpretation of Holy Scripture is important. This is the foundation of our spiritual

[1] Rom. i. 20.
[2] Ps. xix.
[3] Prov. vi. 6.
[4] Matt. xxiii. 37.
[5] Ps. xlii. 1.
[6] Lam. iv. 3.
[7] Luke xii. 27.

edifice, and what gives authority to our preaching. "Thus hath the Lord said unto me,"[1] such was the mission of the prophets; and our Lord Himself said, "My doctrine is not Mine, but His that sent Me."[2] Exposition should be as simple and clear as is possible. There is not much poetry, but plenty of good sense, in some old lines which say,

"Litera facta docet: quid credas, allegoria;
Quid speres, anagogia; quid agas, tropologia."[3]

As to the literal sense of Holy Scripture, that should be studied in the doctors of the Church; but the preacher must know how to give due weight to the words, their special meaning, and emphasis. For instance: Yesterday, as I was explaining the words, "Thou shalt love the Lord thy God with all thy heart, and with all thy soul, and with all thy mind,"[4] I remembered what S. Bernard says, "with all thy heart"—*i.e.* courageously, fervently, because the heart is the seat of courage; "with all thy soul"—*i.e.* affectionately, because the soul is the source of feeling and affection; "with all thy mind"—*i.e.* spiritually, and with judgment, because the mind is the superior and spiritual part, to which appertains discernment, and that "zeal of God" which is "according to knowledge."[5] Again, the word *diligere*[6] should have due weight, because it is derived from *eligo*, and implies that our heart,

---

[1] Isa. xxi. 6.   [2] John vii. 16.

[3] "The letter teaches facts; the allegory what we are to believe; the moral what we are to do; and the anagogia what we are to hope."

[4] Matt. xxii. 37.   [5] Rom. x. 2.

[6] In the Vulgate the words are, "Diliges Dominum Deum tuum ex toto corde," etc.

soul, and mind should choose and prefer God above all things, which is the true "love of appreciation" spoken of by theologians.

Where there is a difference of opinion among the Fathers and Doctors, it is well not to allude to such opinions as are erroneous, for we do not go into the pulpit in order to controvert such men, or to dwell upon their mistakes; but we may fairly produce different interpretations, giving each its turn. Thus, last Lent I gave six patristic interpretations of the words, "We are unprofitable servants;"[1] and again of " It is not mine to give;"[2] each of which was most profitable; but if I am not mistaken, I withheld S. Hilary's interpretation (or ought to have done so), for it is very improbable.[3]

With respect to the allegorical meaning, the preacher must give heed—1. Not to force it, and seek allegory in everything, but to let it come naturally forth, as S. Paul does in the Romans, comparing Esau and Jacob to the Jews and Gentiles; or likening the Church to Sion and Jerusalem. 2. Unless it is very obvious that the type was designed, it is better only to use it as a comparison. For instance, some writers interpret the juniper-tree under which Elijah slept as meaning the Cross. I should prefer saying, that as Elijah fell asleep beneath the shadow of the juniper-tree, so ought we to rest in holy meditation beneath the Cross of Christ. I would rather compare the two things than affirm positively that one meant the

---

[1] Luke xvii. 10. [2] Matt. xx. 23.
[3] Mgr. de Bourges had assisted at the Bishop of Geneva's Lent station at Dijon.

other. 3. If spun out overmuch, such allegorical meanings lose their grace, and become affected. It is needful too that the application be clearly and carefully made. The same rules apply to the anagogic and tropologic meaning; of which the first applies the facts of Holy Scripture to the things of the next world; the last to those of the conscience and soul. To illustrate all four meanings, take the words, "Two nations are in thy womb, and two manner of people shall be separated from thy bowels; and the one people shall be stronger than the other people, and the elder shall serve the younger."[1] These are to be literally understood of Esau and Jacob—that is, the Idumeans and the Israelites—of whom the younger, Israel, became greater than the elder branch, the Idumeans. Allegorically, Esau represents the Jewish people, who were first to know the way of salvation, which was "first preached to the Jews." Jacob is a figure of the Gentiles, who, though the younger, overtook the Jews. Anagogically, Esau represents the body, which is the eldest, inasmuch as it was created, both in Adam and in ourselves, before the soul. Jacob signifies the spirit, which in the next life will altogether master and subject the body to itself. Tropologically, Esau signifies self-love; Jacob the love of God in the soul. Self-love is the eldest—is born with us; love of God the younger, only to be attained through Sacraments and Graces: nevertheless, it must be the master, and where once it enters, self-love will become the subject or inferior. Now these four methods of

---

[1] Gen. xxv. 23.

interpretation supply a good and grand foundation for preaching, and serve admirably to set forth doctrine.

Next to Holy Scripture come the words of Fathers and Councils. I would only say concerning these that they must be quoted briefly, and to the point. When preachers neglect this precaution they are apt to weary their listeners, and are also sometimes inaccurate. Some of S. Augustine's terse sayings are suitable; such as, " Qui fecit te sine te, non salvabit te sine te:" or, " Qui pœnitentibus veniam promisit, tempus pœnitendi non promisit."[1] S. Bernard abounds in such. But having quoted them in Latin, you should give a clear rendering in the vernacular, and proceed to paraphrase their meaning.

Examples or illustrations are very efficacious, and give zest to a sermon; but they should be suitable, well chosen, and better applied. Striking illustrations, clearly put and vigorously applied— as, for instance, Abraham offering up his son, to illustrate how we should withhold nothing from God. He unhesitatingly and without a murmur prepared to offer up this precious only son, while ye, Christians, are so unready to offer, I do not say your child, your fortune, or your life, but even a small alms, an hour snatched from self-pleasing, a little self-indulgence, etc.

Useless and diffuse descriptions are to be avoided; *e.g.* one has heard men describe Isaac's personal

---

[1] " He Who made thee without thine aid, wills not to save thee without it." " He Who promised pardon to the penitent, did not promise time for repentance to the sinner."

beauty, the sharpness of Abraham's sword, the scenery of the sacrificial mount, and the like purely imaginary and irrelevant things. Illustration should neither be so brief as to be pointless, nor so long as to be wearisome. It is well also to avoid putting imaginary words into the lips of scriptural personages; *e.g.* representing Isaac as lamenting his expected death, or intreating his father's mercy; or Abraham struggling with himself as to his proposed obedience. If men have become accustomed to any such process in meditation, they should not introduce it into preaching without great care, giving heed that anything of the kind be very brief, and strictly within the bounds of probability.

Examples from the lives of the Saints are very useful. Similes are profitable both to the intellect and the will. They may be drawn from the actions of men, *e.g.* a comparison between shepherds and Bishops—as our Lord's own parable of the lost sheep shows; from natural history, plants, animals, what not; and similes taken from trivial things are often most instructive, *e.g.* our Lord's parable of the seed; or in the Psalms, "thy youth renewed like the eagle's."[1]

It is useful to the preacher himself to deduce these similes from such parts of Holy Scripture as are but little noticed by the multitude, but this can only be done as the result of much meditation. For instance: David, speaking of the ungodly, says, "Periit memoria eorum cum sonitu."[2] Hence

---

[1] Ps. ciii. 5.
[2] Ps. ix. 6. In the English version this meaning is lost; we have "their memorial is perished with them."

.I draw two similes; when we break a glass, it is destroyed with a noise; and in like manner, when the ungodly perishes, there may be a certain rumour, he may be talked of; but just as the shattered glass is utterly gone, utterly useless, so the wicked man passes away, and is lost for ever.

S. Paul says that he who performs many good works, but without love, is "as sounding brass or a tinkling cymbal."[1] So you may draw a simile between the bell which calls men to church, yet never moves from the belfry itself, and the men whose unloving works are profitable to those around, yet do not help him on to Paradise. In using such similes, you must examine whether the words are in themselves metaphorical; as, *e.g.* "Viam mandatorum tuorum cucurri, cum dilatasti cor meum."[2] Here you must weigh the words "dilatasti" and "cucurri;" considering what things increase their speed when dilated—such as the sails of a ship—which attains the harbour speedily if a propitious wind expand her canvas. Even so, when the Holy Spirit breathes upon the heart of man, he makes rapid way in the ocean of God's Love, and soon attains his desired end. But in all similes you must be very careful to avoid whatever may be unworthy, or in any way suggestive of evil. It is allowable sometimes to apply Scripture words differently to their original meaning, as when S. Francis calls alms "panis angelorum," so applying the words, "Man hath eaten angels' bread."

[1] 1 Cor. xiii. 1.
[2] Ps. cxix. 32. English Bible Version, "I will run the way of Thy commandments when Thou shalt enlarge my heart."

Let all your preaching be shaped upon a method or plan; it helps the preacher, and makes his sermon both more useful and more acceptable to the listeners. I do not agree with those who aim at concealing their method, I would rather have it plain and manifest; otherwise it is useless. There are different methods you can pursue in treating any sacred subject.

I. Take the different persons concerned in it, and draw your teaching from them, *e.g.* in the Resurrection; there are the Maries, the angels, the guard keeping the sepulchre, and Our Dear Lord Himself. In the women I find fervour and devotion, in the angels holy joy and brightness, in the guards I trace the weakness of men when they would withstand God, from Jesus I learn God's Glory, His triumph over death, and the hope of our resurrection.

II. Having considered the principal point of a mystery thus, you may take the events which preceded and followed it, *e.g.* the Resurrection was preceded by Christ's Death, His descent into hell, the Jews' fear that His Body would be stolen away. After it there came the angels and the holy women, and their questions and answers, from all of which you may draw instruction.

III. In every mystery you may consider the following points. Who? Why? How? Who rises from the dead? Our Lord. Why? For His Own Glory and our gain. How? Glorious, immortal, etc. Who is born? The Saviour. Why? To save our souls. How? Amid poverty, cold, and humiliation, etc.

IV. After more or less paraphrasing the subject you can deduce three or four considerations. 1st, What will confirm our faith; 2nd, awaken our hope; 3rd, kindle our love; 4th, excite our imitation in act.

Faith in the Resurrection brings out the Almighty power of God, bursting the bonds of death, and raising the impassible spiritual Body, and from this our faith in the Blessed Sacrament is confirmed—wherein is the same Body, spiritual, yet real. Hope is the fruit of the Resurrection, since we know, as S. Paul tells us, that " He Which raised up the Lord Jesus shall raise up us also by Jesus."[1] Our Risen Lord gives us an example of charity by His return to earth for the edification of His Church. And we must imitate Him as He burst the bonds of death, by rising to new life in contrition and confession. He burst through the rocky tomb, and even so it befits Christians to conquer difficulty and temptation.

If you wish to preach upon some precept of Holy Scripture, consider first on what virtue it bears; *e.g.* " Whosoever humbleth himself shall be exalted,"[2] which of course plainly inculcates humility. In other passages the subject is not so obvious; *e.g.* " How camest thou in hither, not having a wedding garment?"[3] This is charity, but covered with a garment, for the wedding garment is charity. You would then go on to consider in what this virtue consists, its true marks, its effects, and how to acquire or practise it. This has always been my method. There is another, by which you set forth

[1] 2 Cor. iv. 14.   [2] Luke xiv. 11.   [3] Matt. xxii. 12.
De Sales' Sp. L.]

how honourable, useful, and pleasant the virtue in question is, and how greatly to be desired; or again, the benefits to be derived from it, and the evils of the opposite vice; but the first method is the best.

If you are explaining the Gospel (for the day), it is well only to dwell at length on certain selected passages, and to pass rapidly over the rest; but this is not a very profitable plan, and it does not leave sufficiently definite impressions on your hearers.

You can use the lives of the saints in a similar way, considering the leading points of their graces or sufferings; how they resisted the world, the flesh, and the devil; setting forth how we may honour God, by His saints, and His saints in Him; how we should imitate them, etc.

These are enough of methods to begin with; you will, in time, make others for yourself. I should always put Holy Scripture first, arguments next, then similes, and lastly illustrations, if they are sacred; if not, something else must follow—a sermon should always end with some sacred subject. The beginning of a sermon should instruct those who listen; the latter part should move their hearts.

Now as to the manner. The philosopher Aristotle says, that the form of a thing is its being and soul. If you tell the most wondrous truths, but tell them badly, they will profit little. The art is to say but little, and that well. Now to do this in preaching, you must beware of "quanquam,"[1] and pedantic phrases or gestures, which are most pestilential in

---

[1] S. Francis means long rounded phrases.

preaching. You must speak warmly and devoutly, simply, clearly, and with confidence; you must thoroughly love what you teach, and believe what you say. The sovereign art is to be artless. Our sermons should be kindled, not with vehement gesticulations, or an excited voice, but with inward devotion : they should come from the heart rather than the lips. Say what men will, it is the heart which speaks to hearts, whereas the tongue reaches no further than men's ears.

IV. The manner of preaching. As to action. 1. It must be free, without any pedantic or studied effort. 2. It must be dignified, without vehement movements of the hands, or feet, or body, or wild and unmeaning gestures. 3. It must be hearty, not timid, as though you were speaking rather to your elders than to your children. 4. It must be natural, without conceit or affectation. 5. It must be vigorous, not languid, lifeless, or unmeaning. 6. It must be holy, without effeminacy or secularity. 7. It must be grave, without those offensive little wiles of bows and salutations, arranging of surplices, and folding of hands. 8. It must be rather slow, avoiding a short, sharp manner, which reaches the ear rather than the heart. 9. The language should be clear and simple, without any display of Hebrew, Greek, or Latin words.

The composition should be natural and plain ; I like a division into firstly and secondly, so that people may follow the order of your thoughts. To my mind, no one, especially Bishops, should ever flatter any of their hearers, even though they be Kings, Princes, or Popes. There are certain ways of propitiating your people, especially at the outset;—*e.g.* showing your desire for their welfare, giving them your benediction, and expressing your earnest longing for their salvation; but it should be done briefly, heartily, and without affectation. The Fathers, and all those who have done most real work, avoided fanciful conceits and secularities. They speak heart to heart, mind to mind, as good fathers speak to their children. The best form of address is, My brethren, My people (if they are your own), Dear people, Christian listeners. At the end, the Bishop should wear his cap to give the Benediction, and then salute the people. The close of the sermon should be terse, vigorous, and animated. I like a sort of recapitulation, ending with a few earnest words of prayer. I would always have the sermon prepared overnight, and in the morning one should meditate oneself on what one is about to say to others. Grenada says that preparation made before the Blessed Sacrament is specially valuable, and I fully believe it.

I like sermons to breathe love rather than indignation, even against the Huguenots, who should be treated with the utmost tenderness; not flattering but pitying them. All sermons are better short than long, a matter in which I am reforming myself. Half an hour is amply sufficient. I do not approve of any jesting or flippancy: it is most unbecoming. Finally, to preach is to make known God's Will to men by the means of His lawfully appointed channels, in order to teach and move them to serve His Divine Majesty in this world, and to save their souls in the next.

Now I intreat your pardon for this imperfect sketch. I have written *currente calamo,* without study, and without books, for I am away in the country. I have quoted myself, because you wished to know what I think and do in the matter. I will conclude with a most earnest intreaty that you will not allow any sort of consideration to hinder you in preaching. The sooner you begin, the sooner you will succeed; and the best way of mastering the difficulty is practice; you can do this, and you ought: your voice is good, your theology sufficient, your manner favourable, and your position in the Church important. God requires it, and men expect it of you. It is for God's Glory and your own salvation. Be bold, then, for His Sake. Cardinal Borromeo, who has not half your talent, preaches, edifies others, and is himself a saint. It is not our own honour, but God's, that we seek; and meanwhile He will take care of ours. Begin at an Ordination, then at some special Communion, say a few words, a few more, and so on, up to half an hour, and go on to a regular habit of preaching: nothing is impossible to love. Our Lord did not ask S. Peter whether he was learned or eloquent in order to give him the commission "Feed My sheep;" He only asked, "Lovest thou Me?" Real love will suffice. When S. John was dying, he repeated incessantly, "Little children, love one another." He could preach on such words, but we think, forsooth, that we must expatiate in floods of eloquence! Never mind that your predecessor was very able; like you, he once made a beginning. . . . . I would that I could assist you now, as I did at your first mass—in heart and will I shall be with you. Your people await you. Their first impressions are important; begin at once what you ought to do. They will be edified if they see you like their priests, constant at the altar, earnest for their good, speaking the words of reconciliation from the pulpit to them. I never approach the altar without commending you to our Lord, too happy if you sometimes remember me. I am and shall be all my life, faithfully yours, in heart, soul, and spirit, etc.

VII.

To President Frémiot.
On Preparation for Death.

SALES, *Oct.* 7, 1604.

..... YOURS has been a long and honourable life, one of faithfulness to the Church, but still it has been spent in the world, and in worldly affairs, and it is not possible to live in the world, even though we only tread it under our feet, without being soiled by its dust, as S. Leo says, "Necessa est de humano pulvere etiam religiosa corda sordescere."

In patriarchal days, Abraham and his successors were wont to offer water to wash their guests' feet, and so I think the first thing you have to do is to wash your soul, that it may be ready to accept Our Dear Lord's hospitality in Paradise.

It always seems to me unfitting for any mortal man to die without having thought about death, but it is doubly wrong in the case of those who have been blessed by God with the grace of old age; and they are ever best prepared who make ready before the alarm is given, and have not to seek for their arms in confusion and terror. It is well to take leave of the world calmly, and little by little to withdraw one's affections from it. When trees are blown down by the wind, they are not fit for transplanting, because their roots remain in the ground; if you would move them successfully you must loosen their roots and fibres gradually; and as we hope to be transplanted from this miserable world into the world of life, we must withdraw our earthly attachments, and loosen our hold upon them by degrees; not rudely and roughly, but gently and carefully. When people leave a place suddenly, they are excusable if they do not take leave of their friends, and set out unprepared; but those who have foreseen their coming departure should hold themselves ready,—not in order to start before the appointed time, but to await it with calmness. To this end I think you would find great comfort in taking a fixed time daily for consideration, as before God and your Guardian Angel, as to what is necessary to a blessed departure. How would you have your affairs stand if it be near? I know that such thoughts are nothing new to you, but they should be renewed in the Presence of God, made with calm attention, and rather so as to excite the affections than the intellect.

I have benefited by your fine library: from it I would suggest, as your spiritual reading on this subject, S. Ambrose, "De bono Mortis;" S.

Bernard, "De interiori domo," and sundry of S. Chrysostom's Homilies. S. Bernard says that the soul departing to God should first kiss the Feet of the Crucified by purging his affections, and heartily, though gradually, withdrawing himself from the world and its vanities; then His Hands, by the renewal of actions which is the result of changed affections; then His Mouth, uniting himself to his All-gracious Saviour by ardent love. We are told that Alexander the Great, when at sea, discovered Arabia Felix by the scent of its aromatic herbs and trees; even so those who seek a Heavenly Country, while yet on the broad ocean of life, inhale the sweet odours of Paradise, which cheer and encourage them in their voyage thither, but they must ever keep to windward, lest it fail. We owe ourselves to God, to our country, our relations, our friends—to God first, and our Heavenly Country has a stronger claim than our natural·country; then to our relations, but no one is so near a relation as oneself; to our friends, but your closest friend is you. S. Paul says to Timothy, "Attende tibi et gregi;"[1] first "tibi," then "gregi."

Enough, dear Sir, if not too much for this year, which is fast speeding away, and which, in two short months, will be for ever gone, like its predecessors. . . . . May God fill your remaining years with His blessings.

I remain, with a most filial affection, yours, etc.

[1] English Version, "Take heed unto thyself and unto the doctrine."—1 Tim. iv. 16.

[64.] VIII.

To the Abbesse du Puits d'Orbe.
In Sickness.

1604.

. . . . As to meditation, I beg that you will not be disturbed if sometimes, or indeed often, you find no comfort in it;—go on quietly in humility and patience, without straining your mind. Use a book when your spirit grows weary; that is, read a little, and then go on meditating to the end of your half-hour. Saint Theresa began thus, and as we are talking in confidence, I may add that I have tried the plan myself, and find it answer. Take it as a rule that the grace of meditation is not to be won by mental effort, only by a gentle, loving perseverance, full of humility.

As to the hour of going to bed, you must allow me to abide by my opinion; but if you cannot stay in bed as long as the others, I will allow you to get up an hour earlier. Indeed, dear Sister, you cannot think how harmful it is to sit up late at night, or how seriously it weakens the brain. People do not feel this when they are young, but they find it out afterwards, and many have made themselves useless in this way.

I fear the operation on your leg will be very suffering, but be brave—we belong to Jesus Christ, and suffering is His badge. Try and think that the surgeon's knife is one of the nails which pierced His Feet. . . . You say that I may imagine how little you can serve God while confined to your bed, but indeed, my dear Sister, I think otherwise. When did our Saviour offer His greatest service to His Father? Surely when hanging on the Cross, with pierced Hands and Feet. And how did He serve God? By suffering, and offering His sufferings as a sweet perfume to His Father. And such is the service you can offer to God as you lie upon your bed; you will suffer, and offer your sufferings to His Majesty. He will be with you in this trial, and will comfort you.

He sends your cross; embrace, cherish it for love of Him. David said in his trouble, "I became dumb and opened not my mouth, for it was Thy doing;" as though to say, "Were it from some other hand, I should reject it, but being Thine, I am silent, I accept, I revere my sorrow."

Do not doubt but that I will pray our Lord for you, that as He causes you to be a partaker of His sufferings, He will fill you also with His own patience. I shall be with you in spirit through it all. But here is a precious balm to soothe your pain:— Every day take a few drops of the Precious Blood from our Saviour's pierced Feet, and by meditation apply it to your pain, invoking the sweet Name of Jesus, which is "as ointment poured forth;"[1] and the smart will be lessened.

Your obedience to your physician will be accepted by God, and remembered at the day of reckoning.

[1] Cant. i. 3.

IX.

To the Abbesse du Puits d'Orbe.
On Meditation and Prayer.

SALES, *Oct.* 9, 1604.

.... ALWAYS begin meditation by placing yourself in the Presence of God, invoking Him, and offering Him the mystery to be meditated. After the usual considerations always make some effective acts and resolutions; then an act of thanksgiving, of oblation, and prayer. Meditation on the four last things will be useful to you, but, my daughter, I beg that all such meditations may be ended by hope and confidence in God, not by fear and terror —in which case they are dangerous. When you have considered the greatness of Eternity and its pains, and have kindled your fear thereof, and have resolved to serve God better, you should turn to the Saviour on the Cross, and, flying to Him with outstretched arms, embrace His Feet. "I am Thine, O save me!" and leave off filled with this affection, thanking our Lord for His Precious Blood; offering It to His Father, and imploring Him to apply It to yourself. But do not fail always to end with hope, otherwise you will not profit by such meditations; and keep it as a perpetual rule that you should never leave off prayer save with confidence—a virtue most needful to win God's favour, and one which He specially honours.

As to your course of prayer through the day, I think I have said enough before. As you rise very early. you should make your meditation, and the exercise which I called " preparation," the whole not lasting more than three-quarters of an hour. . . . A little before supper, you would find it useful to take a half-quarter of an hour of recollection to go over your morning meditation. . . .

It is always harmful to sit up late ;—most women require six hours' sleep at the least, and those who take less are languid all day.

X.

To Madame Brulart.
On General Confession and Devotion.

. . . As I told you, I found every token of a good, true, solid confession in your general confession. If you omitted anything, examine whether it was knowingly and deliberately ;—in which case you ought doubtless to make your confession over again, if the omission was of mortal sin. But if it was an omission caused by mere forgetfulness, do not be uneasy. You are not obliged to renew your confession, but it will suffice if you tell your ordinary confessor what it was you omitted. Nor do you be afraid that you did not make your general confession with sufficient earnestness, if there was no voluntary omission. . . . . You ask what you should do to acquire a devout and peaceful mind? In truth it is no light query, but I will strive to answer you as well as I can. Devotion is really neither more nor less than a general inclination and readiness to do that which we know to be acceptable to God. It is that "free spirit," of which David spoke when he said, " I will run the way of Thy commandments, when Thou hast set my heart at liberty."[1] Ordinarily good people walk in God's way, but the devout run in it, and at length they almost fly therein. . . . I will give you some few rules to forward you in such paths.

Above all, you must obey the general commandments of God and the Church, which apply to all faithful Christians ;—without this there can be no devotion whatever. But further than this each individual must carefully obey such special points as concern his or her own vocation, without which he cannot attain salvation, though he were able to raise the dead. For instance, Bishops are commanded to feed their flocks, to teach, comfort, guide them, and were I to spend the whole week in prayer, or to fast all my life, I should still be lost if I neglect this duty.

If any married person could work miracles, while yet he broke his vow of marriage, that man "is worse than an infidel."[2] These two kind of commandments must be scrupulously observed as the foundation of all devotion ; but further still, the virtue of devotion lies not merely in observing them, but in doing so willingly and readily. And there are several things to be considered with respect to such readiness.

First, that it is God's Will—and we may well strive to do His Will, for we came into this world for no other end. Alas ! day by day we ask that His Will may be done, and yet when it comes to

[1] Ps. cxix. 32. [2] 1 Tim. v. 8.

the doing, we find it so hard! We offer ourselves so often to God,—we continually say, "Lord, I am Thine, I give Thee my heart," and when He accepts it, we are such cowards. How dare we call ourselves His, if we cannot shape our will to His?

Next, consider how gracious and kind all God's Commandments, whether general or particular, are. What makes them hard to you? Nothing save self-will, which strives to reign within you at any price, so that it rejects the very things when commanded, which it would perhaps seek were they forbidden. Among a myriad of delicious fruits, Eve chose the one which was forbidden, whereas probably but for the prohibition she would not have touched it. In a word, we want to serve God according to our own will, not according to His. So Saul was commanded to destroy all Amalek, and he did destroy all except that which he considered costly enough to offer as a sacrifice; but God declared that "to obey is better than sacrifice."[1] God sends me to serve souls actively, but I prefer contemplation: Well,—the contemplative life is good, but not to the neglect of obedience. We must not choose for ourselves, we must will what God wills, and if He would have me serve Him in one thing, I must not prefer to serve Him in something else instead. God chose Saul to serve Him as a King and a Captain, whereas Saul chose to serve Him as a priest;—doubtless the latter office is the highest, but all the same that did not matter; what God wills is obedience.

God gave manna to the children of Israel, but

[1] 1 Sam. xv. 22.

they despised it, delicious as it was, and longed after the leeks and onions of Egypt. Even such is our wretched nature, which always prefers its own will to that of God. But as we come to have less of self-will, we shall more easily obey His Will. It is well to remember that there is no vocation without its trials, bitterness, and weariness, and without hearty resignation to God's Will every one is tempted to wish he could change his troubles for those of other men. Whence arises this universal dissatisfaction, save from our innate rebellion against constraint, and our perverse disposition to believe every one else better off than ourselves? Nevertheless, turn as we may, hither and thither, no one will be at rest who is not resigned. The fever-stricken patient finds no repose, he would for ever change his bed; but it is not the bed that is amiss, it is his own feverishness. He who is free from the fever of self-will is content with everything, so long as he is serving God. He does not care how God uses him, so long as His Holy Will is fulfilled.

We must go a step further, and to be truly devout, not merely do God's Will, but do it cheerfully. If I were not a Bishop, perhaps, knowing all I know, I would rather not be one; but as I am a Bishop, I am bound, not merely to fulfil the duties of that weighty charge, but to do so cheerfully, and to find pleasure therein. Thus S. Paul says, "As God hath distributed to every man, as the Lord hath called every one, so let him walk."[1] We have each got to carry our own cross, not another

[1] 1 Cor. vii. 17.

man's;—our Lord bids us each renounce himself, that is, our own will. I wish for this or that,—I could do better here or there—all this is temptation. Our Lord knows perfectly what He is doing: let us follow His Will, and abide where He has placed us.

You wish for some practical rule.

I. Make your daily meditation not longer than a good half-hour, and end it with considering our Lord's obedience to God the Father; you will find that all He did was done with reference to His Father's Will; and, studying that, you will seek to acquire a deeper love of that Will.

II. Before entering upon any irksome tasks to which you are called, remember how cheerfully the Saints performed far greater and harder things; how some suffered the loss of all worldly honour, others death itself. S. Francis, and many others, kissed the wounds of those they visited; some lived in deserts, others dwelt amid galley-slaves in order to convert them, and all alike in order to please God. What are any of our difficulties compared with such as these?

III. Remember often that the true measure of all we do is its conformity with God's Will. If I eat and drink because it is God's Will, I am more acceptable to Him than if I suffered death without any such intention.

IV. I would have you invoke God often through the day, asking Him to kindle a love for your vocation within you, and saying with S. Paul, "Lord, what wouldst Thou have me to do?" Wouldst Thou have me serve Thee in the lowest ministries of Thy House? too happy if I may but serve Thee anyhow. And when any special thing goes against you, ask, "Wouldst Thou have me do it?" then, unworthy though I be, I will do it gladly. So doing, you will grow in humility, and acquire a treasure greater than you can possibly imagine.

V. Remember how many Saints have been formed in your vocation,[1] and with what gentleness and resignation they submitted to it :—Sarah, Rebecca, S. Anne, S. Elizabeth, S. Monica, S. Paula, and many more. Our business is to love what God would have done. He wills our vocation as it is: let us love that, and not trifle away our time hankering after other people's vocation. Strive to combine the duties of Mary and Martha; be diligent in your active calling, and often retire within yourself, placing your soul at the Saviour's Feet, saying, "Lord, whether I move onwards or stand still, I am Thine and Thou art mine; all I do shall be done for love of Thee." You will hear Mass daily, and read some spiritual book for half an hour. In the evening make your examination of conscience, and all through the day use ejaculatory prayer. Read the "Spiritual Combat" diligently; I recommend it strongly to you. On Sundays and festivals you can attend vespers and sermon, but not as being constrained to do so. Go every week to confession, and when anything troubles your conscience. As to Communion, if it displeases your husband, for the present abide by the rule I gave you at St. Claude; be firm, and make spiritual Communions; God will accept your

---

[1] *i.e.* of married life.

preparation of heart.[1] Remember what I have so often told you, and do honour to your devotion by making it acceptable to all who know you, especially to your own family, so that every one may be attracted to it. When contradictions arise, resign yourself to them in our Lord, and take comfort, remembering that His favour is upon those who are holy, or who are seeking to become holy. I think much of you. God knows I never forget you or your family in my poor prayers; you are deeply graven in my soul. May God be in your heart and life.

XI.

To Madame de Chantal.
On Intellectual Temptation and Liberty of Spirit.

Oct. 14, 1604.

.... You ask a remedy in the trouble arising from temptations of Satan concerning the Faith and the Church. Such temptations must be dealt with like those of the flesh, without discussion; rather imitating the children of Israel, who were forbidden to break the bones of the Paschal Lamb, which they were to burn whole. You should not answer, or seem even to hear what the enemy says. Let him hammer as he will at the door, do not you ever say so much as, Who is there? You reply that this is true, yet nevertheless he troubles you, and drowns the inner voices you fain would hear.

---

[1] From other letters it appears that M. Brulart objected to his wife's communicating frequently.

Never mind, be patient. Prostrate yourself before God, and remain at His Feet. He will see that you are His, and that you claim His Help, even when you cannot speak. But beware that you never open the door, either to peep out and see what it is, or to drive away the clamour. In time he will be weary of assaulting you, and will leave you in peace. You say that it is time, forsooth, he did! Be brave, it will come. So long as he does not effect an entrance, it matters not. But, indeed, it is a good sign when the enemy storms so lustily at the door; it proves that he is not attaining his end. If he had attained it he would not clamour any more, he would go in and be satisfied. Keep this in mind, so as to avoid scruples.

I will give you another remedy. Temptations concerning the Faith aim directly at the understanding, seeking to draw it into discussion, and to make it question and speculate. Now, while the enemy is striving to scale the fortress of your intellect, do you make a sortie through the gates of the will, and charge him roundly. In other words, when you are tempted to question, How can this be? and if so and so, How can this other be? instead of tampering with your foe by discussing the matter, cry out with heart and voice, Traitor! fallen angel! thou wouldst have me to fall! As thou didst offer the fatal apple to Eve, so now thou biddest me taste thereof! Get behind me, Satan; it is written, "Thou shalt not tempt the Lord thy God." I will neither dispute nor argue; Eve argued and was lost. I believe in Jesus, I cling to His Church.

Do you understand me? I would have you entrench yourself in affections rather than reasons; in passions, rather than considerations. It is true that in such times of temptation the troubled spirit is very dry, but so much the better; its blows will be all the harder to the enemy, who will discover that he is forwarding your progress, and confirming your faith by his assaults. After all, these temptations are like any other trials, and must be borne patiently. Holy Writ says, "Blessed is the man that endureth temptation: for when he is tried he shall receive the crown of life."[1] I have rarely seen any one make much progress without having some such trial, and you must be patient. After the storm God will send a calm. . . . .

In your general rule, if you omit anything I have enjoined, do not be troubled by scruples. Here is the chief rule of our obedience, written in capitals:

LET EVERYTHING BE DONE FOR LOVE, NOTHING FOR FEAR.
LOVE OBEDIENCE MORE THAN YOU FEAR DISOBEDIENCE.

I leave you the spirit of liberty; not such as hinders obedience—that is a carnal liberty—but such as hinders constraint and scruple, or overeagerness. If you love obedience and submission, I would have you look upon any just or charitable call to give up your religious exercises as a sort of obedience, supplying the deficiency by love. . . . .

All good men are free from the constraint of mortal sin, and do not cling to any such attachments. This liberty of spirit is necessary to salvation. But I speak of a different sort of liberty—

[1] James i. 12.

that of beloved children. And that is a thorough detachment from all things, in order to follow God's recognised Will. Let me show you what I mean. We ask God above all things that His Name may be hallowed, His Kingdom come, His Will be done in earth as in Heaven. All this is the true spirit of liberty; for so long as God's Name be hallowed, His Majesty reigning in you, and His Will fulfilled, the spirit cares for nought beside. The first sign that the heart has this liberty is, that it is not attached to comforts, but accepts affliction meekly. I do not say that you will not wish for comfort, but without clinging to it. Secondly, such a free heart will not cleave to spiritual exercises so as to be disturbed if sickness or other causes hinder them. Here again you may rejoice in them, but without excessive attachment. Such a spirit can scarcely lose its cheerfulness, because no privation saddens him whose heart has no earthly attachments. I do not say that he will never lose it, but it will not be for long.

The results of this liberty are great suavity of spirit, great gentleness and indulgence towards whatever is not sin, or leading to sin, a temper easily moved to all that is good and loving. For instance, if you interrupt the meditation of one who cleaves closely to his religious exercises, he will be vexed and worried; but one who has the spirit of true liberty will leave it with an unruffled countenance, and a heart well disposed towards the disturber. To him it is equally acceptable whether he serve God in meditation, or in bearing with his neighbour ; both are alike God's Will, but at this moment the latter is more necessary.

The occasions which call for this liberty are found in whatever happens contrary to our inclination ; he who is detached from self is not impatient when such inclinations are crossed. There are two opposite dangers which beset this liberty; instability or dissipation, and constraint or servility. The first is an excessive freedom, which leads us to change our practices, or our condition, without reason or assurance that such is God's Will. The merest trifle leads us to alter our religious exercises, our object, our rule; the smallest cause disturbs our habit, and in this way we become dissipated and distracted, like an unenclosed garden, whence every passerby can gather the fruit.

The second is a lack of freedom which causes anger or vexation when we cannot do what we had intended, though it may be that we can do something better. For instance : I intend to make my meditation every morning, but if I have an unstable spirit, I shall defer it for the most trifling cause— perhaps a dog has disturbed my night's rest, or I want to write a letter which would do just as well later. On the other hand, if I have the spirit of constraint and servile bondage, I shall refuse to give up my meditation, although some sick person needs my attention, or some important business requires despatch ; and so on. I will give you two or three examples of this free spirit, which will show better what I mean. But first I must give you two rules to prevent errors.

I. No one should leave his ordinary practice and exercises, unless he plainly sees it to be God's Will. Now that Will is manifested in two ways—necessity and charity. I purpose to preach somewhere in my diocese this Lent; but if I fall ill, or break my leg, it is useless to regret it and trouble myself because I cannot preach, inasmuch as it is clearly God's Will that I should serve Him in suffering and not in preaching. Or supposing that I am not ill, but that I am called to some other place, where if I do not go the people are in danger of becoming Huguenots, this again is so obviously God's Will as to change my course.

II. When charity requires us to use freedom of spirit, it must be without scandal or injustice. For instance, I know that I could be more useful in some distant place away from my diocese, but I must not use my liberty in this case, for I should be unjust and cause scandal, inasmuch as I am bound to be here. In like manner, it is a false liberty when married women absent themselves from their husbands under the pretext of devotion or charity, for a true spirit of liberty never interferes with one's vocation; on the contrary, it tends to make everybody happy in their own, because such is God's Will. . . . . Now, as an example of what I mean, I would cite Cardinal Borromeo,[1] who is shortly to be canonized. He was one of the most precise, rigid, austere men possible; he lived on bread and water, and during twenty-four years of his Episcopate, he only twice entered his brother's house when he was sick, and twice went

[1] Carlo Borromeo, Archbishop of Milan.

into his own garden; and yet this severe ascetic used to mix with his neighbours the Swiss, and even join in their carousals, in order to win them to the truth. Surely this was holy liberty in the most austere man of our times! A lax spirit would have done too much; a constrained spirit would have feared to sin mortally; a true spirit of liberty did it out of pure charity.

Bishop Spiridion of old, receiving a pilgrim one Lent, who was almost perishing with hunger, had nothing to give him but some salt meat. The pilgrim refused to eat it, whereupon, out of mere charity, Spiridion ate some of it himself in order to remove the pilgrim's scruple.

Ignatius Loyola, when slightly ill, ate meat directly that his doctor ordered it:—a servile spirit would have contested the matter ever so long.

But I will set before you an instance before which all these grow pale! I have often thought what was the greatest mortification endured by all the saints I ever read of, and after long deliberation, I think it was that which S. John Baptist bore. He went into the desert when he was five years old, and when there he knew that our Saviour and his was born within reach of a day's journey or so. Doubtless he who leapt in his mother's womb for joy and love of that Saviour's expected Birth, must have longed to enter His Earthly Presence. Yet he remained twenty-five years in the desert without coming to see Our Lord, continuing his work of preaching, waiting till his Lord should come to him; and even then, after baptizing

Christ, S. John did not follow Him, but remained at his appointed work. Surely this was a truly mortified spirit! To be so near the Saviour and not to see Him! to know Him close at hand, and not to rejoice in His Presence! What is that but to have a spirit wholly detached from self, and even from God, when He demands it for His better service.? To leave God for God ; not to love Him, in order to love Him better, and with greater purity. I am overwhelmed with the magnitude of such an example!

I had wellnigh forgotten to say that God's Will is known, not only by necessity and charity, but also by obedience ; so that he who receives a command from a rightful Superior ought to hold it as God's Will.

XII.
To Madame de Chantal.
On Temptations of the Will.

. . . . . As to your present cross. . . . . It is a certain incapacity, you say, of your understanding, which hinders it from deriving satisfaction in the consideration of that which is good ; and what grieves you most is that, when you want to make firm resolutions, you do not feel your wonted decision, but you stumble against a barrier which stops you short, and then temptations concerning the faith arise. . . . . You add that meanwhile your will, by God's Grace, desires simply and firmly to cleave to the Church, and that you would willingly die for the faith she has taught you. Thank God, my dear daughter, "this sickness is not unto death, but for the Glory of God."[1] You are like Rebecca, when two peoples struggled within her womb, but the younger was destined to prevail. Self-love only dies with our natural death; it has a thousand wiles whereby to keep a hold within the soul, and we cannot drive it forth. It is the first-born of the soul; it is upheld by a legion of auxiliaries—emotions, actions, passions; it is adroit, and knows how to employ endless subtleties. On the other hand, the love of God, which is the later born, has also its emotions, actions, inclinations, and passions. These two struggle within us, and their convulsive movements cause us infinite trouble. . . . . You do not feel firm, constant, or resolute. You say that there is somewhat unsatisfied in you, though you know not what. I wish I knew what it is, my dear daughter, so that I might tell you. Perhaps some day, when we can talk at leisure, I shall be able to discover. But meanwhile, may it not be that your mind is obstructed by a multitude of desires? That is a malady from which I have suffered. The bird which is chained to its perch is not conscious of its captivity until it wants to fly, and it is much the same with an unfledged nestling.

One remedy, then, is not to struggle, or be over-eager to fly; be patient till your wings are grown. I fear very much that you are too vehement in pursuit, too headlong in your wishes and attempts to fly. You see the beauty of spiritual light and

[1] John xi. 4.

good resolutions; you fancy that you have almost attained, and your ardour is redoubled; you rush forward, but in vain, for your Master has chained you to your perch, or else it is that your wings are not grown; and this constant excitement exhausts your strength. You must indeed strive to fly, but gently, without growing eager or restless.

Now examine yourself in this matter. Perhaps you will find that you limit your aim too much to the delight which your soul experiences in firmness, constancy, and resolution. You are firm—what is it but having the will to die rather than to sin against the Faith? But you have not the feeling or sentiment of firmness which would impart great delight. Now pause; do not be in a hurry; you will be all the better for it, and your wings will grow the faster. Your over-eagerness is a defect, and this *je ne sais quoi* unsatisfied, arises from a lack of resignation. You do resign yourself, but it is always with a BUT: you want this and that, and you struggle to get it. A simple wish is no hindrance to resignation; but a palpitating heart, a flapping of wings, an agitated will, and endless, quick, restless movements are unquestionably caused by deficient resignation. But be of good cheer, my dear sister; if our will is given to God, we are surely His. You have all that is necessary, although you have not the consciousness thereof; but that is no great loss.

Do you know what you must do? You must be willing not to fly, since your wings are not yet grown. You remind me of Moses, who, when on Mount Pisgah, saw the promised land before his eyes,—the land after which he had longed for forty years, amid all the murmurs of his people, and the trials of the desert. Now he beheld the land, but he might not enter in—he died looking upon it. The cup was raised to his lips, but he might not drink. What must have been his longing! Yet Moses died a more blessed death than many of those who were permitted to enter the promised land, since God vouchsafed Himself to bury him. . . . . Well, and if you were called upon to die without tasting of the well of Sychar, what would it signify so long as your soul is admitted to drink for ever at the fountain and source of eternal life? Do not be so eager with your vain desires, do not even be eager in avoiding eagerness;[1] go on quietly in your path—it is a good path.

I am writing amid many interruptions, and if what I say is confused, no wonder. But would you ascertain whether what I say is true, namely, that what is wanted in you is entire resignation? You wish to take up the Cross, but you want to choose your Cross; you would have it a bodily one, or some other according to your fancy. But what is this? No, my dear daughter; I desire that your Cross and mine may be solely the Cross of Christ; and as to its kind, or the way it is laid upon us, God knows what He does, and why: it is all for our good. He gave David his choice as to the rod with which he should be smitten, but it seems to me that I would rather not have chosen, leaving it all to His Divine Will. The more wholly a Cross comes from God, the more we ought to prize it

[1] "Ne vous empressez pas à ne vous empresser point."

. . . . . Let us bear all dryness, all barrenness possible, so long as we love God.

But with all this you are not yet in the land of total darkness—at times you see light, and God visits you. Is He not very Good? Does not the very trial make you taste His sweetness better? I am quite willing that you should pour out your trouble to your Dear Lord, only lovingly and without over-eagerness. He likes us to tell Him how He is grieving us, so long as we do it humbly and lovingly, and to His own Ear, like little children who have been punished by a tender parent. But you must suffer a little longer in patience. I do not think it is amiss to say to our Lord, "Come into our souls." . . . .

Serve Him as He wills,—some day you will find Him doing all and more than you can ask.

. . . . . Do not be troubled by S. Bernard's saying that hell is full of good intentions and wills. There are two kinds of goodwill. One says, "I would fain do well, but it is hard to do, and so I shall not do it." The other says, "I mean to do right, but I have less strength than goodwill, and that hinders me." The first of these fills hell, the second Paradise. The first only begins to wish, but does not go on to will ;—such wishes have no courage, they are mere abortions, and thus they help to people hell. But the second results in earnest, well-formed desires ;—and thus Daniel is called "a man of desires."[1] May God vouchsafe

---

[1] In the English Version it is, "O Daniel, a man greatly beloved ;" but in the Vulgate, "Daniel, vir desideriorum." Dan. x. 11.

to give us the perpetual aid of His Holy Spirit, my very dear daughter and sister.

XIII.

To Madame de Chantal.

Feb. 18, 1605.

I PRAISE God for the constancy with which you bear your trials. Nevertheless, I see some lingering remains of anxiety and over-eagerness, which hinder your entire patience. "In your patience possess ye your souls," the Son of God has said.[1] The effect of patience, then, is to enable us to possess our souls, and the more perfect it becomes, the fuller and better will that possession be. Now that patience is most perfect which is least mingled with anxiety and eagerness. May God deliver you from these inconveniences, and you will soon be delivered from all else.

Courage, I intreat you, my dear Sister! You have borne the discomforts of your way but three years, and you crave for rest! Remember that the children of Israel were forty years in the desert before they arrived at the promised land, although six weeks would easily have taken them thither; yet they were not allowed to inquire why God led them by such winding ways, and through so many difficulties; and all who murmured died before arriving. Remember, too, that Moses, who was nearest to God of the whole band, died on the borders of that land, beholding it only, and not entering in.

[1] Luke xxi. 19.

Would to God that we could pay but little heed to the road we tread, rather fixing our eyes on Him Who leads us, and on the blessed country towards which we travel! What does it signify whether we pass through desert places or pleasant fields, so long as God is with us, and that we reach Paradise? Believe me, you had better forget your pain as much as possible, and if you feel it, at all events do not dwell upon it,—the sight will cause you more fear than the feeling causes pain. It is the custom to blindfold those who are about to undergo a severe operation. It seems to me that you dwell rather too much upon the thought of your trouble.

As to what you say, that it is a great trial to have the will and not the power to act, I might say that one must will what one can perform; as also that it is a great matter in God's Sight to be able to will. Consider the utter desolation of our Master in the Garden of Olives; see how that Dear Son asked consolation at His Father's Hand, and knowing that He willed not to give it Him, endured all in patience and tranquilly, asking no more, but stedfastly and heroically carrying out the work of our Redemption. . . . When you have prayed that God would comfort you, if He does not will so to do, cease to seek it, but gird yourself up to work out your salvation on the Cross, as though you were never to come down thence, never again to live in a clear untroubled atmosphere. What would you have? We must speak with God amid the storm and the whirlwind; we must see Him in the burning bush, and in order to do this, we must indeed, like Moses, put our shoes from off our feet, and make a hearty abnegation of our will and affections. But God's Gracious Goodness has not called you on so far, without strengthening you for all this. It is His to finish His work. He may be long about it, seeing your needs; only be patient.

In short, for God's Glory, accept His Will entirely, and never suppose that you could serve Him better in any other way. You can never serve Him well, save in the way He chooses. And He chooses you to serve Him without sweetness, without emotion; rather with repugnance and mental convulsions. Such a service does not please you, but it satisfies Him—it is not according to your liking, it is according to His.

Supposing that you were never to be set free from such trials, what would you do? You would say to God, "I am Thine—if my trials are acceptable to Thee, give me more and more." I have full confidence in our Lord that this is what you would say, and then you would not think more of it—anyhow you would not be anxious. Well, do the same now. Make friends with your trials, as though you were always to live together; and you will see that when you cease to take thought for your own deliverance, God will take thought of it for you; and when you cease to help yourself eagerly, He will help you.

Madame B. inquires through you whether she may wait for the arrival of her spiritual father,[1] to accuse herself of something forgotten in her general confession, and apparently she wishes much to do so. But tell her, I beg, that that cannot be; I

[1] Himself.

should be a traitor to her soul, if I permitted such an abuse. She must accuse herself of this forgotten sin or sins at her very next confession, in all simplicity and honesty, without repeating any other part of her general confession, which was very good, and then, in spite of these omissions, she must not be troubled. Try to remove the mistaken feeling which troubles her in this matter. In truth, the first and foremost point of Christian simplicity consists in frankly and without pretence confessing one's faults, not shrinking from our confessor's knowledge of them. It is his office to hear of sins, not virtues; ay, and of sins of every kind too. Let her, then, bravely conquer this fear, by means of a great humility and self-contempt, not shrinking from laying bare all her weakness to him by whose means God wills to heal her. . . . But if she feels an excessive shame or fear in going to her ordinary confessor, she may go elsewhere; but I would have it all done with perfect simplicity, and in truth I believe that what she has to say is, after all, no great matter, and that timidity alone makes it appear alarming. Tell her all this very tenderly, and assure her that if I could yield to her wish I would gladly do so. If afterwards, the first time she sees her spiritual father, it is any comfort or benefit to her to tell him these faults, she can do so, although it be not necessary. But by her last letter she seems to wish it, and I think it may be useful to her to make another general confession with very careful preparation. . . .

Be firm, I pray you. Let nothing move you. It is night as yet, but the day is coming, and will not tarry. Meanwhile let us follow David, "Lift up your hands in the sanctuary, and praise the Lord."[1] Let us bless Him with all our heart, and intreat Him to be our guide, our vessel, our haven. I will only answer some of the most urgent points of your letter.

You cannot believe, my very dear daughter, that temptations against the Faith and the Church come from God; but whoever told you that they did? Darkness, powerlessness, grovelling, absence of all vigour, lack of spiritual perception, interior bitterness, all these may come from Him, but blasphemous, doubting, unbelieving thoughts, never! He is all Pure and cannot create such things.

Shall I tell you what He really does? He permits the wicked maker of lies to present such abominations to us, in order that by despising them we may bear witness to our love for heavenly things. And if so, my dear Sister, must we be troubled or upset because of them? Surely no. It is the devil who walketh about our minds, hunting for some loophole to enter in Even so he dealt with Job, with S. Anthony, S. Catherine of Sienna, and an infinitude of pious souls whom I have known, as well as with my own worthless soul, which I do not know. But you must not be grieved at it. Let him work his own confusion, and keep every avenue carefully closed; he will grow weary at last, or God will constrain him to raise the siege.

Remember what I think I have said to you before. It is a good sign when the devil makes

---

[1] In the Vulgate it is, "In noctibus extollite manus vestras in sancta, et benedicite Dominum."—Ps. cxxxiv. 2.

such a stir without; it proves that he has not got
within. Take courage, dear soul; so long as we
can say resolutely, though without excited feeling,
Hail, Jesus! we need not fear. Do not tell me
that you feel as if you said it like a coward, without
strength or courage, and only by doing violence to
yourself. This is just that very violence which
takes Heaven by storm. Indeed, my daughter, it
is a sign that the enemy has taken the fortress, all
save the impenetrable, immovable watch-tower,
which cannot be lost unless it betray itself. Such
violence is in the free will, which, bare and open
before God, dwells in the highest and most spiritual
part of the soul, depending wholly upon God and
upon itself; so that, when all other faculties of the
soul are vanquished by the enemy, this alone
remains self-controlled and unrelenting.

You will find souls aggrieved because the enemy
takes possession of all other faculties, and makes
a frightful tumult therein, while the higher will, in
spite of its clearer voice, scarce can be heard. In
truth, the vulgar clamour of the one drowns the
other. Finally, remember this—so long as you are
grieved at the temptation there is nothing to fear,
for why does it grieve you save because your will
does not consent to it? In truth, these troublesome
temptations come from the devil's malice, but the
pain and suffering they cause us come from God's
Mercy, Which causes a holy tribulation to spring
forth from the wiles of the enemy, thereby to refine
the gold He destines for His treasury. I repeat,
then, your temptations are of hell and the devil;
but your troubles and afflictions are of God and

Paradise. Despise the temptation, embrace the tribulation.

XIV.

To a Lady.
On Conformity to God's Will.

June 10, 1605.

.... GIVE heed, my dear child, to become daily more pure in heart. Now this purity consists in weighing everything in the scales of the sanctuary, and that is the Will of God. I intreat you not to love anything too ardently, not even virtues, which are sometimes lost in an immoderate pursuit. Do you understand me? I allude to your eager wishes. Let us be what we are, and strive to be that well, in order to do honour to Him Who made us. Let us be whatever He wills, so long as we are wholly devoted to Him, but let us not be what we will contrary to His intentions; for were we the most perfect denizens of Heaven, of what use were it, unless we be such according to God's Will?

XV.

To Madame Brulart.
On Submission to her Husband.

.... YOU must yield to their will (her father and husband), and bend to the utmost without breaking through your good rules,—such submission is acceptable to our Lord. I have told you before, the less we live according to our own taste, the less we choose for ourselves, the better and more solid our devotion will be. There are times when we must leave our Lord to please others for love of Him. My dear daughter, I must tell you all I think, and you will appreciate my sincerity. Perhaps you have given your good husband and father some grounds for being annoyed at, and interfering with, your religious practices? Perhaps you have been rather too eager and busy, and have sought to press or to restrain them? If so, that is why they react upon you now. We must strive, if possible, that our devotion should be troublesome to no one. I will tell you what to do now. When you can communicate without annoying them, do so, according to your confessor's advice; but when you fear to cause vexation, be content with a spiritual communion, and believe me, this spiritual mortification, this privation, will be highly acceptable to God, and will strengthen His hold upon your heart. "*Il faut quelquefois reculer pour mieux sauter.*" I have often admired the intense resignation of S. John Baptist, in remaining so long near our Lord, without eagerly seeking or following Him; even after His Baptism letting Him go without cleaving to His bodily Presence. Surely it was because the Baptist knew that he was really serving the Lord by bearing this privation of His Presence. And so you will serve God if, in order to win those who are set over you, you endure the privation of actual Communion. It will be a great comfort to me to know that you are not distressed at this advice. Believe me, this resignation, this abnegation, will be extremely useful to you. . . . Mortify yourself cheerfully, and in proportion as you are hindered in doing the good you wish, be more diligent in doing that which you do not wish. You do not wish to give up these things, but something else. But those sacrifices which you do not want to make are worth most, be sure. . . . Keep your heart open, ready to receive all manner of crosses, sacrifices, and abnegations, for the love of Him Who bore so many for us. His Holy Name be ever blessed.

XVI.

To Madame Brulart.
On the Sanctification of Married Life.

. . . . You earnestly desire Christian perfection : it is the noblest wish you can have : nourish it so that it may grow daily. There are various ways of attaining perfection, according to different vocations; for religious, widows, and married people ought all to seek after it, but not all in the same way. For you who are married, the means are union with God and your neighbour. Union with God you will attain chiefly through the sacraments and prayer. As to the former, you should never allow a month to pass without communicating; and after a time, as you advance in God's service, and subject to guidance, you should communicate oftener. As to confession, I would advise you to have more frequent recourse to that, especially whenever your conscience is troubled by any imperfection, such as often happens in the beginning of the spiritual life. Nevertheless, if you cannot go to confession, contrition and repentance will supply the deficiency. Be diligent in prayer, especially meditation. . . . And offer constant ejaculatory prayers to our Lord, at all times and in all society, always seeing God within your heart, and your heart in God. I would have you give half an hour daily to spiritual reading. Such are the chief means of union with God. As to those which concern our neighbour, they are many. I will only suggest some few. We should look at others through God, Who would have us love them. Thus S. Paul bids servants see God in their masters. We ought to cultivate this love of other men, even when it is contrary to our inclination, so that habit and good intention may conquer the repugnance felt by our lower nature. We should turn our prayer and meditation to this subject, and after asking to learn to love God, ask also to learn to love our neighbour, especially those to whom we are not attracted.

I should advise you to take some trouble to visit in the hospitals, to comfort the sick, and to pray for them while ministering to them. But in all this be very careful not to inconvenience your husband, relations, or servants, whether by too long seasons spent in church, too much retirement, or neglect of your household. Do not be meddlesome in other people's business, or hold in contempt society where your own rules of devotion are not exactly observed. In all such matters we must be guided by charity, and yield to the will of our neighbour, whereinsoever it is not opposed to the Will of God.

You should not only be religious and love religion; you should make religion attractive, useful and agreeable to every one around. The sick will like your religion if it leads you to tend them, your family will be attracted to it if they see you more careful in your duties, more patient, more diligent, more gentle in finding fault. If your husband sees that, as you become more devout, you are also more affectionate to him, more tenderly submissive, he will be won to your religion. In a word, let your religion be as winning to others as possible.

XVII.
To the Abbesse du Puits d'Orbe.
On Little Troubles.

Nov. 16, 1605.

BE careful to preserve your heart in peace and tranquillity; let the waves and storms beat about your bark, without fear, for God is there, and consequently salvation. Dear Sister, I know that little vexations are more trying, through their multiplicity and their importunity, than greater things;—home troubles harder to bear than such as come from without; but I also know that the victory over such is often more acceptable to God than many other victories which have a greater show of merit in the world's eye. . . . Be as cheerful as you can in well doing; there is a double grace in good actions when they are done cheerfully and brightly.

XVIII.

To Madame de Chantal. On Abjection.

Aug. 6, 1606.

MAY God aid me to answer your letter of July 9 profitably. I desire greatly to do so, but I foresee that I shall not have leisure to express my thoughts. You are right, my daughter, to speak quite openly to me, as to one whom God has given to you wholly. You say that you are putting your hand somewhat to the work;—thank God. That is a great comfort to me. Go on doing so, put your hand somewhat to the work, spin every day some little, whether it be in the day by the light of interior sweetness, or at night by the lamplight of helplessness and barrenness. The Wise Man says of the virtuous woman, "Her hands hold the distaff."[1] I could say much about these words. Your spindle is a mass of good desires; spin every day a little; carry out the thread of your wishes into execution, and you will do much. But beware of hurry; that would lead you to make knots in your thread, and spoil your work. Let us go on quietly; however slowly we advance, we shall make great progress really.

Your powerlessness hinders you;—because, you say, it prevents your recollectedness, and nearness to God. But this is not the right way to put it: God places us where we are for His greater Glory, and our own profit. He would make our misery

[1] Prov. xxxi. 19.

the throne of His Mercy;—our powerlessness the seat of His Omnipotence. Did not God cause Samson's great power to lie in his hair, ordinarily the weakest part of his frame? Let me hear no more of this from a daughter who seeks to serve God according to His Divine Pleasure, not according to her own tastes and likings. Job said, "Though He slay me, yet will I trust in Him." No, my daughter, this want of power does not hinder you from recollecting yourself; it only hinders you from self-satisfaction.

We are for ever wanting this and that, and although our Dear Lord rests within our bosom, we are not satisfied; yet surely that is all we can desire. One thing only we need;—to be near Him.

My dear daughter, you know that at the Nativity the shepherds heard the Angels' song of triumph;—but we are not told that Our Lady and S. Joseph, nearest of all as they were to the Holy Child, either heard the angelic song or saw the supernatural light. Rather they heard the new-born Babe weep, and by some wretched lantern they saw the Infant God shivering with cold. Yet would you not rather have been with them in the manger, than with the shepherds who were abiding in the field? "It is good for us to be here," S. Peter said, as on this very day, on the Mount of Transfiguration; but your Mistress (the Blessed Virgin) was not there. She was on Mount Calvary, surrounded by the nails, the thorns, the thick darkness, the utter desolation, and death.

Enough, my daughter; love God amid all darkness. Abide by Him. Love your abjection. Do you? You reply, What do you mean? What I mean is this. If you continue humble, calm, gentle, trustful amid obscurity and powerlessness; if you are not impatient, not hurried, or eager;—if you take up your cross simply and cheerfully, that is loving abjection. What is it to be abject but to be obscure and helpless? If you love such a lot, for His Sake Who wills it to be yours, you are loving abjection.

The Latin word implies humility; and when Our Lady says, "He hath regarded the lowliness of His Handmaiden,"[1] she means that God has looked mercifully upon her abjection. Still, there is a difference between humility and abjection, inasmuch as humility is the acknowledgment of abjection; and the highest point of humility is, not merely to recognise one's abjection, but to love it, and this is what I would have you do.

To speak more plainly : Our troubles are of two kinds—honourable and abject ; and while many resign themselves to the first class of sufferings, very few submit gladly to such as are abject.

For instance, a Capucin monk goes about with a torn habit, shivering with cold. Every one respects his worn habit, and pities his discomfort. But a poor artisan, or scholar, or widow, bears the like inconvenience unpitied, and so their poverty is abject.

A Religious takes a rebuke from his Superior patiently, and we call it obedience and mortification. But a gentleman who accepts something similar for

[1] Vulg.: "Respexit humilitatem ancillæ suæ."

the Love of God is called a coward. This is an abject virtue. One man has a cancer in his arm, another in his face—the first conceals it, and has only the pain to bear; the other cannot hide his disease, and has to bear the external humiliation as well as the pain. But I say that we must learn to love the abjection, as well as the pain. Further, there are abject virtues, and creditable virtues. For the most part, patience, gentleness, mortification, and simplicity in the world, are abject virtues; whereas almsgiving, courtesy, and prudence, are creditable virtues.

Almsgiving and forgiveness of injury are both works of charity, but the former is honourable in the world's eyes, while the latter is abject. I am taken ill among people who look upon my illness merely as an inconvenience; there is an abjection added to suffering. Or your quiet widow's dress is condemned as affected by worldly-minded ladies, or perhaps they say that it is studied with the intent to attract; or men will not believe that I do not wish for a higher position and rank than I possess, or that I heartily delight in my vocation. All these are cases of abjection.

On the other hand, you and your Sisters go forth to visit the sick, among whom the most wretched are allotted to you. . . . In the world's judgment this is the most abject part. But if those better off are assigned to your care, you have the most abject lot in God's Sight—for He and the world do not agree as to what is honourable in these things. The best thing is to rejoice in whichever part falls to you. If you are sent to the worst cases, say,

"They suit me best." If to the best, say, "I am not worthy to minister to those who need more."

If I am guilty of some folly, it makes me abject, or I stumble, and give way to uncontrolled anger; in so doing I displease God, and deserve to be esteemed as vile and abject. Nevertheless, my daughter, beware of one thing: while we love the abjection following upon what is evil, we must not slacken in trying to remedy the evil. Whatever I can do to avert having cancer in the face, I am bound to do; but if it comes, I am bound to welcome the abjection. So in moral concerns: I have been disobedient, ill-regulated, and I am grieved at it, even while I accept the consequent abjection; and if the two things were separable, I would gladly retain the abjection, while I shun the sin.

Again, we must not forget charity, which sometimes requires that we put abjection aside for our neighbour's sake; but in such a case, we must only hide it from his eyes, lest he be scandalised, not from those of our own heart. "I would rather be a doorkeeper in the house of my God, than to dwell in the tents of the ungodly."[1]

Finally, my daughter, you ask what are the best abjections? I answer such as are not self-chosen, and are least welcome; those for which we have least inclination; in a word, those which pertain to our vocation or profession.

For instance: Some think any abjection preferable to that of marriage; some Religious would

---

[1] Ps. lxxxiv. In the Vulgate, "Elegi *abjectus* esse in domo Dei mei, magis quam habitare in tabernaculis peccatorum."

obey any Superior save the one to whom she is subject; or you might say you would rather be worried by any possible religious Superior, than by the father-in-law with whom you dwell. But I answer that the abjection laid upon each of us is the most profitable, and choice takes away half the merit thereof. Who will give us grace, my daughter, to love our own abjection? None save He Who so loved His Own abjection as to die therein. Surely that is sufficient for us.

Full of hope that you might shortly enter the religious life, you fear to have run counter to obedience. But I did not tell you not to think or hope for it. I would not have you trifle with it, because most assuredly nothing so hinders us in what we are doing as to be longing after something else; in so doing, we leave off tilling our own field to drive the plough through our neighbour's land, where we must not look to reap any harvest; and this is mere waste of time. If our thoughts and hopes are elsewhere, it is impossible for us to set our faces steadily towards the work required of us. Jacob never really loved Leah while he was longing for Rachel. But remember, I do not say that you are not to think and hope; I only say that you are not to trifle with such matters. We may look to the place where we fain would be, but on condition that we always look onwards. The Israelites could not sing in Babylon, because they were looking back homewards, but I would have you able to sing always.

. . . . Fear is a greater pain than pain itself. O thou of little faith, what dost thou fear? Be not afraid; you walk indeed on the waves, amid the storm, but it is with Jesus; why should you fear? But if terror should come over you, cry out aloud, "Lord, help me!" He will stretch forth His Hand; hold it tightly, and go on joyfully. In short, do not philosophise over your troubles; do not argue; go on in all simplicity. God will not let you perish while you are stedfast in resolution. Let the world be turned upside down, let it be in utter darkness, in smoke, in tumult, so long as God be with us; we know that on Sinai He was surrounded with thick darkness, with thunder and lightning, and He is still near to us.

XIX.

To a Young Lady. Concerning her Vocation.

Dec. 14, 1606.

I AM very glad to hear that you are growing in the love of our Lord, as M. de N—— tells me is the case, though he only spoke generally, mentioning no details save that you wish to become a Religious. The wish is a good one, doubtless, but you must not let it disturb you, as for the present it cannot be carried out. If our Saviour wills that it should be fulfilled, He will bring it about by means of His own, which as yet we know not.

But meanwhile, do the work which concerns you at the present moment; that is to say, go on quietly with your spiritual exercises; give yourself up many times each day, both heart and mind, into God's Hands, commending your work heartily to

Him; consider what daily opportunities you have of serving His Divine Majesty, whether by your own advance in holiness, or by promoting that of your neighbour, and make a faithful use of all such. You will profit greatly, my daughter, by this practice, in the Love of God. I know that you grieve sorely at being forsaken by your father; but you must say with your heart, as well as with your lips, "When my father and my mother forsake me, the Lord taketh me up."[1] Doubtless it is a cross, my child, to be thus forsaken of men, but it is a very holy cross, and one most specially calculated to win the Love of God. You must be very brave in the strength of this blessed Love, and trust wholly in the assurance we have that our Heavenly Bridegroom never fails those whose hope is in Him.

I send you a little cross, in the midst of which the martyr, Saint Thekla, is represented, to encourage you in suffering willingly for our Lord. It is not a return for your beautiful gift, but only in remembrance of the affectionate love which I bear through our Lord for your soul. I pray you commend me often to Him, as your most humble and faithful in our Holy Cross, etc.

XX.

To Madame Brulart.

ANNECY, *Jan.* 30, 1607.

YOU ask whether you may communicate two days running, when festivals come after your ordinary

---

[1] Ps. xxvii. 10.

days for receiving the Blessed Sacrament. . . If it is a great festival, it should certainly be celebrated by an extra communion; for how can we keep a great day without that holy Feast? . . .

The multitude of thoughts which trouble you should not be separately handled, you would never be able to conquer them one by one. Only from time to time (I mean several times a day) give them the lie collectively, and reject them all together, and then let the enemy make what clatter he will outside your heart, it matters not, so long as he does not come within. Be in peace yourself, though surrounded with war, and be not afraid. God is on your side. I pray Him to draw you more and more to Himself. Amen.

You are right in accusing yourself of superfluity or excess, but aim at a wise moderation, keeping to the rule of neither being less liberal nor handsome in your reception of your friends than is suitable to your position and theirs, nor on the other hand exceeding that which is duly liberal. I am myself inclined to this latter fault, and have to watch against it, though of course I am in a great measure guarded and guided by ecclesiastical rules.

XXI.

To Madame de Chantal.

Feb. 11, 1607.

. . . . I SEE that all the seasons of the year are represented in your soul; one while you endure the winter of barrenness, distraction, repugnance weariness; another time you taste the sweet dews of May, and the pleasant scent of holy blossoms; another while the warmth of an earnest desire to please our Dear Lord. Nought remains save autumn, of which you say that the fruits are scanty; but very often when the corn is threshed and the grapes pressed, we find more result than the harvest promised.

You would fain have nothing but spring and summer, but, my dear daughter, there must be vicissitudes in the interior life as well as in that which is external. Only in Heaven shall we find perpetual spring as to beauty; perpetual summer in love; perpetual autumn in fulfilment of desire. There will be no winter there, but here winter is necessary that we may practise self-abnegation, and a thousand minor graces which spring forth in the time of barrenness. Let us go on steadily, though slowly; so long as our affections are firm and good, we shall not go wrong.

No, my dear daughter, it is not necessary, in order to practise Christian graces, to be always dwelling consciously on each; such a process would confuse and hamper both your thoughts and feelings. Humility and love are the main links, to which all else is bound. Keep steady to these—the highest and lowest, for the whole building depends upon the foundation and the roof. If your heart is kept in the stedfast practice of these, you will not find other graces very difficult. They are the parents, and all other virtues follow them as little chickens follow their brooding mother.

I am very glad that you are taking the part of

schoolmistress. God will reward you for it. He loves little children;—as I said the other day when catechising, wishing to urge our ladies to interest themselves for the girls, their guardian angels have a special love for those who bring up little children in the fear of God, and our Saviour threatens such as hinder them through any scandal with the wrath of those guardians.

. . . . No, you are not disobedient because you raise your heart to God less often than I bade you, or because you do not exactly follow all my advice. These things are counsels, profitable to you, but they are not commandments. When one lays commands on anybody, one does it in unmistakable terms. Do you know how counsels should be dealt with? They should not be despised, but rather loved; that is quite enough, they are not in any way binding.

Be of good cheer, my daughter. Let your heart be warmed this Lent. We must not doubt;—Jesus Christ is ours. As a little girl said the other day to me, " He is more mine than I am His, more than I am my own."

XXII.
To one of the Bishop's Married Sisters.

July 20, 1607.

. . . Do not be eager, but believe me that the true way to serve our Lord is in careful stedfast quietness. Do not try to do everything; be content to do something, and doubtless you will do a great deal. Practise such mortifications as come most in the course of things before you ; they need our first attention, and afterwards we can seek others. Embrace heartily these crosses which our Lord Himself has put into your arms—do not stop to consider whether they are made of precious scented woods ; all the better as crosses if they be common and unsavoury. These thoughts are ever with me ; I am perpetually singing this song. In truth, my dear sister, it is the Song of the Lamb—somewhat sad, perhaps, but lovely and full of harmony. "Father, not my will, but Thine be done." Magdalene sought the Lord while in truth she touched Him ; she inquired for Him of Himself, for she did not behold Him under the form she sought, and therefore she was not satisfied, and strove to find Him elsewhere. She looked to see Him in His robes of glory, not in the earthly garb of a gardener; but so soon as He called her by her name, "Mary," she knew Him.

Now, my dear sister, you meet our Lord in His gardener's garb in the daily vexations and mortifications which offer themselves to you. You would prefer grander, more attractive mortifications ; but, indeed, those are not the most profitable. Do you not believe that He calls you by name? "Mary, Mary." But before you see Him in His Glory, He wills to plant many a little lowly flower in your garden, after His own fashion, and therefore He comes to you in such a garb. May our hearts be eternally united to His Heart, our wills to His Will. I am for ever and without bounds, my dear sister, your loving brother, etc.

Be of good cheer, and do not let yourself be cast down. Let us belong solely to God, for He is ours. Amen.

XXIII.

To a Curé. On Abiding in his Work.

MY VERY DEAR BROTHER,   SALES, *Sept.* 25, 1607.

Forgive my delay in answering the first letter you ever wrote to me. It shall not be so in future if I have the pleasure of hearing from you, but I was so occupied at the time of my departure as to have no leisure whatever for this duty. I persist in telling you that you ought to serve God where you are, "et facere quod facio." Not, dear brother, that I would forbid the increase of your good works, or the continual purification of your heart, but "fac quod facio, et melius quam facio," for what God said to Abraham, He says in him to all the faithful, "Walk before Me, and be thou perfect,"[1] and again, "Blessed are all they that fear the Lord, and walk in His ways,"[2] "they will go from strength to strength."[3]

Be of good courage, then, in cultivating your vineyard, contributing your little work towards the spiritual good of souls, as one of those who have not bent the knee to Baal, though "dwelling in the midst of a people of unclean lips."[4] Do not marvel that the fruits of your labour do not as yet appear: "Be stedfast, unmoveable, always abounding in the work of the Lord, forasmuch

[1] Gen. xvii. 1.   [2] Ps. cxxviii. 1.   [3] Ps. lxxxiv. 7.   [4] Isa. vi. 5.

as ye know that your labour is not in vain in the Lord."[1]

Indeed, dear sir, God has fed us with the milk of consolation, in order that, having come to years of discretion, we may strive to help in rebuilding the walls of Jerusalem, whether by carrying staves, by mixing mortar, or by wielding the hammer. Believe me, abide where you are. Do faithfully and heartily whatever you have moral power to do, and you will realise the promise, "If thou wouldst believe, thou shouldst see the Glory of God."[2]

If you would go on well, count any suggestion that you should change your place as a temptation; for while your mind is looking elsewhere than upon your actual work, it will never be thoroughly given to do the best where you are.

I beg you to consider all this as said in the confidence with which your letter inspires me, and with that sincere friendship which I bear you "in visceribus ejus cujus viscera pro amore nostro transfixa sunt." I pray Him to confirm you more and more in zeal for His Honour, and am most heartily yours, etc. etc.

XXIV.

To a Lady at Court.

MADAME,   ANNECY, *Sept.* 27, 1607.

It is unnecessary to make any excuse for writing to me; your letters are a consolation to me in the Lord, in Whom I love you sincerely. I see that

---

[1] 1 Cor. xv. 58.   [2] John xi. 40.

you are alarmed at the prospect of being established at the Castle, fearing lest you be deprived of your present opportunities of serving God, but you must not be discouraged. Even if you have less of external aid, so long as your wishes and resolutions to be wholly devoted to God remain stedfast, the Holy Spirit will help you with a hidden power, which will supply all deficiencies, as well as the religious exercises which you give up only to serve Him in another way.

I think your communions will be permitted; I do not see how that could be denied you. And you can surely have half an hour daily for mental prayer, in addition to the appointed prayers in which you join Madame; you may fairly be satisfied with that, supplying other services with frequent and fervent ejaculatory prayer, and uplifting of spirit to God; replacing sermons by diligent, attentive reading of some good book.

As for the rest, being under restraint and obliged to live with others, will give you a thousand opportunities for real mortification, and bending your will, which is no slight means of perfection, if you use it with gentleness and humility. These must be your cherished virtues—as specially set before you by our Lord—as also an exceeding purity of heart, and great sincerity in your words, especially in confession. No society, no trammels, can prevent your speaking often with our Lord, His Saints and Angels, or hinder your pacing the streets of the Heavenly Jerusalem, or from listening to the words preached within your heart by Jesus Christ and your guardian Angel, or from daily Spiritual

Communion. Do all this in a cheerful spirit, and for my part, accepting the confidence you have in me, I will pray His Divine Majesty to fill you with the grace of His Holy Spirit, and to make you more and more wholly His. Yours, etc.

XXV.

To Madame de Chantal.
On the Death of Jeanne de Sales.[1]

MY DEAR DAUGHTER, *Nov. 2, 1607.*

Is it not reasonable that God's Holy Will be done in the things we prize as in all else? But I must at once tell you that my dear mother has accepted this cup with a most Christian courage, and highly as I always thought of her goodness, it has gone beyond my expectations. On Sunday morning she sent for my brother the Canon, and having noticed the night before that he and my other brothers were all very sad, she began by saying, "I have been dreaming all night that my daughter Jeanne is dead. Tell me, I intreat you, is it so?" My brother had sent for me (for I was on a Visitation tour), and was waiting till I should come to tell our mother, but when so good an opening arose, he answered that it was true, and then he was unable to say any more. My dear mother only said, "God's Will be done," and then she wept freely for some time, but after a while,

---

[1] Mme. de Chantal had taken this young girl with her into France, at the earnest request of the Bishop and his mother, Mme. de Boisy. Jeanne died very shortly afterwards of a severe and rapid illness.

calling Nicole (her maid), she said, " I must get up and go to the chapel to pray for my dear child." And so she did. Not one word or look of impatience, nothing but giving God thanks, and resignation to His Will. I never saw a more tranquil sorrow ;— plenty of tears, but all flowing from mere tender grief, without a shadow of bitterness, and yet this was her very dear child. Have I not good reason to love such a mother?

Yesterday, being All Saints' Day, I was Confessor to all the family, and sealed my mother's heart against all sorrow with the Blessed Sacrament. Meanwhile she thanks you exceedingly for the care and motherly love which you showed to the little one that is gone, as much in truth as though God had willed that it should have saved her. All the family join in this expression ; they have all shown the utmost good feeling in this sorrow, especially de Boisy, and I love him all the more for it.

I know that you want to ask how I have borne the sorrow. Alas, my daughter, I am a mere man, and nothing better—and my heart has melted more than I should have looked for. In truth my mother's grief and yours have touched me ; I feared for you both. But as to the rest, Hail, Jesus ! I bow to God's Providence, Which does all things well, and disposes everything rightly. Surely it is well for the dear child to be " speedily taken away, lest that wickedness should alter her understanding, or deceit beguile her soul."[1] Some fruits are gathered earlier than others—let us leave God

[1] Wisd. iv. 11.

to reap His own harvest in His own field. He takes nothing out of season.

You may imagine, my dear daughter, how dearly I loved this child. I was her father in the Lord, for I baptized her fourteen years ago with my own hand. She was the first on whom I exercised my priestly office. I was her spiritual father, and I looked to making a very choice creature of her; I loved her too, because she was your charge. But amid all my earthliness, which feels this death so keenly, there is a sweet restful peace in God's Providence, which comforts me not a little.

Tell me how you have borne the trial. Has your magnet pointed all through to its guiding star, its God? What has your heart done? Have you given any scandal to those who have seen you in this affliction? Tell me honestly, my daughter. ... No, my dear daughter, we must not merely be willing to accept God's stroke, we must also be willing that He shall strike where He pleases. We must leave the choice to God, it is His right. David offered his life for Absalom, but it was for his soul's sake, and that is different. In temporal losses, let God strike what chord He will in our lute, the harmony can never be amiss. Lord Jesus, Thy Will be done in father, mother, child, in everything and everywhere; without a reserve, without a BUT, an IF, or a limit. Indeed I do not say that we may not wish and pray for their preservation, but as to saying to God, Take this, and leave that, my daughter, it must not be. Nor will we say so, by the help of His Grace.

I can see you, my dear daughter, with your

vigorous heart, loving and willing strongly; and I am glad that it is so, for withered, half-dead hearts are good for little. But you must make a special practice, at least once a week, of accepting and loving God's Will more heartily, more devotedly, in all things, supportable and insupportable. You will find much help in the "Spiritual Combat," which I have so often recommended to you.

It is an exalted lesson, my daughter, but God, for Whom we learn it, is very great. You have a father, brother, children, a spiritual father whom you love. They are all dear to you, and rightly so. But if God were to deprive you of them all, were it not enough that you would still have God? and if we had nothing save Him, is it not enough? The Son of God, our Dear Jesus, had scarcely that, when hanging on the Cross; through love and obedience He was forsaken of His Father. One with the Father, His Human Nature lost the sense of that Presence for a brief moment;—a trial never laid on any other soul, for none beside Jesus could endure it.

If God were to take all else from us, He will never deprive us of Himself so long as we desire Him. And, moreover, all our losses and separations are but for a moment. Surely we may well be patient. . . . .

As to Jeanne's burial let it be very simple. . . . You know that I like simplicity both in life and in death. . . . .

XXVI.

To Madame de Chantal. On Spiritual Hunger.

Jan. 24, 1608.

You say that you hunger more than usual after Holy Communion. There are two kinds of hunger —one which proceeds from a good digestion, the other from a perverted appetite. Humble yourself, and kindle your soul with the Holy Love of Jesus Christ Crucified, in order that you may be able to digest this celestial food; and, inasmuch as he who complains of hunger surely craves for bread, I would say, communicate this Lent on Wednesdays and Fridays, as well as on Lady Day and Sundays.

Do you know what I mean by rightly digesting this spiritual food? In the natural life a good digestion assimilates the food we eat, so that it invigorates the whole system. And even so those who spiritually digest the Blessed Sacrament, will find that it spreads its sacred influence throughout body and soul. Brain, heart, eyes, hands, tongue, ears, feet, all will be partakers of their Saviour. He makes all that is crooked straight, purifies all that is soiled, mortifies what is redundant, animates everything. The heart lives through Him, the brain thinks through Him, the eyes see, the tongue speaks, through Him. He is All in all, so that "it is not I that live, but Christ liveth in me." Oh, my daughter, when will that be? My God, when will it be?

Now I will tell you at what we must aim, though

indeed we must be content to attain it by very slow degrees. Let us be very humble, and communicate boldly ; little by little our spiritual digestion will learn to assimilate the celestial food. It is a great matter to be well supplied with good food; the digestion works better when such is the case. Let us desire our Lord only, and I trust it may be so with us.

XXVII.
To Madame de Chantal.

Feb. 5, 1608.

. . . . . WHY do you get up so very early in the morning? Indeed it is not well to enfeeble the mind by overworking the body. S. Francis used to tell his disciples this. I do it sometimes, it is true, but only out of sheer necessity, and I would have you make the same rule. My last letter was written at midnight, but I had not been up so late for long. People must not do that sort of thing without good cause, women especially ; one is good for very little all the next day.

It seems to me, my daughter, that your mind has been quite in an entanglement these first two or three days of Lent. I am not at all surprised, for your mind is so sensitive and so jealous over any resolution you have made, that whatever crosses the thread touches you deeply. I have told you a thousand times that it will not do to be so fastidious in our work. . . . I wish that the skin of your heart was rather tougher, and less accessible to flea-bites.

Faith, hope, and charity, which are very parts of ourself, are subject to gusts of wind, though they cannot be blown over; and why should we expect our resolution to be exempt from all such trials? I marvel, my daughter, whether you expect not only that your tree should be well and firmly planted, but that not a leaf should ever rustle in the breeze? Meet all such misgivings by definite acts of love of God and confidence in His Grace. And after all do not be afraid that these trifles will shake your resolution. These are vain fears. If Satan's minister, buffeting S. Paul with all manner of temptations, could not soil his purity, why should our good resolutions suffer from passing emotions? . . . .

March 7.

. . . . I will tell you what you do. When some trifle disturbs your mind, you are vexed because of it, and afraid. This fear weakens your mind, and makes it limp, sad and unsteady; it displeases you, and so begets another fear lest the first be wrong, and thus you get more and more confused. You fear being afraid, and then you are afraid of fearing; you are vexed at the vexation, and then you are vexed at having been vexed. I have seen people in the same way get into a passion, and then be angry because they had lost their temper! just like the circles on water when one throws in a stone, one spreading beyond the other without end. The remedy, my daughter, is not to be so susceptible. Put aside all these entanglements, do not dwell upon them, laugh at them, distract your attention by active employment.

XXVIII.
To a Lady. On Interior Peace.

MADAME, *April* 8, 1608.

I have received your first letter with special satisfaction, as a good beginning of the spiritual intercourse which is to exist between us, to the advancement of God's Kingdom in our hearts. May God help me to guide you wisely.

It is not possible that you should so quickly become mistress of your own soul, or control it thoroughly at the outset. Be content if from time to time you gain some little victory over your besetting sin. It is a duty to bear with other people, but first of all we must learn to bear with ourselves, and to have patience with our own imperfection.

My dear child, are we to expect to win inward peace without going through ordinary contradiction and difficulty? Now attend to these rules.

Every morning compose your soul for a tranquil day, and all through it be careful often to recall your resolution, and bring yourself back to it, so to say.

If something discomposes you, do not be upset, or troubled, but having discovered the fact, humble yourself gently before God, and try to bring your mind into a quiet attitude. Say to yourself, "Well, I have made a false step, now I must go more carefully and watchfully." Do this each time, however frequently you fall. When you are at peace use it profitably, making constant acts of meekness, and seeking to be calm even in the most trifling things. Our Lord says, "He that is faithful in that which is least is faithful also in much."[1] Above all, do not be discouraged; be patient; wait; strive to attain a calm, gentle spirit. God will uphold you with His Hand, and if He should let you stumble it will only be to show you that without Him you would fall altogether, and to teach you to hold His Hand the tighter. Farewell. May you be His wholly, solely, irrevocably.

XXIX.

To Madame Brulart.

June 25, 1608.

.... You speak of your impatience. Is it real impatience, or only natural repugnance? But as you call it impatience, I will take for granted that it is such, and till I can talk with you more fully on the subject, I will tell you freely that, judging from your letters, more than from the little conversation we have had, yours seems to me a heart which clings too vehemently to the objects it desires.

I know that your chief desire is the Love of God, and to attain that we must make use of means, exercises, practices. Now I think that you cling vehemently to such means as are to your taste, and would have everything yield before them, so that you are uneasy when anything hinders or disturbs you. The remedy is to endeavour to rid yourself

[1] Luke xvi. 10.

of this restless feeling; God would have you serve Him as you are, in actions suitable to the position to which He has called you; and while endeavouring to perform these, you must strive to accept both your actual position and the duties attached to it, for His Sake Who has called you to them. But, my dear sister, it is not enough merely to give a passing thought to this; it must abide in your heart, and be graven there by recollectedness and meditation. Believe me, all that is opposed to this habit of mind is mere self-will.

As to Holy Communion, I approve of your wish to receive it frequently, so long as your wish is duly submitted to your confessor, who is the best judge of the present state of your soul.

The fluctuations of your mind, both in and out of prayer, now earnest, then languid; one while attracted to the world, and the next disgusted at it;—all these are God's way of rendering you very humble and gentle, for you see what you are of yourself, and what under the guidance of His Hand; but there is nothing in this which ought to discourage you. . . . . I commend you continually to our Dear Lord; your progress is very near my heart, and I will remember you at the Holy Sacrifice.

XXX.

To a Lady in Sickness.

Sept. 29, 1608.

I UNDERSTAND, my dear daughter, that your illness

is more suffering than dangerous, and I know that such sickness is apt to make people disobedient to their doctors, so I wish to tell you that you must in no way refuse to take anything prescribed for you, whether rest, medicine, food, or recreation. You can accept all these in a spirit of obedience and resignation, which will be most acceptable to our Lord, for all these are crosses and mortifications, which you have neither chosen nor sought. God has laid them on you with His Own Holy Hand: receive them, embrace them, love them; in truth they carry an atmosphere of grace with them. Farewell, my dear daughter. I feel tenderly for you, and would say more had I time, for I desire exceedingly that you may be faithful through all these vexatious little trials, and that in small and great things alike you may always say, Hail Jesus! Yours, etc.

XXXI.

To Madame de Chantal.

ANNECY, *Sept.* 29, 1608.

.... YOUR wishes as to this life are good, provided they do not become more urgent than their object warrants. It is right, no doubt, to wish for the life of him whom God has sent as your guide. But, my dear daughter, God has a hundred, I would rather say endless, means of guiding you, apart from me. It is He Who leads you like a sheep of His pasture. I intreat you to keep your heart fixed on high; bind it irrevocably to the Sovereign

Will of our loving God and Father. May He, and He only, be ever obeyed by us. Nevertheless, I shall take care of my health as I promised. . . . . My dear daughter, so long as God wills that you remain in the world, I would have you remain there willingly and cheerfully. Many people quit the world without forsaking self: they really seek to indulge their taste for rest and quiet, and such persons grow very restless, for the self-love which rules them is ill-regulated, eager, and turbulent. Let us not be like these: let us forsake the world in order to serve God, to follow Him, to love Him; and in the same spirit, so long as He wills us to serve Him in the world, let us abide in it heartily and cheerfully. We do nothing save to serve Him, and we are satisfied to be wherever we can do that. Then be at rest, my daughter, and do that well for which you are dwelling in the world: do it heartily, and believe that you are more acceptable to God while so doing, than you could be by leaving the world of your own will. . . . . Be at rest, keep the Crucified Saviour in the midst of your heart. Not long ago I saw a girl carrying a pail of water on her head, into the midst of which she put a piece of wood. I asked why she did that, and she answered that the wood steadied her pail, and prevented the water from being spilt. Even so, I said to myself, we must carry the Cross in the midst of our heart to hinder it from swaying to and fro, and from overflowing with the anxieties and disturbances of this restless life. I like to tell you my stray cogitations.

XXXII.

To Madame de Mienury. Against a Troubled Mind.

MADAME, *Nov.* 4, 1608.

Write to me as often as you please, in perfect confidence, and without ceremony; such freedom befits our friendship. I beg you to despise all these foolish, self-conceited thoughts which flit across your mind concerning your good deeds; they are really no more than troublesome flies, which can do no worse than tease you. Do not spend time in examining whether or no you have consented to them; go on with your work as though such things were no concern of yours.

Do not try to force yourself to pity or compassion when meditating on the Passion; it is enough if, in our meditations, we form good resolutions as to our amendment of life, and stedfastness in the Love of God, without sighs and tears, or conscious tenderness. There is a wide difference between that sweetness of devotion which we desire because it is agreeable, and that resolution of heart which we ought to desire because it renders us true servants of God. Again, do not take any notice of the impure thought which troubles you. Only say to our Lord in your heart, "Lord, Thou knowest that I honour Thee above all things, I am Thine," and go on without arguing against the temptation.

Do not be disturbed at the faultiness of your self-examination. It cannot be very great when you have a true desire to purify your conscience, and it is not well to torture the soul while conscious of the wish to be faithful to God. When your ordinary Confessor is out of reach, do not fail to go to some one else, thinking only of God, and not of the man who confesses and absolves you. Continue to go frequently to confession, and may God ever dwell in your heart. In Him I am, madame, yours, etc.

XXXIII.
To a Married Lady. On Quietness of Mind.

MADAME, *Jan.* 20, 1609.

Doubtless you would be able to explain yourself much better verbally than in writing, but till such time as God enables you to do so, we must use such means as are available. All this heaviness and languid dulness cannot exist without depressing you, but so long as your mind and will are firmly resolved to serve God, you need not fear. Such troubles arise from natural imperfection, and are rather diseases than sin, or spiritual faults. All the same you must rouse yourself, and strive to be as brave and as vigorous as you can possibly be.

Yes, indeed, my daughter, death is a very hideous thing, but the life beyond it, which God of His Mercy gives us, is yet more precious, and we must not be afraid; for wretched as we are, His Mercy is far greater than our weakness, and He has promised it to those who seek to love Him, and whose hope is in Him. When Cardinal Borromeo was at the point of death, he asked for a picture of the Dead Christ, that the sting of death might be taken away in remembering how Christ died for him. The best remedy against your fear of death is meditation on Him Who is our life : never think of one without going on to think of the other. My dear child, do not scrutinize so closely whether you are doing much or little, ill or well, so long as what you do is not sinful, and that you are heartily seeking to do everything for God. Try as far as you can to do everything well, but when it is done do not think about it ; try rather to think of what is to be done next. Go on simply in the Lord's way, and do not torment yourself. We ought to hate our faults, but with a quiet, calm hatred, not pettishly and anxiously. We must learn to look patiently at them, and win through them the grace of self-abnegation and humility. For want of this, my child, and through looking at your imperfections in an unreal way, they become more subtle, and do but increase upon you. Nothing so causes our tares to prosper as disquietude and impetuosity in striving to uproot them.

There is a great temptation to be disgusted at the world, when we are constrained to dwell in it ; but God's Providence is wiser than we are. We fancy that if we changed our position, we should do better : possibly, if we changed ourselves ! But I am a stedfast foe to all such useless, dangerous, evil desires : even when what we wish for is good in itself, the desire is evil, since God denies us that particular good thing, and chooses rather to prove us in some other way. He wills to speak to us as to Moses, from a burning bush, and we would fain hear Him in a still small Voice, as when He spoke to the Prophet Elijah. May His Goodness ever keep you, my child; be only constant and courageous, and rejoice in that He has given you the will to be wholly His. In Him I am, yours, etc.

XXXIV.
To a Lady in Sickness.

May 3, 1609.

. . . . . As to meditation, the doctors are right: while you are feeble, you must often abstain from it; but to make up for this, you must redouble your ejaculatory prayers, and offer all to God, by perfect acquiescence in His good pleasure; He in no way separates you from Himself, by letting you be thus hindered in meditation; He designs rather to unite you more firmly to Him by the practice of a holy, calm resignation.

What does it matter to us whether we are with God in one way or another? Of a truth, since we seek Him Only, and find Him no less in mortification than in prayer, especially when He lays sickness upon us, we ought to be equally satisfied with either. Ejaculatory prayer, and the upward glances of the soul, are a most true and continual worship, and the endurance of pain is a most worthy offering to Him Who saved us through suffering. Let some good book be read to you, from time to time, that will supply the lack of meditation in a manner. As to Communion, go on as usual. . . . . Do not be disturbed because you cannot serve God in your own way; you serve Him, while accepting your infirmities, in His Own way, which is far better. May He be ever Blessed and Glorified. Yours, etc.

XXXV.
To his Sister, Madame de Cornillon.
On the Death of their Youngest Sister, Jeanne de Sales.

MY DEAR SISTER AND DAUGHTER, *May 15, 1609.*

Let your religion be that of joy. How happy you will be if you can follow this out! Our dear little sister, who has gone hence so suddenly and in so Christianlike a way, has rekindled my soul to the love of that Sovereign Good, to Which everything in this brief life should be referred. Let us love one another fondly, my dear sister, and together seek the Saviour of our souls, through Whom Alone we can find happiness. I am full of hope that you will go on serving, obeying, and adoring our Dear Lord more and more faithfully, and I can wish you no greater blessing.

The many troubles in your household (of which my good brother told me the other day) will tend to your edification, if you strive to bear them all in gentleness, patience, and kindness. Keep this ever before you, and remember constantly that God's Loving Eye is upon you amid all these little worries and vexations, watching whether you take them as He would desire. Offer up all such occasions to Him, and if sometimes you are put out, and give way to impatience, do not be discouraged, but make haste to regain your lost composure. Bless those that afflict you, and then, dear child, God will bless you. I pray Him most heartily so to do, my beloved sister and very dear child, to whom I am most entirely devoted.

XXXVI.

To a Lady. On the Distractions of a Busy Life.

May 19, 1609.

I REMEMBER that you told me how heavily your various affairs pressed upon you ; and I told you that it was a good way of acquiring real and substantial virtue. A multiplicity of business is a real martyrdom; just as sometimes travellers in summer suffer more from the teasing flies which buzz around than from the journey's toil, so a multitude of disconnected affairs is more wearing than troubles which might be really heavier.

You greatly need patience ; and I hope God will grant it you if you diligently ask it of Him, and strive to cultivate it faithfully. Make special application of some point in your daily meditation to this subject, and then be persistent in summoning up your patience all through the day, as often as you feel that it is wavering. Never let slip any occasion, however trifling, of practising the grace of gentleness towards those around. . . . Do not trust to your own industry for success, but lean wholly on God's Help ; rest in Him, believing that He will do whatever is best for you so long as you, on your part, are quietly in earnest and gently diligent. I say this because impetuous activity hurts both our business and our soul, and is really a hindrance.

Dear madame, we shall soon be in Eternity, and then we shall see how trifling all the things of this world are, and how little it mattered what became of them ! Yet now we are as eager over them as if they were all-important ! When we were children, we used to be eager in collecting bits of wood and tile and mud, to build our play-houses; and if they were knocked down, we were sorely grieved, even to tears ; now we know that this was all child's play. Even so, when we reach Heaven, we shall see that all these earthly interests were but child's play too. . . . .

I do not want to set aside our care for the trifling details of this world ; God gives them to us to train us during our earthly life ; I would only moderate the eagerness of such care. Let us pursue our child's play while we are children, but do not let us be engrossed by it, and if our baby houses and castles fall to pieces, do not let us grieve overmuch. When the evening comes, and we must needs seek shelter, we shall not be able to find it in any such makebelieve dwellings, but only in our Father's Home. . . . Be diligent in your business, but bear in mind that the most serious business of all is your salvation, and your progress in true devotion.

Be patient with every one, but above all with yourself. I mean, do not be disturbed because of your imperfections, and always rise up bravely from a fall. I am glad that you make a daily new beginning; there is no better means of progress in the spiritual life than to be continually beginning afresh, and never to think that we have done enough.

Commend me to God's Mercy, as I pray Him that you may abound in His Holy Love. Amen.

Yours, etc.

XXXVII.

To Madame de Chantal. On the Presence of God.

Jan. 16, 16.0.

. . . . . To abide in the Presence of God, and to place oneself in that Presence, are, it seems to me, different things. In order to place oneself before the Presence of God, it is needful to call the soul from every other object, and fix the attention solely on Him as Present; but having once placed oneself there, one can abide in It, while making acts either of the understanding or the will; while gazing upon Him, or upon other objects for Love of Him; or while simply speaking to Him, even while merely remaining where He has placed us, as a statue abides in its niche. And if we can add to this simple abiding some consciousness of belonging to God, and of Him as our All, we ought to be most thankful for such grace.

Suppose a statue in its niche capable of speech, and ask of it, "Wherefore art thou here?" it would reply, "Because my master, the sculptor, placed me here." "Wherefore art thou motionless?" "Because he willed me so to be." "Of what use art thou? What does it profit thee to be there?" "I am not here for my own sake, but solely because it is the will of my master." "But thou canst not even see!" "No, but he sees me, and chooses that I should abide here." "Wouldst not thou fain have the power to move, and go nearer thy master?" "Not so, unless he willed it." "Hast thou no wishes?" "None, for I am where my master placed me, and his pleasure is the sole object of my existence."

My daughter, what better prayer, what better way of abiding in God's Presence, than to give oneself up to His Will and Pleasure? I think Magdalene was as a statue in its niche when she sat motionless, silent, maybe without even gazing upon Him, at her Saviour's Feet, listening to His gracious words when He spoke, no less attentive and earnest when He was silent. A little child asleep on the breast of its sleeping mother is in the best and happiest of all conditions, although it does not speak to her, or she to it.

Happy indeed are we when we seek to love our Lord. Let us love Him, without striving to inquire too inquisitively what we are doing for love's sake, so long as we know that our aim is to do all things in and through that Love. I believe that we may abide in God's Presence even while we sleep; we fall asleep in His Sight, because it is His Will; He lays us on our bed, as a statue in its niche, and when we awake we shall find Him there yet. He has never left us, or we Him; we have been all the time in His Presence, although our eyes were closed.

XXXVIII.

To Madame de Chantal. On his Mother's Death.

MY DEAR DAUGHTER, *March 11, 1610.*

Must we not in all things and everywhere adore God's Holy Providence, every act of which is loving, gracious, and blessed? And even so now that it has pleased Him to call from out this miserable life our most excellent and dear Mother, taking her, as I trust, to be ever with Him, at His Own Right Hand. Let us, my beloved daughter, confess that " He is gracious and His Mercy endureth for ever :" "Righteous art Thou, O Lord, and true is Thy judgment." His Will is "good, acceptable, and perfect."[1]

And yet for my part, daughter, I own that I feel this parting deeply. I must needs confess my own weakness, while I confess the Goodness of God; nevertheless, it has been a very peaceful, though a keen grief—I can say with David, "I became dumb, and opened not my mouth, for it was Thy doing." But for that I should doubtless have cried out beneath the blow, but how could I presume to murmur beneath the Fatherly Hand Which has taught me to love Its dealing from my youth upwards?

Probably you would like to hear how that excellent woman ended her life. I will tell you,—you, to whom I have given her place in my daily memorial at mass, without taking away the place

[1] Rom. xii. 2.

you already filled. My dear mother came here this winter, and during a month's stay she made a general review of her soul, renewed her aspirations with most earnest love, and went away full of affection for me, saying that she had got more comfort from me than ever before. She continued in this happy mind until Ash Wednesday, when she went to the parish church at Thorens, where she made her confession and communion most devoutly, and heard three masses and vespers. When she went to bed, my mother was not able to sleep, and she bade her maid read three chapters of the "Vie Dévote" to her, in order to keep up devout thoughts in her mind, noting the "*protestation*," which she meant to make the next morning. But God accepted the will for the deed, and ordered it otherwise, for the next morning she rose, but while dressing she suddenly fell as one dead.

My poor brother, your son,[1] was still asleep, but he was summoned, and hastened to our mother. He had her lifted up, and tried all sorts of remedies, so that she was roused, and tried to speak, but almost unintelligibly.

I was sent for, and went at once with the doctor and apothecary, who found her paralysed on one side, and very lethargic; but it was easy to rouse her, and when roused she had full possession of her mind, as was proved by the words she strove to say, and the motion of the hand that was not struck ; for she spoke most clearly of God and her soul, and felt about for her crucifix, (she was unable

---

[1] Bernard de Thorens, who had married Madame de Chantal's eldest daughter.

to see,) and kissed it. She took nothing without making the sign of the cross, and thus she received Extreme Unction.

When I arrived, although she was blind and half asleep, she caressed me tenderly, and said, " This is my son and my father ;"[1] and kissed me, putting her arm round my neck, first kissing my hand. My mother continued in this state for nearly two days and a half, after which we could not really rouse her at all, and on March 1st she gave up her soul gently and peacefully to our Lord; her countenance was more lovely than ever before, and she was the most beautiful of any dead I ever saw. I must tell you that I had courage to give her the last blessing, and I closed her eyes and gave her a last kiss of peace directly after she departed ; after which my heart swelled within me, and I wept over this dear mother more than I have ever wept since I took Holy Orders, but, thank God, it was without any bitterness of spirit. This is all that took place. By the way, I must not forget to speak of the admirable goodness of your son, who gratified me exceedingly by the care and devotion he showed to our mother. I should have been struck with it, even if he were not my brother. I think he is greatly improved, both as to worldly matters, and above all, those which concern the soul.

[1] " C'est mon fils et mon père, celui-ci."

XXXIX.

To a Lady, involved in Legal Affairs.

MY VERY DEAR DAUGHTER, *Sept. 19, 1610.*

I have heard of all your troubles, and I have commended them to our Lord, asking Him to bless them with that sacred benediction which He gives His chosen servants, so that they may all turn to the sanctification of His Holy Name, and of your soul.

I must confess that to my mind, of all afflictions and evils, lawsuits excite my pity most, because they are so dangerous to the soul. How many people I have seen bearing the sting of sickness or the loss of friends patiently, who yet have lost their inward peace under the harass of legal affairs or lawsuits! The reason, or more correctly the cause, is this;—we are not ready to believe that God makes use of such a trial to prove us, because it seems to come direct from the hand of man; and while we dare not kick against an All-wise, All-good Providence, we do kick against the fellow-creatures who trouble us, and are wroth with them, not without great risk of a loss of charity, the only loss we need really fear in this life. Well now, my dear daughter, when can we better testify our faithfulness to our Saviour than on such occasions? What fitter time for bridling heart, judgment, and tongue, than when we are toiling along such crooked paths, and going so near the edge of a precipice? For God's Sake, my dear daughter, do not let slip a time so eminently calculated for spiritual progress without laying in a fresh store of patience, humility, gentleness, and love of abjection. Remember that our Lord never spoke one word against those that condemned Him; He did not judge them; but, although unjustly condemned, He was gentle as a lamb, and His only revenge was prayer for His enemies. But we judge every one,—our antagonists and our judges;—we bristle with complaints and reproaches. Believe me, dear daughter, we must be stedfast in loving our neighbour — I say this with my whole heart, without any consideration as to your individual opponents or anything concerning the matter, caring for nothing save your perfection. But I must stop, nor did I mean to say so much. You have God always with you, if you will. Does not that make you rich enough? May His Will be your rest, His Cross your glory.

I am, ever yours, etc.

XL.

To a Gentleman, going to the Court.

SIR, *Dec.* 8, 1610.

So at last your sails are spread, and you are about to enter the high seas of the world and the Court. May God vouchsafe to guide and keep you in His Holy Hand!

I am not so timid as some people, nor do I hold this manner of life to be the most dangerous for well-trained souls who are bold and brave. There are but two great perils to dread;—vanity, which is the ruin of sensual, indolent, self-indulgent, effeminate characters; and ambition, which destroys presumptuous, audacious minds.

Vanity implies a lack of courage: the vain man has not strength to seek after real, well-earned approbation, and so he is satisfied with what is unreal and hollow; whereas ambition is courage carried to excess, which goes headlong in pursuit of glory and honour, regardless of all reason and rule.

So vanity leads a man into the frivolities which are acceptable to foolish women and other weak persons, but which are despicable in the eyes of nobler spirits; and ambition makes him grasp at honours which he has not earned—it makes him put too high a price upon himself, and upon the merits of his forefathers, on which he strives to build his fabric.

Now, dear sir, as you wish for my advice, I would say, strengthen your mind against all this, by spiritual and sacred food, which will enable you to resist both vanity and ambition.

Be stedfast in frequent communion; believe me, nothing will so tend to confirm you in the right way; and for the better use thereof, place yourself under the guidance of some good confessor, and ask him to call you to account for any neglect you may ever fall into in this matter. Let your confessions be humble, and made with a real and express purpose of amendment.

I intreat you never to omit asking upon your knees for the Help of our Lord before you go forth in the morning, and in like manner ask forgiveness of all your faults before going to bed at night.

Especially avoid bad books;—let nothing induce you to be led away by the writings which captivate certain weak minds by their vain subtleties; such works I mean as those of Rabelais and others, who affect to throw doubt and contempt on everything, and scoff at all our venerable doctrines and precepts. Keep books of a solid character, especially Christian and spiritual works, at hand, and refresh yourself with them from time to time.

I would have you cultivate a gentle, sincere courtesy, which offends no one, but wins everybody;—being more ready to seek love than honour;—never jesting at the expense of another, never sarcastic, never affronting or being affronted.

Take care not to get involved in flirtations, and do not allow your affections to carry you away against judgment and reason. Once let feeling get the lead, and it is apt to make a sorry slave of the judgment, and leads to results you are sure to repent of.

In manner, appearance, conversation, and all such things, I would have you make an open profession that you purpose to live virtuously, wisely, and stedfastly, as a Christian should. Virtuously, so that no one may attempt to lead you into any debauchery;—wisely, without any exaggerated outward demonstrations; steadily, because unless you show that you have a stedfast will and even mind, evil men will seek to tempt and delude you; and as a Christian should, because some men profess a philosophic virtue, which is but a mere phantom at best. We who know that we can have no possible goodness save through the grace of our

Lord, are bound to live by the rules of piety and religion, or else all our virtue will prove a shadow and an empty imagination.

It is most important that you should let it be known from the first what you mean to be; there should be no doubt about the matter; and it will help you much if you have some like-minded friends, with whom to exchange counsel and sympathy. Unquestionably the intercourse of right-minded people tends not a little to keep us straight.

I think you will easily find some worthy friend among the Jesuits, the Feuillants, or in some other not necessarily monastic quarter, who will be glad if you occasionally seek him to repose yourself, and take breath, so to say, in a spiritual sense.

There is one special point on which you must permit me to touch. I dread, sir, lest you should again take to gaming. It would be an exceeding evil, and in a few days would lead to complete dissipation, withering the bloom of your good desires. It is but an idle pursuit, at best . . . . not to dwell upon the angry passions, the dishonesty, and despair, from which few gamblers are exempted. I would wish for you a vigorous heart, and a disposition to avoid bodily ease, whether in food, sleep, or anything else. A really noble mind despises mere luxury and self-indulgence. But I touch upon this point because our Lord says, "They that wear soft clothing are in kings' houses;" not as meaning that all dwelling there must be luxurious, but that many found in such quarters are so disposed. Of course I am not alluding to the exterior, but to the interior life. In short, I would have you keep the body in hand, and make it sometimes forego pleasant things, and endure hardness and abstinence, so that the higher nature may assert and maintain its superiority over that which is lower.

Imagine for a while that you are a courtier of Saint Louis (your little King may be considered holy in his innocence[1]), he liked those about him to be brave, courageous, generous, cheerful, courteous, open-hearted, but, above all, he would have them to be good Christians. If you had been about S. Louis, you would have seen him laugh merrily, speak boldly, maintain a brave outward show of royal dignity, like King Solomon, and the next moment he would be ministering to the sick and poor in hospital. In short, he combined civil and religious virtue, majesty and humility. And this is what you must aim at; to be no whit less brave because you are a Christian, no whit less a Christian because you are brave. But this implies being a very earnest Christian, that is, devout, pious, spiritually minded; as S. Paul says, "He that is spiritual judgeth all things,"[2] *i.e.* he knows the right time and place for a due practice of every virtue.

Often call to mind the thought that in this world we hang between Heaven and hell, and that our last step will land us in one or the other. Remember, too, that we do not know when we shall make that last step, and that he who would make it well must needs strive to make every step in the fear of God.

O blessed, endless Eternity! and blessed are they that rightly ponder it! All that we do here for a brief uncertain time is but as child's play. It

[1] Louis XIII., then not nine years old.   [2] 1 Cor. ii. 15.

were less than worthless, save that it is the passage to Eternity. But for that reason we must give good heed to our time and its use here, in order through a right use thereof to win our lasting good.

Think of me, I pray you, as wholly yours, as in truth I am in our Lord, wishing you all happiness in this world, but still more in the next. May God bless you, and have you in His Holy keeping.

To end as I began—you are taking to the high seas of life, but do not change your captain, your sails, your anchor, or your breeze. Ever keep Jesus for your Captain, His Cross for your mast, whereon to spread the sails of good resolutions; let your anchor be a deep unfailing trust in Him, and then—go gaily on.. May the propitious breeze of heavenly grace fill your sails more and more, and carry you safely and happily into the haven of a blessed Eternity. Such is the very hearty wish of, dear sir, yours, etc.

XLI.

To a Married Lady.

April 3, 1611.

.... LIVE wholly to God, my dear daughter, and since you are obliged to be much in society, strive to make yourself useful to your neighbours by the means I have often set before you. Do not imagine that our Lord is any farther from you amid the weariness and temptation of your present position, than He would be were you enjoying a calm and peaceful life. No, my very dear daughter, it is not a peaceful life which brings Him into our hearts—

but the fidelity with which we love Him; not the conscious sense we have of His sweetness, but our ready consent to His most Holy Will. It is better that It should be fulfilled in us, than that we should fulfil our will in Him.

XLII.

To a Married Lady.

April 8, 1611.

.... N. was quite right to go to the Carmelites, for it seemed to be for God's Glory, but since the Superiors send her away, she must believe that though God accepts her attempt, He wills her to serve Him elsewhere, and she will do wrong if, after the first disappointment, she does not become calm and resolve firmly to live to God in some other way. There are various roads to Heaven, and so long as the fear of God is our guide, it matters not much by which we travel, although some may be more desirable than others, when we have a choice. I do not see why you should be distressed about this matter. You placed the poor girl in that holy place of refuge out of charity, but if it is not God's Will that she should abide there, it is not your fault. You must acquiesce in what His Sovereign Providence orders. He is not obliged to consult our wants and wishes. God will provide a home for N——, in which she can serve Him, either through consolation or tribulation, as He sees fit. ... The Carmelites are quite right not to receive a person who is not calculated to observe their rule.

My dear daughter, the little annoyance to which you have given way on this occasion ought to be a warning to you that self-love is alive and strong in your heart, and that you must keep a careful watch lest it become your master. May God in His Goodness never let it be so, but may He ever reign in us, over us, against us, and for us, with the strength of His Holy Love.

XLIII.

To Madame de Chantal.
When absent on Family Business.

THONON, *Sept.* 10, 1611.

. . . . I INTREAT you, my dear daughter, keep close to Jesus Christ, and Our Lady, and your good angel, in all your business, so that the multiplicity of affairs may not overwhelm you, or their difficulty trouble you. Attend to them one by one, as best you can, and to do this, give your mind steadily to your work, though quietly and gently. If God vouchsafes you success, we will bless Him; if He does not do so, we will equally bless Him. It is enough that you sincerely do your very best; neither our Lord nor common sense will call us to account for results or events; we are only responsible for steady, honest diligence in our work; that does depend upon ourselves, success does not.

God will bless your good intention in this journey and in your undertaking to order matters well and wisely for your son; He will reward you either by a successful end to your labour, or by a holy humility and resignation under disappointment.

XLIV.
To a Lady. On withheld Communion.

Feb. 11, 1612.

.... You are right in obeying your confessor, whether he deprives you of the comfort of frequent communion in order to test you, or whether he does so because you are not sufficiently earnest in correcting your impatience. I should be inclined to think that he has both objects in view; and you must persevere in patience so long as he sees fit thus to deprive you, feeling sure that he does nothing without due consideration. If you obey humbly, one communion will be really more profitable to you than several made in a different spirit; food is never so nourishing as when we are hungry with exercise, and the exercise of mortifying impatience will invigorate your spiritual digestion.

But be gentle in your humiliation, and often make an act of love thereof. Put yourself a while in the attitude of the Canaanitish woman, unworthy to eat the "children's bread," and say, "Yes, Lord, I am truly as a dog—I, who am prone to wound my neighbours by my impatient words. But even as the dogs gather up crumbs under their masters' table, so I ask of Thee, dear Lord, if not Thy Blessed Body, at least the blessing Its Presence confers on those who come near in loving reverence." Some such mind you should have, my dear child, on those days when you would have communicated if you were allowed. . . .

Your feeling of being wholly God's is not an illusion, but you must be rather more diligent in the practice of virtue, and specially in those points where you are most deficient; warm feelings in prayer are good, but it will not do to rest in them to the neglect of good deeds, or the mortification of our passions.

XLV.

To Madame de Chantal. On Spiritual Dryness.

March 28, 1612.

. . . . Now as to the inward trial, about which you write. It is a downright insensibility, which deprives you, not only of consolation and inspiration, but even of faith, hope, and charity, you say.

Nevertheless you have these really and fully, only you do not enjoy them; you are as a child whose guardian deprives him of the disposal of his property, so that, while really his, he has no power over it, but, as S. Paul says, "differeth nothing from a servant, though he be lord of all."[1] Even so, dear daughter, God withholds from you the disposal of your faith, love, and hope, and does not allow you to enjoy them, only to use them when actually necessary. But in truth, my daughter, we are very happy to be thus held and restrained by our Heavenly Guardian! and we may well adore His Loving Providence, and cast ourselves unques-

[1] Gal. iv. 1.

tioning into His Arms. No, Lord, I ask no conscious enjoyment of Thy gifts, save that I may be able to say in all honesty, though without sweetness or feeling, that I would die sooner than give up faith, hope, and love. If it be Thy good pleasure, Lord, that I should have no enjoyment in exercising the graces Thou givest me, I would heartily acquiesce, however much my will may be thwarted thereby.

The highest point of holy religion is to be content with bare dry acts, performed solely by the superior will ; just as it would be the highest degree of abstinence to be content to eat, if not with positive disgust, at all events without any taste or relish.

You have clearly explained your trial, and there is no remedy but that which you already use, making frequent protest to our Lord that you are willing to bear a living death, and to take your spiritual food without taste, feeling, or consciousness.

That Dear Lord would have us so entirely His, as that nothing should remain ours, but that we may give ourselves up wholly, unreservedly to His Providence. Let us abide patiently amid the darkness of the Passion. Amid the darkness ;— for bethink you that when Our Lady and S. John were at the foot of the Cross, surrounded by the marvellous darkness which came on, they could neither see nor hear the Saviour ; nothing was left them but distress and bitterness ; and though they had full faith, it too was plunged in deep darkness, inasmuch as they shared in the Saviour's desolation when He was forsaken of His Father. Happy we, who are the slaves of that God Who became a slave for us! It is time for my sermon.—Farewell.

XLVI.
To a Young Lady, who wished to join the Order of the Visitation.

MADEMOISELLE, ANNECY, *July* 3, 1612.

You are inclined to believe that your wish to leave the world is not according to God's Will, because it does not coincide with that of certain of those who have a right to guide you in worldly matters. If you mean those persons to whom God has given a right and authority to guide your soul, you are right to obey; but if you mean only those whose authority applies but to domestic and temporal questions, you deceive yourself. If friends and relations were always to be consulted in spiritual matters, we should find but few people ready to seek Christian perfection.

Secondly, as you continue to wish to leave the world, in spite of worldly attractions and hindrances, it may be received as a sign that God wills you to do so. . . . . And I think you are wrong in thinking that the hindrances which arise prove it to be His Will to keep you back. . . . . If your wishes have been too eager, you must rather correct and restrain than give them up. I have been told that you have offered half your fortune to this house. But this is too much, considering that you have a sister burdened with a large family, to whose needs, in due course of love, you ought rather to apply your property. Now repair this error, and bring to the Order only such a portion of your money as is needful for your support, giving the rest to whomsoever you will, and even reserving that which you bring for their benefit after your death. You may thus set things right, without altering your intention, and everything will go on cheerfully, quietly, and religiously.

Finally, be brave and come to an absolute decision ; for although these weaknesses and uncertainties are not sinful, they certainly are great hindrances to all progress, and to true comfort of soul.

I have told you my opinion plainly, hoping that you will kindly not be annoyed at my doing so. May God give you all the blessings I wish for you, as well as the sweet co-operation of heart which He demands. In Him I am yours, Mademoiselle, in all sincerity, etc.

XLVII.
To a Lady under Trial.

MADAME, *July 20, 1612.*

Your letters afford me a special satisfaction, for I see that amid many hindrances and contradictions you hold fast the will to serve our Lord, and, in truth, if you remain faithful amid all these vexations, your consolation will much more abound, in proportion to the greatness of your difficulties. I think of you when you least imagine it, and watch you with tender compassion, knowing amidst how many collisions and worries you live, which might easily distract you from that holy devotion to God at which you aim. Consequently I never cease to commend your needs to His Divine Goodness, but neither would I fail in urging you to turn these trials to your spiritual progress.

There is no reward without victory, no victory without war. Take courage, and turn your troubles, which are without remedy, into material for spiritual progress. Often turn to our Lord, Who is watching you, poor frail little being as you are, amid your labours and distractions. He sends you help, and blesses your affliction. This thought should enable you to bear your troubles patiently and gently, for love of Him Who only allows you to be tried for your own good. Raise your heart continually to God, seek His Aid, and let the foundation-stone of your consolation be your happiness in being His. All vexations and annoyances will be comparatively unimportant while you know that you have such a Friend, such a Stay, such a Refuge. May God be ever in your heart, my very dear daughter.

XLVIII.

To a Lady living in the World.

Sept. 29, 1612.

YOU should proportion the length of your prayers to the quantity of your engagements : and as it has pleased our Lord to place you in a way of life which involves you in perpetual distractions, you must accustom yourself to make short devotions, which should become so habitual as never to be given up save under the greatest necessity. In the morning you can always kneel down in adoration, make the sign of the Cross, and ask God's Blessing upon the day just beginning. If you can, you will hear mass devoutly; in the evening, before supper, or thereabouts, you can easily make time for a few fervent prayers, casting yourself before your Lord; you can scarcely be so fettered with engagements as not to be able to ensure such a brief interval of leisure. And at night, when you go to bed, wherever you are, or whatever you may be doing, you can make a general review of what you have done through the day, ending by kneeling down to ask God's forgiveness for the faults you have committed, and asking Him to watch over you and bless you, all of which you may do briefly. But above all, I would have you turn your heart to God on every occasion, all through the day, in ejaculations of faith and love.

As to your mental anxieties, my dear daughter, you will not find it hard to discriminate between such as can be remedied and such as cannot. Where a remedy is possible you should try to use it, gently and calmly; where the evil is irremediable strive to bear it as a mortification laid on you by our Lord in order to make you more wholly His. Beware of giving way to complaints; rather train your heart in patient suffering; and if you have been overtaken by any sudden outbreak of impatience, so soon as you become aware of it strive to regain peace and composure. Believe me, dear daughter, God loves those souls who are tossed by the storms and tempests of the world, so long as they accept everything from His Hand, and, like valiant warriors, strive to maintain an unshaken fidelity to their trust amid it all.

I must stop, and go to try and settle a hot dispute which should be hindered. I am, most heartily, yours, etc.

XLIX.

To a Lady. On the Death of her Child.

Jan. 3, 1613.

I ASSURE you, my dear daughter, your affliction has touched me very deeply, for I know how severely you will have felt it; the rather that our earthly minds, unable to see the end and object of trials, receive them less as what they really are, than as what we feel them to be for the moment.

And now, my dear daughter, your little son is safe; he has attained eternal salvation, he has for ever escaped the danger of losing that to which so many are exposed. Might he not have grown up in evil ways? Is it not possible that, like so many other mothers, you might have had great cause for anxiety in his future life? But now God has taken him out of all peril, giving him victory before the battle, and granting him grace to reap the harvest without bearing the toil and heat of the day.

Will you not grant, my dear daughter, that your prayers and desires are fulfilled? You prayed for your child, asking that he might remain with you in this vale of misery, and our Lord, Who knows what we really need better than we ourselves, has heard and granted your prayers, but at the cost of that earthly happiness for which you longed.

Indeed I approve of the confession you make, that it is by reason of your sins that your child is taken from you, as a proof of humility, but, nevertheless, I do not think that it is true. No, dear daughter, this trial is not sent to chastise you, but out of love to the little one whom God has so early called and saved. You feel all the sorrow and loss, but to the child it is an infinite gain; and for your temporal grief he receives an eternal gladness. When our own end comes, and the veil falls from our eyes, we shall see how worthless this life is, and that it was not well to regret those to whom it closed early. The shortest life is the best, if only it leads to Eternal life.

And now your little one is amid angels and holy innocents in Paradise. He remembers lovingly all that you did for him while he was here with you, especially your prayers for him, and in return he prays to God for you, and pours out many a petition that your life may become more and more conformed to God's Will, and that through it you may attain to that life in which he now rejoices for ever. Be at rest, my daughter, and fix you heart in Heaven, where your dear little saint is gone before. Persevere in striving to love the Saviour's Holy Will even more and more. May He ever be your True Consolation. I am always, yours, etc.

L.

To a Lady.

MY DEAR SISTER, *Jan.* 7, 1614.

I have just received your letters, explaining the nature of your distress, which I see is very great by reason of the numerous accidental circumstances added to your first trouble. But, my dear sister, these mists are not so thick but that the sun can scatter them, and God, Who has led you so far, will uphold you with His Holy Hand. Only you must cast yourself with perfect confidence into the Arms of His Providence; now is the time for doing that. Almost any one can trust in God amid the peace and comfort of prosperity; but His children only know how to trust absolutely in Him through the storm and tempest. If you can do this, dear sister, you will be amazed, some day, to see how all that now you dread will melt away from before your eyes. He expects this of you, for He has drawn you to Him in a very special way. As to the man whom you consider to be partly guilty in this matter, speak but little of him, and that very conscientiously. I mean, avoid complaining; and, if you must speak, do not say anything but what you know to be exactly true, without conjectures, and expressing yourself doubtfully as to what is doubtful. As far as may be, soothe the minds of your relations gently and wisely. In such cases, to make the best of things does more to heal the mischief in an hour than resentment can do in a year. After all it must be mainly God's doing.

LI.

To M. de Rochefort. On the Death of his Son.

DEAR SIR, *Jan.* 20, 1614.

Judging of your grief by my own feelings, I know how deeply you are mourning. I remember the delight with which you spoke to me about your son, and I was deeply moved at the thought of your exceeding sorrow at his death. At first I was not sure if the tidings were true, and now it seems late to speak words of consolation, when I believe that your heart will already have conquered the first bitter grief of this loss. I know that you will have felt that this dear son was more God's property than yours, to whom he was but lent by a Divine bounty; and if God saw that the time for recalling His loan had come, you could not doubt that it was for His child's gain; and a father's heart accepts such gain to his son patiently. This world is not so charming that we need greatly pity those who lay down its burthen; and for his own sake, meseems, your son is the gainer by quitting it almost before he has really entered upon it. We shrink at the word death, as we use it—saying, "Your dear father or your son is dead"—but Christians should rather say, "Your father or your son is gone to his Home and yours, and, in order to reach it, he must needs pass through death, but he did not stop there." In our better judgment we cannot prize our home in this life very greatly, when we compare it with the Heavenly Home in which we hope to dwell eternally. We are journeying thither, and we are more certain that we shall find there the dear ones gone before, than we can be of enjoying the presence of those yet among us, for they await us, and we are going to them ; whereas the others we leave behind, and they may linger yet.

If you are still sorrowing over the departure of that gentle soul, cast your heart down before our Crucified Lord, and ask His aid : He will assuredly give it, and will fill you with the desire and firm resolution to prepare for the time when you too must make the dreaded journey, and arrive joyfully there, where we believe our happy one to be already.

LII.

To Madame de Chantal. On Simplicity.

Dec., 1614

TELL the dear Marie, whom I love so much, and who loves me so well, to speak freely of God wherever she thinks it will be useful, regardless of what those who listen may think or say of her. In a word, I have already told her that while we ought neither to do nor say anything in order to obtain praise, no more ought we to leave anything undone or unsaid because we may be praised for it. Nor is it hypocritical to act less perfectly than we talk; of a truth, were it so, we should all be in a bad plight! In that case I must be silent for fear of being a hypocrite, since, if I speak concerning perfection, it follows that I count myself perfect! No, indeed, my dear daughter, in speaking of perfection I no more reckon myself to be perfect than I suppose myself to be a native of Italy because I speak Italian; but I use the language appertaining to perfection, having learnt and studied the subject.

Tell Marie to powder her hair if she will. Her intention is good, and the matter is unimportant. It is not well to entangle the mind amid all these cobwebs. This good girl's mind needs as much disentangling as her hair! That is why she worries herself! It is not good to be so punctilious, nor to distract oneself with so many little questions which do not concern the things of our Lord. Tell her to go on sincerely, holding fast to simplicity and humility, and to cast aside all these subtleties and perplexities. . . . .

LIII.
To Madame de Chantal.

Jan., 1615.

. . . . Do not be disheartened: God will never lose sight of you or your flock so long as you trust in Him. The door of consolation is strait, but the reward surely follows. Do not let yourself be disgusted, my dear daughter, or allow contradictions to weaken your mind. Whenever was God's service free from contradictions, especially in the beginning of good works? I must, however, tell you honestly that what I fear most in all this is a temptation to set up dislike and aversion between you and N——— It is a common temptation where two people are brought thus into collision; it is a temptation incidental to the most angelic minds on earth, as we see by its arising even among the greatest saints. Our folly, as children of Adam, will be the ruin of us all, unless we are saved from it through charity.

When I see two Apostles like SS. Paul and Barnabas separating because they cannot agree concerning a third companion, I look indulgently upon these little dislikes, so long as they do not hinder the work, even as the Apostles parting asunder did not hinder their mission. If some such thing happens between you two women, it is no great marvel, always supposing that it does not last. But, all the same, my dear daughter, brace your mind anew, and be sure that what you do is of great consequence. Bear patiently, do not be pettish, soften all asperities; remember that this lady is intending to serve God according to her light, as you are according to yours; and recollect that you ought both to bear with and help one another for the love of Christ. Two or three years will soon pass by, but eternity remains.

Your bodily ailments make the matter worse; but you will be strengthened if you call to mind the help promised to those who suffer. Finally, be on your guard against discouragement. Believe me, we must sow in labour, in perplexity, in anguish, if we would reap in joy, in consolation, in happiness. Holy confidence in God softens everything, penetrates everything, establishes everything. I am assuredly yours wholly, my dear daughter, and I do not cease to pray that God will make you holy, strong, stedfast, and perfect in His service. I salute our dear sisters cordially, and intreat them to pray for my soul, which is for ever bound up with yours and theirs in the joy of our Lord and Saviour, Jesus.

LIV.

To Madame de Chantal.

Feb., 1615.

As I behold the tears of our poor Sister N—— it seems to me that all our childishness proceeds from this one fault : namely, we forget how the Saints tell us that we ought daily to begin anew our endeavours after perfection; if we did remember this we should not be so surprised at finding so much that is wretched and needs correction in ourselves. The work is never done; we must perpetually begin afresh, and always begin heartily afresh. What we have done so far is good, but what we are going to begin will be better; and when that is finished we will begin again better still, and so on, until we leave this world altogether, to begin another life, which will know no end; inasmuch as there can be nothing better. So we must not begin to weep because we find things going wrong with us, but we must rouse up fresh courage to go on anew, never stopping to look back; and where it is necessary to cut off superfluities, we must remember that "the word of God is sharper than any two-edged sword, piercing even to the dividing asunder of soul and spirit, and of the joints and marrow."[1]

Your mind and mine, dear Mother, are one on this point. But let us not forget the precept of the Saints, who have all taught us that those who would follow their steps should speak but little of themselves or the things which concern them. Do not fancy that because you are at Lyons you are dispensed from the compact we made, namely, that you were to be as discreet in speaking of me as of yourself. Unless our Master's Glory requires more, be ever brief, and observe a most strict simplicity. Self-love often dazzles us, and it is very difficult to see ourselves fairly. Therefore it is that the great Apostle exclaims, "Not he that commendeth himself is approved, but whom the Lord commendeth."[2]

LV.

To a Religious. On Self-love.

1615.

.... IN reply to your letter;—self-love may be mortified, but it never dies within us; from time to time, and on sundry occasions, it puts forth fresh shoots, which prove that, though cut down, it is not rooted up. This is why we do not find the satisfaction that we ought to have in seeing others do well; we do not altogether rejoice in good works which are not to be found in ourselves, whereas

[1] Heb. iv. 12. [2] 2 Cor. x. 18.

we greatly admire all that is our own, and that because we love ourselves so exceedingly. But if we had a perfect charity, which causes us to be of one heart and soul with our neighbour, we should rejoice unfeignedly in whatever of his is good and perfect.

This same self-love leads us to do certain things because we choose them for ourselves, although we would not do them at another's bidding, or from mere obedience. If things are our own originating we like them, but not when they come through other people. Self is for ever seeking self, self-will and self-love; but if we were perfect in the love of God, we should prefer to obey, because in obedience there is more of God and less of self.

As to finding it easier to do disagreeable things oneself than to see them done by others, that may arise from charity, or because self-love secretly fears that other people may equal or surpass us. Sometimes we feel more at seeing others suffer than in suffering ourselves, out of genuine kindliness; but sometimes it is because we think ourselves more enduring and more able to bear suffering, thanks to a good opinion of ourselves. . . . . But I am sure that these are only the feelings of your natural mind; the higher, supernatural mind rejects them all. The only remedy is to disown all such thoughts, striving after obedience, and resolving to prefer it, in spite of all things, to self-pleasing; thanking God for whatever good we see in others, and asking Him to increase it fourfold.

We must never be surprised to find self-love alive within ourselves; it is ever there. At times it sleeps like a crafty fox, but then suddenly it dashes out anew. We must keep a steady watch over it, and be always on the defensive, though gently and patiently. If sometimes self-love wounds us, and we are forced to unsay what we have said, to disown what it has made us do, we shall be partly cured.

LVI.

To a Religious—the Bishop's Niece.

Oct. 12, 1615.

WHAT is in the heart of my very dear child, who is so near to my heart? I think that it is very closely united to the Heart of our Lord, and continually says to Him, "The Lord is my Light and my Salvation, of whom then shall I be afraid?" Dear child, cast all your thoughts into the Bosom of your Lord and Saviour; He will bear you and strengthen you. "Cast thy burden upon the Lord, and He shall nourish thee." If He calls you (as He actually does) to a kind of service which is according to His Will but not according to your taste, you must not go to it with less, rather with more courage and energy than if your taste coincided with His Will. The less of self and self-will there is in anything we do the better.

My dear niece, my dear child, you must not let your mind give way to self-contemplation, or dwell upon your own strength, or your inclinations; rather fix your eyes on God's Good Pleasure.

You must not amuse yourself with going from

side to side, when duty calls you straight on; nor make difficulties, when the real thing is to get over them. Gird up your reins vigorously; let your heart be full of courage, and then say, "I shall succeed. Not I, but the Grace of God which is with me."

The Grace of our Lord Jesus Christ be with your spirit. Amen.

LVII.

To the Mère de Chastel.

SS. Simon and Jude, 1615.

INDEED, my dear daughter, you gratify me by calling me your father; for my heart has a most paternal feeling towards your heart, which I do not cease to love, although I see plainly that it is rather weak under these common little contradictions which it encounters. At times it seems about to lose courage on account of passing words and rebukes, but the poor little heart has not really failed, for God upholds it with His Strong Hand, and in His Mercy He never yet forsook His feeble children. Be sure, my dear daughter, that He never will forsake you; you may be tormented and wearied with vexations, temptations to be downcast and pettish, but your will is fixed in Him.

Indeed, my dear daughter Marie, you say truly that there are two beings in you. The one is a Marie, who, like S. Peter, is tender, sensitive, ready to be irritated by a touch. This Marie is a daughter of Eve, and so her temper is frail. The other Marie wills to be wholly God's; and in order so to be, she wills in all simplicity to be humble and gentle towards every one, and she would fain imitate S. Peter after he was converted. This Marie is the child of the Blessed Virgin.

These two diverse Maries come into collision, and the bad one is so bad that often the other scarce knows how to defend herself, and then, perforce, she fancies herself beaten, and believes the bad Marie to be stronger. But not so, my poor dear child; the bad one is not stronger than you. She is more perverse, more enterprising, more obstinate, and when you lose heart and sit down to cry she is pleased, because it is so much time lost for you; and if she cannot make you lose eternity, at all events she will try to make you lose time!

My dear daughter, rouse your courage; arm yourself with patience, such as we all need with ourselves; often wake up your heart, that it may be on its guard against surprises; be watchful of your enemy; tread cautiously for fear of the foe; if you are not on your guard against her, she will be too much for you. Even if she should take you by surprise, and make you totter, or give you a slight wound, do not be put out—call upon our Dear Lord and Our Lady. They will hold out a helping hand, or if they leave you awhile in trouble, it will but be that you may be led to cry out more earnestly for help. Now do not be ashamed of all this, my daughter, any more than S. Paul was when he confessed that there were two beings in him, one rebellious against God, the other obedient to

Him. Be perfectly simple, do not be angry, humble yourself without being disheartened, be bold without presumption. Remember that our Lord and His Mother, having placed you amid the worry of a household, see and know that it does worry you, but they will not cease to love you so long as you are humble and truthful. But, dear daughter, do not be ashamed because you are somewhat dusty and soiled ; so long as you humble yourself, everything will turn to good. Pray for me, and may God always be your Love and your Protector. Amen.

LVIII.
To a Religious of the Visitation.

Dec., 1615.

.... It is thus, my daughter, that we must steadily thrust the hand into all the folds of our heart, and tear thence the foul excrescences which come forth from self-will, thanks to our evil tempers, our inclinations and aversions.

It is a real satisfaction to my paternal heart to hear a beloved child denounce herself as vexatious and malicious. That is a happy fault which is followed by such a hearty confession ! The hand which traced that letter is as brave as ever was that of Alexander ! Now, my dear child, carry out all that your heart dictates. Do not be astonished at what has happened. . . One great step towards perfection is to bear with one another in our mutual imperfections ; there is no better way of exercising love of our neighbour.

LIX.

To one of the Bishop's Spiritual Children.
1616.

WHEN will our mere natural ties, common courtesies, and civilities, all our sympathies and graces, be purified and reduced into perfect subjection to the pure love of God's Good Pleasure? When will self cease to crave for visible, external tokens of earthly love, and when shall we be fully satisfied to rest in the unchanging promise of God's Presence? What can a visible presence add to the love which God has created and sustained?

When shall we all overflow with gentleness and kindness to our neighbour? When shall we see our neighbour wholly in the Sacred Heart of the Saviour? Alas, those who do not behold Him in this light run the risk of failing to love Him purely, faithfully, or evenly. But if we see Christ in our fellow-man, who would not love and bear with him? Who would not tolerate his failings with patience? Who would be peevish or weary of his neighbour? But it is so, and we ought never to forget that Christ so loved that neighbour as to die for him of very love.

LX.

To a Married Niece.
March 5, 1616.

Do not think, my dear niece, that it has been forgetfulness or want of affection that has made me delay writing so long. Indeed the earnest desire to serve God faithfully, which I saw in your soul, kindled an equally earnest desire in mine to help you as far as lies in my power, to say nothing of the affection I have always borne you, and the good opinion I have had of you from your childhood.

Well, my dear niece, you must carefully cultivate this precious heart of yours, and spare nothing which will advance its real happiness. This can be always done, but the present season is most suitable. It is a great grace, my dear child, to begin serving God while youth makes us very susceptible to impressions, and the tree which bears flowers as well as its first-fruits is a choice offering.

Strive to keep stedfast in the resolutions with which God inspired you as you knelt before me in His Presence. If you do but keep them throughout this life, they will keep you throughout the life to come. To this end you can follow the counsels I have written down in the *Introduction*, but as you wish it, I will further briefly specify what I wish you to observe.

I. Go to confession every fortnight, and receive the Blessed Sacrament. Never go to either of these heavenly mysteries without renewing a fervent resolution to amend all your failings more and more, and to acquire an ever-increasing purity of heart. If you feel drawn by a devout spirit to communicate weekly, do so; and especially if you find that through receiving that sacred mystery your faulty tendencies and the imperfections of your daily life are lessened. I only fixed a fortnightly communion as the longest interval.

II. Let your spiritual exercises be brief and fervent, so as not to weary yourself by over-length. You should always follow the morning exercise given in the *Introduction*, but you may thank God for having preserved you through the night in ejaculatory prayer, whilst dressing; and you may follow the second and third points either then or even before getting up; but then, as soon as you are able, kneel down for the rest. And so with self-examination, you may begin wherever you are, provided the latter parts are said upon your knees. Hear mass reverently and fervently; it is better not to go to church than to do otherwise.

III. Learn constantly to offer up ejaculatory prayer, and raise your heart to God.

IV. Be careful always to be gentle and affable to every one, but above all at home.

V. When you can, dispense your alms yourself; it adds greatly to their grace to be given by your own hand.

VI. Visit the sick in your village diligently. This is one of the good works which will be remembered by the Lord at the Day of Judgment.

VII. Read a few pages of some spiritual book daily, so as to keep alive a devotional spirit; and on festivals read a little more, instead of a sermon.

VIII. Be very dutiful to your father-in-law. It is God's Will that you be so; and love your husband heartily, doing all you can to please him in all gentleness and simplicity. Be patient in bearing with the faults of every one, especially in your own home.

I think there is nothing more to be said, except

that when we meet again you shall tell me what progress you are making in this devout life, as, if there is anything to be added, I will then do so. Live cheerfully in and for God, my very dear child, and believe that I cherish you most tenderly, etc.

LXI.

To a Religious of the Visitation.

MY DEAR DAUGHTER, *April 17, 1616.*

There are two kinds of good desires, those which increase grace and goodness in God's servants, and those which are fruitless. To exemplify the first;—" I wish to give alms, but I do not, because I have not wherewith to give;" such a wish tends to increase charity and to sanctify the soul; or again, holy souls wish for contempt, crosses, and even martyrdom, but these are withheld from them. The second kind of desire takes a different shape; " I would gladly give alms, but I am not going to give at present;" and as there is no impossibility in the matter, only indifference and want of love, all such desires are useless, neither fostering grace nor sanctifying the soul. It is of such good intentions and desires as these that S. Bernard says hell is full.

Fully to remove your difficulty, you must bear in mind that these desires are alike apt to be mistaken one for the other. For instance, no servant of God but must desire to serve God better than he does; and, inasmuch as we may always be going on from good to better, it might seem that such a wish

De Sales' Sp L.] K

could only be hindered by the lack of stedfast resolution. But it is not so. Such good desires are hindered by the inevitable conditions of this mortal life, in which it is not so easy to do as to wish, and such desires as these for the most part are profitable, advancing the soul, warming and stimulating it in spiritual progress.

But when some individual opportunity arises for carrying these wishes into effect, and yet we stop short in the mere wish ;—as, for instance, when some occasion for forgiving an injury presents itself, or for giving up my own will, and, instead of doing so, I am content with saying, "I would fain be forgiving, but I cannot ; I would gladly give up my own will, but it is out of the question to do so;" who can fail to see that such wishes are wholly unreal? Indeed I am the more guilty, in that I have so decided a tendency to do what is right, and yet have not will enough to carry it out. Such wishes are easily mistaken for those of the opposite character.

I think these observations will solve your difficulty, but if not, write to me, and I will answer you sooner or later, with all my heart. . . .

LXII.

To the Père Fabre,
SUPERIOR OF THE VISITATION AT LYONS.

Sept. 10, 1616.

. . . IF our Mother has had time she will perhaps have told you how much I fear lest the "little foxes" should creep into our new vineyard and spoil it; I mean dislikes and aversions, which are the temptation of saints. Stifle all such in their birth. Let your charity be blindfold, and be suspicious of whatsoever is at all contrary to entire unity, mutual forbearance, and that reciprocal respect which you ought to feel for one another. Beware of earthly prudence, which our Lord counts as folly; work on peacefully, gently, trustingly, simply. . . .

Oct. 8.

These dislikes and repugnances of which I hear trouble me. Oh, when shall we duly estimate the importance of bearing patiently with our neighbour! It is the last and most important lesson in the doctrine of the Saints, and blessed is the soul which has learnt it! We wish to be borne with in our infirmities, which always appear to us worthy of indulgence, while we esteem those of our neighbour to be of a wholly different character, and not to be endured.

May God make you and all your flock holy, my dear daughter, and may His Glory be set forth through all your weakness and faults, etc.

LXIII.

To a Lady who feared Death.

MADAME, *April* 7, 1617.

I take the earliest opportunity of fulfilling my promise of setting before you some ways of diminishing that fear of death which has so greatly troubled you in your confinements and other illnesses. There is no sin in such a fear, but it is a hindrance to your soul, which, while harassed by this dread, cannot rise in such fervent love to God as it would otherwise do.

First of all, I would assure you, that if you persevere, as you are doing, in the habit of devotion, this trouble will gradually diminish, and that because, as your soul becomes more free from evil affections, and more closely united to God, it will be less tied down to this mortal life and the happiness to which we cling therein. Therefore be stedfast in leading a devout life, and go forward in the good way, and by degrees your terror will cease to be so distressing.

Secondly, dwell often upon the thought of the exceeding love and pity with which God the Father and our Dear Saviour watch over those departing souls who in life have trusted in God, striving to serve and love Him, according to their vocation. "How great is Thy mercy, O Lord, upon them that fear Thee."

. Thirdly, lift up your heart continually, in holy trust mingled with humility, towards our Redeemer, saying, "I am frail and worthless, O Lord, but Thou wilt receive my frailty into the Bosom of Thy Mercy, and bring me to Thine heritage. In Thee, O Lord, have I put my trust; let me never be put to confusion. I am poor and in misery, but the Lord careth for me."

Fourthly, kindle in your heart as much as possible a love of Paradise and the Life Eternal; often meditating on this subject, (you will find meditations thereon in the "Vie Dévote,") for the more you realise and love Eternal Life the less you will fear to quit this brief, fleeting life.

Fifthly, do not read books or such parts of books as treat of death, judgment, and hell. Thanks be to God, you have heartily resolved to live to Him, and do not need being urged thereto by the terrors of the Law.

Sixthly, make frequent acts of love for Our Lady, the Saints and Angels; accustom yourself to familiar thoughts of them; the more friends you number among the citizens of the Heavenly Jerusalem, the less you will mind leaving those who are as yet but the denizens of this world.

Seventhly, praise and bless the Crucified Lord for His Holy Death, putting all your trust in Him and His Merits, to grant you a happy death, often saying, "By Thine Own Precious Death, O Jesus, lead me gently through the gates of death." S. Carlo Borromeo found comfort on his deathbed by having a picture of the Sepulchre to look at, as well as in the Saviour's words on the Mount of Olives.

Eighthly, remember thankfully that you are a member of the Church Catholic; such of her children as strive to live according to her laws will die a happy death; as S. Theresa says, it is a great comfort at the last hour to be a child of the Catholic Church.

Ninthly, let all your prayers end with an act of trust and confidence. "Be merciful unto me, O God, for my soul trusteth in Thee." "Who ever trusted in the Lord and was confounded?" "In

Thee, O Lord, have I trusted; let me never be confounded." And in your ejaculatory prayers throughout the day, as also in receiving the Holy Sacrament, be frequent in love and hope: "Thou art my Father and my God. Thou art the joy of my soul, the delight of my heart. O Jesus, my beloved Master, my Help, my Refuge."

Tenthly, accustom yourself to think of those persons whom you love best, and from whom it would cost you most to part, as the very persons with whom you are to dwell for ever in Heaven, as, for instance, your husband, your little Jean, and your father. "This dear little son will, by God's Blessing, one day share that eternal happiness with me, rejoicing in my felicity, as I in his, never to part through all Eternity." You can the better do this, that all your nearest and dearest love and serve God. And as you are somewhat disposed to be melancholy, read what I have said about that and its remedies in the "Vie Dévote."

I think, dear Madame, that I can say no more at present on this subject. With great affection, and begging you to commend me to God's Mercy, as I will never fail to seek His Blessing for you, I am, yours, etc.

LXIV.

To a Lady.

Sept. 12, 1617.

I HAVE been really ill, my dear child—very ill, though without danger. What more could you have done, if you had known it? for I know you constantly pray for me, as indeed I ever remember you in my poor prayers, and when celebrating Mass. I am still somewhat languid, and have not shaken off the signs of illness, though able to return to my usual duties.

Be stedfast, my dear child; aim at being God's servant as perfectly as possible. Be very watchful as to gentleness. I do not bid you love that which you ought to love, I know you do so, but I bid you strive to be even, patient, and gentle. Control the ebullitions of your natural temperament, which is somewhat over-quick and eager.

I do not know why you should be dissatisfied as to your confessions; you make them very properly. Now be at peace before God, Who has so long loved you, filling you with His Holy Fear and Love. If hitherto you have not sufficiently corresponded to His Grace, there is ample remedy for you in doing so more heartily in future. You should not be surprised at your own weakness and frailty, God knows it all; and He never rejects the frail, but rather turns their weakness to His Glory.

I wish I had a heavy hammer wherewith to pound away the edges of your mind, which are too sharp for your spiritual progress! I have often told you that devotion must be pursued in good faith, and on a broad scale. If you do well, thank God for it; if ill, humble yourself. I know that you would not willingly do ill, and our other faults ought only to be a cause for self-humiliation.

Now do not be fearful any more, and do not fret

your poor conscience. You know that all you need is to seek the Lord's Love, and to give Him yours.

Do this, my dear child, and diligently cultivate gentleness and inward humility. I ceaselessly wish every blessing for you ; above all, that you may be humble, gentle, and kind, and that you may turn your troubles to good by accepting them lovingly for love of Him Who has suffered so much for love of you. In Him I am, my dear child, yours msot affectionately, etc.

LXV.
To a Lady.

Oct. 1617.

.... I CANNOT understand why those who have given themselves up to God and His Goodness are not always cheerful, for what possible happiness can be equal to that? No accidents or imperfections which may happen ought to have power to trouble them, or to hinder their looking upward. Be tranquil, and abide in gentleness and humility of heart. You have heard of all our little sorrows, which I might well have called great but for God's special graces to the souls He has taken away--my brother died like a Religious among soldiers, my sister like a saint among Religious.

LXVI.

To Madame de Chantal. On the Death of M. de Sainte Catherine.[1]

MY VERY DEAR MOTHER, *Jan. 25, 1618.*

When I was called from you it was to go to M. de Sainte Catherine, but I supposed it was merely an attack as before. However, it proved that I had to help him to say "Hail, Jesus!" some ten or twelve times, and make a firm protest that all his hope was in the Saviour's Death, which he uttered with great earnestness and strength; and then he went to the Home we all seek, under the shadow of the great Saint Paul. God, Who gave him to us for His Own Service, has taken him away for His Glory. "The Lord gave, and the Lord hath taken away; blessed be the Name of the Lord."[2]

Let us remain tranquilly at the Saviour's Feet, ready to live for Him, and by His Grace to die for Him. God will make up to us for this loss, and will raise us up labourers to take the place of these two whom He has been pleased to call forth from His vineyard, that He may cause them to sit down at His Table. But be of a calm spirit—that is absolutely necessary: and remember what we are told in the Book of Wisdom, namely, to "weep a

---

[1] M. de Sainte Catherine, so called to distinguish him from his brother, M. Coëx, was the intimate friend of both the Bishop of Geneva and Madame de Chantal. He was a Canon of Geneva, and also for long, Francis de Sales' ordinary Confessor.

[2] Job i. 21.

little" over the dead, and then to take comfort in God, Who is our Hope and our Salvation. Amen.

LXVII.

To a Superior of the Visitation. On Spiritual Dryness.

ANNECY, *Feb.* 18, 1618.

Do you ask, my dear daughter, whether our Lord thinks of you, and whether He looks upon you with love? Yes, indeed, He looks upon you, and upon every hair of your head; "the very hairs of your head are all numbered."[1] This is an article of faith, and must in no way be doubted. Indeed, I am sure that you do not doubt it; it is only a way of expressing the dryness and insensibility which at the present moment oppresses your soul on the natural side. Jacob said, "Surely the Lord is in this place, and I knew it not;"[2] *i.e.*, "I did not perceive Him, or feel Him; I was unconscious that He was so near." I have dwelt upon this at length in the "Traité de l'Amour de Dieu," in speaking of resignation and the destruction of self-will, but I do not remember in what book. But, in truth, you have no reason to doubt that God looks upon you with love; He looks thus even upon the most grievous sinners if they have any sincere desire to turn to Him. Now tell me, dear daughter, do you not fully purpose to be God's child, and to serve Him faithfully? And who spires you with this purpose, save He Himself,

[1] Matt. x. 30.   [2] Gen. xxviii. 16.

through His great Love? You must abstain from closely searching out whether your heart be pleasing to Him; but you may examine whether His Heart satisfies you, and if once you contemplate that Heart, it cannot fail to satisfy you; it is so loving, so tender, so pitiful towards His weak creatures, provided they will but acknowledge their weakness; so gracious, so good to all penitents! Who would not love this Heart, Which is as that of father and mother combined towards us all?

You say truly, my daughter, that these temptations arise from a want of tenderness in your heart towards God, because if you experienced such tenderness, you would be comforted, and if you were comforted your troubles would be at an end. But, dear daughter, the Love of God does not consist in tenderness or consolation, else our Lord had been without that Love when, in His extreme "sorrow unto death," He cried out, "My God, My God, why hast Thou forsaken Me?" whereas rather that moment was the crowning act of His Love. The fact is we always want sugar in our food—that is, we want to enjoy conscious love and tenderness, and their pleasantness, just as we would fain be free from all imperfections; but, my dear daughter, we must patiently bear with our nature, which is human, and not angelic.

I do not mean that we are to rest satisfied with our imperfections; rather we should say with the great Apostle, "O wretched man that I am! who shall deliver me from the body of this death?"[1] But we ought not to be discouraged or surprised;

[1] Rom. vii. 24.

we should learn submission, humility, and mistrust of self from our failings;—never despondency and sadness, much less mistrust of God's Love for us. He does not love our imperfections or our venial sins, but He loves us in spite of them. Just as a mother grieves over her child's weakness and faultiness, but still loves him most tenderly, so God cherishes us, notwithstanding all our frailty; even as David cries out, " Have mercy upon me, O Lord, for I am weak."

Enough, my daughter. Be cheerful. Our Lord looks lovingly upon you, and the weaker you are the greater is His tenderness. Do not allow your mind to dwell upon anything contrary to this. If vexatious thoughts arise, do not dally with them; turn away, and look to God with a brave humility; dwell upon His Infinite Goodness, Which has regard to our frail, needy human nature, in all its infirmity. Pray for me, and commend me to all your dear novices. I am wholly yours in our Lord. May He ever live in all our hearts.

LXVIII.

To a Superior.

Feb. 19, 1618.

I SEE, my dear daughter, that you are quite suffering and ill, because of the illnesses and sufferings of your children. It is not possible to be a Mother without cares. S. Paul says, "Who is weak, and I am not weak?" Some of the Fathers, writing upon this passage, say that a hen is always greatly troubled while leading about her brood, and they liken S. Paul to one, gathering her chickens under her wings. But, my dear daughter, the same Apostle says, "When I am weak, then am I strong," and "God's strength is made perfect in weakness." So do you be strong amid the trials of your house. These long illnesses are a good school for charity to those who nurse the sick, and of loving patience to such as have to bear them. The first are like Our Lady and S. John, standing at the foot of the Cross, in tender watchfulness; the others share our Lord's Passion, and hang with Him upon the Cross. . . . . . Lift up your heart, my daughter; amid all your troubles grow in courage, and ever behold our Great Redeemer leaning down from Heaven towards you, watching you amid these trials, and holding your heart by an invisible thread, so that it may never break loose from Him.

Dear daughter, you are the bride, not as yet of Jesus Christ Glorified, but of Jesus Christ Crucified; your rings and ornaments are the cross, the nails, and thorns; the feast to which He calls you is of gall, hyssop, and vinegar. In Heaven we shall find the rubies, emeralds, and diamonds; the milk, honey, and manna. I do not say this to dishearten you, but rather because I would share your grief and sadness in loving sympathy. Do not say that you presume upon my kindness by writing such long letters; I am very glad to have them.

That good father calls me a flower and a phœnix, but in truth I am a foul raven, a mere dunghill. Nevertheless, continue to love me, my daughter, for, indeed, God loves me, and gives me an exceeding desire to serve and love Him in purity and holiness. After all we are but too happy to be able to aspire after a glorious Eternity, through the Merits of our Saviour's Passion, Who raises up our weakness in order to clothe it with His Mercy. To Him be honour and glory, world without end. Amen.

LXIX.

To a Lady, who had praised the Bishop extravagantly.

April 22, 1618.

VERY DEAR CHILD OF MY HEART,

Do you know that I have a child who writes that my departure tears her asunder, that her eyes rain down tears as copious as the torrents of the skies, and similar rhapsodies ! She goes further still, and says that I am not a mere man, but a divinity, sent on earth to be loved and admired, and adds that she could say yet more if she dared ! What think you, my child ? Is she not very wrong to use such language ? Are not such words most extravagant ? Nothing can possibly excuse her save her love for me, which I believe to be a holy love, although it is expressed in such terribly worldly language. Now, dear child, will you tell her that she must never, in any way whatsoever, apply the word Divine to mere weak men ; and that to give way thus to unmeasured commendation shows an ill-regulated mind, or, at best, a most disorderly manner of expression. Tell her that it is even more needful to guard against vanity in words than in dress and *coiffure;* let her language henceforth be simple, and not frizzed out! All the same, tell her this kindly and gently, and ask her to accept this reprimand in a loving spirit, for, as you know, it comes from a heart full of fatherly love for her; she is a very dear child, and I have great confidence in her. May God ever be our chief object of affection, my very dear daughter, and may we live in and for Him eternally. Amen.

LXX.
To a Lady. On Prayer.

MY DEAR DAUGHTER, *June 20, 1618.*

The Mother told you truly—I am overwhelmed, not so much with business as by many hindrances. Nevertheless, I would not have you desist from writing to me when you wish to do so. Your letters are an interest and a recreation to me, only you must be somewhat indulgent if I am tardy in replying. . . .

Your method of meditation is good, better than if you went more into considerations and colloquies, which are only useful when they kindle the affections; and, therefore, if God pleases to give us warm affections without their aid it is a great grace. The secret of secrets in prayer is to follow the leadings of your heart in all simplicity. You will find all that you require concerning meditation in the seventh book of the "Traité de l'Amour de Dieu."

I remember that once you told me in confession

what you did, and I approved of it, and told you that if, while meditating on any point, God led you to special affections, you should quit all formal points, and follow His leading. The quieter and simpler these affections the better — they make more impression.

But, my dear daughter, do not indulge yourself while meditating in any attempts to find out whether you are praying well; the best prayer or meditation is that which so fixes our mind on God that we do not think of ourselves, or of what we do. If we want to reach God we must approach Him in all simplicity, without artifice or self-consciousness, seeking only to love and know Him. True love deals but sparingly in systems and methods.

LXXI.
To a Lady.

PARIS, *Jan.* 16, 1619.

. . . . . I WAS afraid you were made anxious by your father's illness. . . . . Indeed we need to learn the lesson, that this life is given us only that we may attain to eternal life. For lack of remembering this, we fix our affections on the things of this fleeting world, and when the time comes that we must quit it, we are all aghast and terrified!

Believe me, dear child, if we would pass contentedly through our pilgrimage, we must keep the hope of arriving at our true Home ever before our eyes, else we shall continually be halting. God calls us to Him, and He watches us as we go, and allows nothing to happen save what is for our real good; He knows what we are, and when we come to rough places He will always uphold us with His Fatherly Hand, so that we be not hindered. But to correspond to this grace we need an absolute trust in Him.

Do not look forward to the changes and chances of this life in fear; rather look to them with full hope that as they arise, God, Whose you are, will deliver you out of them. He has kept you hitherto, do you but hold fast to His Dear Hand, and He will lead you safely through all things; and when you cannot stand, He will bear you in His Arms. What need you fear, my child, remembering that you are God's, and that He has said, "All things work together for good to them that love Him." Do not look forward to what may happen to-morrow; the same Everlasting Father Who cares for you to-day, will take care of you to-morrow, and every day. Either He will shield you from suffering, or He will give you unfailing strength to bear it. Be at peace, then; put aside all anxious thoughts and imaginations, and say continually, "The Lord is my strength and my shield; my heart hath trusted in Him, and I am helped."[1] He is not only with me, but in me, and I in Him.

What can a child fear surrounded by such a Father's Arms? Be truly as a child, my daughter. You know children do not trouble themselves with looking forward; they leave that to others, and are perfectly content so long as they are near their

[1] Ps. xxviii. 7.

De Sales' Sp. L.]

father. Do this, my dear child, and you will be at rest. Amen.

LXXII.
To a Gentleman.
On the right use of Holy Scripture.

SIR, *July 2, 1619.*

It is quite true that Holy Scripture contains fully and clearly all doctrines necessary to salvation; we do not doubt it. It is also true that it is very useful to interpret Holy Scripture by comparing passages together, and bringing the whole into an analysis of doctrine. But I must always believe and affirm that, notwithstanding the admirable perspicuity of Holy Scripture in all things necessary to our salvation, the human mind does not always find its right meaning, but is liable to err, and practically does very often err in interpreting passages which are of great importance to the confirmation of the Faith. Witness the Lutheran and Calvinistic writers; they, though leaders of the so-called Reformation, are involved in irreconcilable differences as to the meaning of the words of institution of the Holy Eucharist; and while each side maintains that they have diligently and faithfully studied the sense of those words, taking them with the context of Holy Scripture generally, and comparing the whole with the analogy of Faith, nevertheless they come to very different conclusions. The Word of God is clear enough, but our human minds are cloudy, and, like bats, cannot face the light.

The method of which we speak is good, but our human minds are not able to use it. It is the Holy Spirit of God Who has given us the Scriptures; the same Holy Spirit opens their true meaning to us, and that only through the Church, which is the temple and pillar of Truth: the Church, by whose means the Holy Spirit has kept and preserved the true letter of Scripture; the Church, which alone has the gift of the Spirit of Truth to interpret it. And therefore he who would seek the real meaning of that Heavenly Word, apart from its guardian the Church, will never find it; he who would seek it independently of her, finds a vain delusion instead of the truth; he is misled by the evil one, who knows how to transform himself into the appearance of an angel of light. It was this which all the heretics of old did, pretending to a better interpretation of Holy Scripture than that taught by the Church, to whom her Crucified Spouse has committed the precious trust. This, sir, is in substance what the Fathers have ever taught.

LXXIII.

To Madame de Chantal. On Self-renunciation.

Aug. 9, 1619.

OH, Dear Lord, what a blessing and consolation it is to me to see our Mother thus renouncing herself before Thee! I have long felt the most intense sweetness when I sing the response in the holy office, "Naked came I out of my mother's womb, and naked shall I return thither: the Lord gave, and the Lord hath taken away, blessed be the Name of the Lord."[1] How blessed it must have been to S. Joseph and the Holy Virgin as they journeyed towards Egypt, to see nothing save their gentle Jesus! The object of the Transfiguration, my dear Mother, is to see neither Moses nor Elias, nought save Jesus Christ. And the delight of the Bride is to be alone with her King, to say, "My Beloved is mine, and I am His."[2] We must strive to be stripped of all things, and to let our affections be so wholly and solely united to God that nothing may cling to us as of ourselves. Joseph was very happy in wearing his robe so loosely, that when sin seized and would have held him by it, he left it behind him and fled.[3]

I stand in wondering love before the Saviour of our souls, Who came forth naked from His Mother's womb, and, dying naked on the Cross, was once more laid in her lap to be made ready for His burial. I ponder that Mother's readiness to despoil herself of all things, even of her Son, "The Lord hath given, the Lord hath taken away; blessed be the Name of the Lord." Yes, dear Mother, I bless the Lord, Who has stripped you. My heart rejoices to see you in so hopeful a state, and with Isaiah I say, "Walk naked and barefoot before the Lord;" do not heed making acts of devotion unless they arise within you heart; be content to say, "Naked came I forth from my mother's womb, and naked shall I return thither." Do not constrain yourself, but go, as you determined yesterday; "hearken and incline thine ear, forget also thine

[1] Job i. 21.   [2] Cant. ii. 16.   [3] Gen. xxxix.

own people, and thy father's house,"[1]—"so shall the King have pleasure in thy beauty,"—in your simple self-renunciation. Abide therein, and ask no more. Amen.

LXXIV.
To a Lady, who had lost her only Son.

Aug. 23, 1619.

KNOWING your sorrow, my dear daughter, my soul has been touched in proportion to the sincere love for you with which God has inspired me. I can see you, very grievously afflicted, a poor mother losing her only and most dear son. Nevertheless, I doubt not but that you are well assured that this parting is not for long, inasmuch as we are all travelling fast towards the country where your son has already arrived, as we hope, and rests within the Arms of God's Mercy. And it is your duty thus to soften, as far as may be, the bitterness of your natural grief. But I hardly need say this to you, my dear daughter. You have so long striven to serve God, and have so diligently studied in the school of the Cross, that you will not only accept this sorrow patiently, but gladly and lovingly too, I am certain; remembering Him Who bore His Cross even to the death, and her who had like you an Only Son, (and such a Son as none else ever had,) Whom she saw dying on the Cross, her heart full of grief, her eyes running down with tears, yet with a most tender, holy grief, for her grief was the

---
[1] Ps. xlv. 10.

salvation of the world. Well, my dear daughter, you have given up the most precious possession you had. Bless the Name of the Lord, Who gave it and has taken it away. He will be more to you than many children. As for me, I have prayed earnestly for the departed soul, and will continue to do so by reason of the love I bear your soul, which may our Lord of His Eternal Goodness ever fill with heavenly blessings.

I am, my dear daughter, wholly yours, etc.

LXXV.
To a Young Lady.

MY VERY DEAR CHILD, *Sept.*, 1619.

I say Adieu to you with all my heart; may you be *à Dieu* for ever in this mortal life, serving Him faithfully amid the trials we must meet in carrying our cross after Him; and in the life to come may you worship Him for ever with His Heavenly Host. The great blessing of our souls is to be God's; the greatest of all is to be His only.

He who is God's only is never sorrowful, save when he has displeased God, and then his sorrow turns to a deep, but gentle, calm humility and submission, from out which he rises up with true loving confidence, free from all vexation and disturbance.

He who is God's only seeks none save God, and, inasmuch as he is God's child as much in tribulation as in prosperity, his grace is never destroyed, come what may. He who is God's only thinks often upon Him, amid all the varying occupations of this life. He who is God's only would have it known by all that he is the servant of Christ, and strives in every way to live accordingly.

My dear child, be God's only; seek to please Him alone, and His Creatures in Him, through Him, and for Him; what greater blessing can I wish you? So with this I will say adieu, and, bidding you commend me often to His Mercy, I am, etc.

LXXVI.

To a Religious.

My Dear Daughter, *Sept. 9, 1619.*

Strive to keep your heart in peace, and to preserve an even temper. I do not say *do it*, but *strive* to do it; let this be your chief aim. Above all, beware of being disturbed because you cannot all at once conquer the excitability of your temper and its many moods.

Shall I tell you what a monastery is? It is an academy for a minute education, in which each soul must learn to be manipulated, repaired, and polished, so that, having been finished and perfected, it may be fitted into precisely that position which has been assigned to it by God's Will. There is no surer sign of perfection than a willingness to be corrected; the best fruit of humility is a knowledge that we stand in need of correction. A monastery, again, is a hospital of spiritual invalids who seek to be cured, and who are ready, to that end, to endure the lancet or the knife, as well as all other necessary treatment. In the early days of the Church monks were called by a name which signified "one who heals." Now, my daughter, do you be all this, and put away whatever self-love may say to the contrary; only let your resolution so to do be quietly and lovingly made. Say, "I must either die or be healed, and inasmuch as I would not die spiritually I must be healed; and in order to be healed I will bear cure and correction, and I will intreat the physicians to spare me no suffering which is needful to such a cure."

My dear daughter, I hear that you are afraid of spirits and ghosts! The Sovereign Spirit of God is everywhere, and without His Will and permission no spirit has any power at all. Whoso fears His Holy Spirit need fear none besides. You are safe under His Wings, like a chicken beneath those of its brooding mother. When I was young I shared somewhat in this fancy, and in order to get rid of it I forced myself by degrees to go alone into the places which were alarming to my imagination, armed with trust in God; and I grew so completely out of the terror that now I delight in the darkness and solitude of night, in which the Presence of God seems more especially near. His good Angels, too, are around you, as a guardian band. "He shall give His Angels charge over thee; thou shalt not be afraid for any terror by night."

You will gradually win this confidence, as God's Grace waxes stronger in you; for grace brings forth trust, and "hope maketh not ashamed." May God ever reign within your heart. In Him I am, yours, etc.

LXXVII.

To the Abbess Angélique Arnaud, of Port Royal.

Sept. 12, 1619.

I HOPE that God will strengthen you more and more, and that the thought, or rather temptation, of despondency as to you fervour will not last. When it arises, answer resolutely that you know those who trust in God will never be confounded, and that spiritually, as well as in all temporal things, you have cast your care upon the Lord, confident that He will sustain you. Let us serve God diligently to-day, and He will provide for to-morrow. Sufficient unto the day is the evil thereof. Take no thought for the morrow; the Same God Who disposes of events to-day will dispose of them to-morrow. . . .

Beware, my dear daughter, of calling men fools; remember our Lord's words, " Whosoever shall say to his brother, Raca," etc. Learn by degrees to tame your eager spirit, and bring it into the subjection of patience, gentleness, and kindliness amid the follies, childishness, and feminine imperfections of your Sisters, who are a little self-indulgent, and apt to worry their Mother. Do not take so much delight in the affection of an earthly father; seek above all the Heavenly Father, Who loves you, and gave His Son for you.

Sleep well; by degrees you can return to six hours' sleep only if you wish it. But to eat little, to work a great deal amid considerable mental anxiety, and then to refuse sufficient sleep to the poor body, is neither more nor less than to expect a worn-out horse to work without his food. . . . I wish you had not ridiculed and laughed at those people, but that you had rather edified them by your modest simplicity and kindliness, as our Lord has taught us to do. . . . Farewell: study to win humility and a kindly spirit. . . . Abide in God. I am, etc.

LXXVIII.

To a Superior of the Visitation. On her Duties.

MY VERY DEAR DAUGHTER, *Oct. 2, 1619.*

Beware of being disheartened by any little murmurs, or by any fault that may be found with you. Indeed, dear daughter, I can assure you that the art of fault-finding is very easy, and that of amending most difficult. Very little talent is needful to pick holes in those who govern, or in their administration; and when we are reproved, or our defective system of rule is set before us, we ought to listen meekly to everything, and then lay it before God, taking counsel with those who are our coadjutors in the work; after which the right thing is to do what seems for the best, with a holy confidence that God's Providence will turn all things to His own Glory.

Do not be hasty in making promises, but take leisure to think well over any matter of importance. This is necessary, both for the wellbeing of the work, and for your personal humility. S. Bernard, writing to a certain Arducius (who was a predecessor of mine in the See of Geneva), says, "Do everything subject to the advice of but few persons, giving heed that they be peaceable, wise, and good." You should consult with those under you so discreetly as not in any way to lessen the respect which they bear you, or to make them imagine that you cannot do without them; rather they should feel that you consult them out of modesty and humility, and because it is in accordance with your constitutions. You understand, my dear daughter, that as far as possible the love our inferiors bear to us ought not to lessen their respect, nor should their respect lessen their love.

If there is any Sister who does not hold you in sufficient reverence, let it be mentioned to her by any one of the other Sisters through whom you think it will come best, not as from you, but as of herself: but your gentleness must not run any risk of being mistaken for timidity; therefore, if any Sister should be intentionally wanting in due respect, it would be well for you privately and gently to admonish her that it is her duty to honour your office, and to co-operate with the rest in maintaining the dignity of that which binds the whole community together as one body and one soul. . . .

Now, my dear daughter, hold fast to God, and be humbly courageous for His Sake. Moreover, I pray you often commend my soul to Him. I cherish your soul most exceedingly, and wish it a thousand blessings. When I say do not show this letter, I mean, do not show it indiscriminately. If it is a comfort to you to show it to any special person, pray do so. Yours, etc.

LXXIX.
To a Lady. On the Death of her new-born Child.

MY DEAR CHILD, ANNECY, *Dec.* 2, 1619.

The Father Confessor of Sainte Claire de Grenoble has just told me that you have been exceedingly ill. . . . I can imagine your dear heart accepting all these trials as blessings with a perfect submission to His Divine Will, from Whose Fatherly Hand they come. Oh, how happy that little babe is to have taken flight like an angel to Heaven, almost before it had lighted upon earth! What a precious pledge for you up there, my dear child! But I know well that you have communed not a little with your Saviour, heart to heart, over all this trial; He has before now soothed all the shrinking tenderness of your mother's heart; and you have many a time poured out your childlike trust in His own words, "Even so, Father, for so it seemed good in Thy Sight." Oh, my dear child, if so you are most blessed, you are "dead' with your babe in Christ, "and your life is hid in Him with God, and when He, Who is our life, shall appear, then shall ye also appear with Him in glory."[1] So speaks the Holy Ghost in Holy Scripture.

We groan, we suffer, we die with those we love, by reason of our great love for them; and when they suffer and die in our Lord, and we accept

[1] Col. iii. 3, 4.

their suffering and death for love of Him Who suffered and died for us, we are indeed "dead" with Him and them. These are the true spiritual riches, my dear child, and we shall realise it one day, when for our "present light afflictions" we receive "an eternal weight of glory."

And now, dear child, as you have willingly accepted your illness, because it was God's Will, strive in like manner to accept your recovery cheerfully, inasmuch as He wills you to recover. I cease not to pray, my dear child, that we may all be His without exception or reserve, in health and in sickness, in sorrow and in joy, in life and in death, in time and in Eternity. With all best wishes to your very filial heart, I am, yours, etc.

LXXX.
To Madame de Chantal.

ANNECY, *Dec.* 13, 1619.

. . . . THE other day, as I made mention of S. Joseph during Mass, I bethought me of his perfect calmness when he found himself, as it seemed, deceived in his espoused wife. And so I commended these good gentlemen and their minds and tongues to him, that, if it might be, they may acquire some of his meekness and charity. Then, too, it came upon me how in all that perplexity Our Lady said nothing, made no self-defence, and was not dismayed, and then God made it all plain; so I commended this present trouble to her, and resolved that I would be silent. One gains nothing by going forth to encounter the winds and the waves, rather one is apt to be covered with foam! Indeed, my dear Mother, you must not be so sensitive about me. You must be willing to hear me censured; if I do not deserve it for one thing I do for another. The Mother of Him Who deserved nought save infinite adoration did not proffer one word when He was overwhelmed with reproach and shame. "Blessed are they which are persecuted for righteousness' sake, for theirs is the Kingdom of Heaven." Dear Mother, you are too sensitive in what concerns me. Am I only, of all the world, to be exempt from reproach? I can assure you that nothing in this matter has pained me so much as to see how it pained you. Be calm, and the God of peace will be with you, and will "tread the lion and the adder under His Feet." Nothing will disturb our peace if we are His true servants. My dear Mother, depend upon it there is a great deal of self-love in the wish to be loved by everybody, and esteemed by everybody. . . . Many remembrances to Sœur Marie Anastasie. She is a little Jacobite,[1] for the Lord has touched her in His Love, but I trust she will go better along the path of perfection with her lameness than she would have done without it. I salute our new novice, and all who are my dear Sisters and daughters in the Lord. . . .

[1] Alluding to Jacob, when the angel touched him, and he "went halting."

LXXXI.
To a Superior of the Visitation.

Dec. 19, 1619.

OH, my dear child, God has been very good to you in recalling your heart to a loving patience towards your neighbour, and in having so mercifully mingled the balm of gentleness with the wine of your zeal! You see I am answering, though somewhat tardily, the letter you wrote, after I had passed through N——. I write briefly but lovingly to my dear child, whom I have loved, so God willed it, from her cradle.

This was all you needed, my dear child; your zeal was admirable, but it had the fault of being rather sharp, rather bitter, rather excessive. But now all that is purged away, and henceforth it will be a gentle, benignant, gracious, patient, enduring zeal. Contemplate the Holy Babe of Bethlehem, in all His incomparable zeal, how humble, how meek, how loving He is!

Be brave, and be joyful, my dear child, and that in the very depth of your soul, for the angels who announce our Saviour's Birth tell us in their song that there is joy, peace, blessedness, to "all men of good will," in order that all may know that we need nothing to receive Him save good-will, and that even although our good-will has as yet borne no fruit, He came to shower blessings on that good-will, and by degrees He will render it fruitful, so long as we give it up freely to His guidance, as

I hope you and I mean to do, my child. So be it.
Always wholly yours.

LXXXII.

To a Religious of the Visitation.

WHAT abundant blessings God will shed forth upon your heart, and what consolation on mine, my dear daughter, if you continue to grow in the more perfect practice of Divine Love. Sometimes the Holy Spirit delights to bring about His gracious work gradually, and the vocations He inspires are very real and stedfast.

The man of whom we read in the Gospel bade one son "go work in his vineyard, but he answered and said, I will not, but afterward he repented and went. And he came to the second and said likewise. And he answered, I go, sir, and went not. Whether of them twain did the will of his father?" our Saviour asked. Doubtless, my daughter, it was the first.

You have too brave a heart not to do perfectly whatever is required of you by Him Who will have an undivided service; go on thus, dear daughter, your mind fixed on God, gazing stedfastly upon your Heavenly Bridegroom, set to do all things according to His Will, and doubt not but that He will fill you with His Own Grace, and give you strength equal to all that which He may require of you.

Christ holds the gift of prayer, ready to bestow it

on you so soon as you are emptied of self; that is to say, the love of your own flesh and your own will. As soon as you are really humble, He will fill your heart with that gift. Be content to advance patiently by slow degrees, till the time when He gives you feet to run, or rather wings to fly. Accept willingly yet a while your position as a mere embryo. You will soon be full grown. Cast yourself in loving abasement before God and men;— He speaks chiefly to humble ears. "Hearken, O daughter," He says, "and consider, incline thine ear, forget also thine own people, and thy father's house."[1] Even the Only Beloved Son fell on His Face as He prayed to the Father. God will fill your vessel with precious balm if He sees that it no longer contains this world's perfumes. But, my dear daughter, beware of saying, like him we read of in the Gospel, "I go, sir," without a firm desire to go.

LXXXIII.
To a Superior of the Visitation.
On Unwise Abstinence.

Jan. 11, 1620.

... THIS good child is right in believing her inclination to fast to be a real temptation. It is, and will be such while she continues to abstain in this manner, which doubtless enfeebles her body, but on the other hand strengthens her self-will. She weakens the body, but meanwhile she feeds

[1] Ps. xlv. 10.

her heart with a most poisonous self-esteem and self-love.

When abstinence is opposed to obedience, it simply transfers what is sinful from the body to the soul. Let this person strive to control her own will, and she will soon shake off these phantoms of piety to which she clings with so much mere superstition. She has consecrated her physical strength to God, and she has no right to ruin it, save when God may will that it be ruined; and she cannot know His Will save through obedience to those whom He has placed in authority over her. If necessary, you must help her in this temptation by calling in the advice of some faithful servant of God; more help than mine may be needed to uproot these fanciful notions concerning external holiness, to which self-love clings so closely.

LXXXIV.

To a Religious.

(Probably the person alluded to in the last letter.)

Jan. 11, 1620.

I UNDERSTAND the suggestions made by your enemy, my dear child, with a view to hindering your progress, and I also see that the Holy Spirit of God is giving you grace to stand firmly and stedfastly in the path in which He would have you go. My dear daughter, the Evil One cares not how much you macerate your body, provided you nourish your self-will. It is not austerity which he fears, it is obedience. What greater austerity is there than the constant subjection of the will to obedience?

Be honest with yourself; you delight in these voluntary penances, if indeed that may be called penance which is the work of self-will. But when after much intreaty and much consideration you took the habit, you entered the school of obedience and abnegation of self-will, instead of being guided by your own private judgment. Now do not allow yourself to be upset,—abide where our Lord placed you. No doubt you find much to mortify your heart, through your own imperfection, which so often needs to be corrected and set right; but what ought to be your aim save true mortification of self, and a constant sense of your own unworthiness? Do you reply that you are not allowed to carry out the penitence you desire? But tell me, dear child, what better penitence can a faulty heart practise than that of bearing the cross of a renounced self-will? Enough: God will uphold you in the vocation to which He has called you with the Same Hand Which placed you in it, and the enemy will not prevail over you; but having been tried by temptation you will be crowned with perseverance. I am, my dear child, yours wholly.

LXXXV.

To the Abbess Angélique, of Port Royal.

ANNECY, *Feb.* 4, 1620.

.... IT is something gained that you are more exact in the observance of your rule. God formed man first of the dust of the ground, and afterwards He breathed into his nostrils the breath of life, and man became a living soul. Our Lord teaches us that humiliations often are the means of leading us to humility. If you are stedfast in what is external, by degrees the interior spirit will follow.

Indeed, my daughter, I understand how you are enthralled by all these suggestions of vanity; they are fostered by the fertility and subtlety of your imagination, but why need you trouble about them? When the birds of the air swooped down upon the sacrifice which Abraham offered to God, he "drove them away."[1] And so, my daughter, a simple utterance of some holy words will drive away these thoughts, or deprive them of all their power to hurt. "O Lord, forgive this child of the old Adam, for she knows not what she does." Or sing softly, "He hath put down the mighty from their seat, and hath exalted the humble and meek." But make all such acts quietly and simply, as for love, not in a spirit of strife.

Accustom yourself to speak quietly, to walk quietly, to do everything quietly and gently, and you will see that in three or four years all this eagerness and hurry will be quite overcome. But to do this you must make a habit of doing things quietly, even when there is no particular reason for being eager: going to bed, getting up, sitting down, eating, talking with your Sisters; in short, never allow yourself intentionally to set aside the rule.

I know very well that you will break it many times a day, and that your impetuous temperament

[1] Gen. xv. 11.

will burst forth often; but never mind so long as it is not deliberate, or with the consent of your will, and that so soon as you become conscious of your excitement you strive to still it.

Be very watchful as to whatever can give offence to others; if you fail in this respect, strive to repair the mischief as promptly as possible. All these little jealousies are unimportant; indeed, they may be useful, because they show you your own love of self, and teach you to make acts of the opposing virtue.

LXXXVI.
To Mademoiselle de Froubille.

ANNECY, *Aug.* 9, 1620.

IT is an unspeakable delight to me, my dear daughter, to see the heavenly working of the Holy Spirit in your heart, as testified by your resolute, generous renunciation of the world. This is true supernatural wisdom, my child, and shares the spirit which moved Our Lady to "rise up and go into the hill country." Such readiness to do God's Will is a powerful means of obtaining great and wondrous graces for the fulfilment of any good work. You, my dear daughter, after the first severe shock to your heart, of tearing away its natural inclinations and tempers, have found comfort and peace in the resting-place you have chosen, wherein to sing ceaseless praises to your Saviour and Creator.

Dear child, I would have you often raise your

thoughts to the eternal reward which awaits you in Heaven for having acted thus. It is all as nothing (and I know you feel this), when compared with your duty, or with the everlasting reward held out to you by God. What are all the trifles which we despise and forsake for His Sake but poor little pretences of liberty, more binding in reality than His chains? ceaseless anxieties, empty longings, never to be gratified, which disturb the mind with endless fears and cares, and make life restless and unsatisfied. Yet it has pleased God that whosoever will forsake these mere fleeting trifles and vain delights should receive in exchange eternal happiness; a bliss in which, to love Him ever more and more, will be to the soul one ceaseless flood of joy.

In truth, dear daughter, I should not have ventured to bid you trample down your feelings, your fears, and anxieties and repugnances, if I had not fully believed that the Heavenly Bridegroom, of His great Goodness, would give you strength and courage to maintain His cause against natural likings. And now, my child, you have quietly died to the world and the world is dead to you. This is but a part of your sacrifice: you have yet to be a victim—you have to tear self from out your heart, cutting off and rooting up all the little failings left by nature and the world's training; and then you must burn all that remains of self-love upon the altar, until your whole soul is consumed with the flames of Divine Love. But, my very dear child, this is not to be done in a day. He Who graciously enabled you to make the first step will enable you to go on; His is a Father's Hand, and

He will either lead you unconsciously to yourself, or He will give you that constancy and joy which He gave to the saint we commemorate to-day (S. Laurence). Therefore, fear nothing ; " I am confident that He Which hath begun a good work in you will perform it until the day of Jesus Christ."[1] Only "be faithful in a few things, and He will make thee ruler over many things."

You promise that, if it is allowed, you will write me a history of your blessed Retreat, and I can promise you that it will be allowed, and that I shall greatly delight to receive your report. May God be ever blessed, praised, and glorified, my very dear child. In Him and for Him, I am in all sincerity, yours, etc.

Your good Carthusian uncle will rejoice when he hears that you have become a Religious.

LXXXVII.

To a Lady, expecting her Confinement.

MY DEAREST DAUGHTER, *Sept.* 29, 1620.

I am no ways surprised to hear that your good resolutions seem to be weary and heavy ; it is an unquestionable fact that our souls are habitually affected by the condition and circumstances of our inferior nature,—that which is purely physical, I mean, and subject to physical infirmities. So a delicate frame, oppressed by discomfort and pain, cannot but hinder the soul from being as lively and vigorous, as ready for exertion, as it would be at

[1] Phil i. 6.

another time. Still, all this does not really counteract the true life of the superior nature; its acts are as acceptable to God as they would be were you in the most cheerful, easy condition— rather more so, being made with greater effort and struggle to yourself; but of course they are not so acceptable to her who makes them, because of that very effort and struggle.

My dearest daughter, we must not be unjust, or exact more than is possible of ourselves. When we are weighed down with ill-health or bodily weakness, we must only require the soul to make acts of submission and acceptance of its weariness, uniting our will to God's Good Pleasure; while as to external acts we must do the best we can, and be satisfied often to perform such things *à contre cœur*, languidly and wearily. But in order to turn all this weariness and languor to good account, so that it may advance the Love of God in our heart, it is needful to face it honestly, and to accept, and even love, the humiliation it brings. By so doing you will change the heavy leaden weight which oppresses you into gold, and that a finer gold too than anything you have known in your brightest hours. So be patient with yourself. Let your superior being bear calmly with the infirmity of your inferior nature, and do not fail continually to offer up to your Creator's Glory the little one whose existence He wills to create by means of you.

My dear daughter, we have a Capucin artist at Annecy, who, as you may imagine, paints nothing save what is for God and His temple. While painting, his mind is so wholly given to his work that he cannot pray at the same time, and often he is very much absorbed and wearied by his work; nevertheless, he does it heartily, as advancing God's Glory, hoping that his pictures will promote His Worship among men. So, my dear daughter, the child you bear is created in the image and likeness of God, but the physical discomfort involved wearies and oppresses you, so that you are unable to perform your wonted religious exercises heartily and with enjoyment; but accept all this weariness and exhaustion lovingly, as your contribution towards God's Work, remembering that your babe is destined one day to be an inhabitant of the Heavenly Jerusalem, to be the cause of joy to God, to men, and angels, that the Saints will give thanks because of its eternal blessedness, and you, too, when you are permitted to share it with your child. So be patient for a while, though you feel lifeless and weary, clinging firmly to the Holy Will of our Dear Lord, Who, in His Eternal Wisdom, has so willed and ordered events. I cannot say how earnestly my soul desires that yours may grow in all perfection. God has planted you very deeply in my heart. May His Divine Goodness guide both you and me according to His Good and Holy Will, and bless all your family abundantly, especially your dear husband, whose I am, as well as yours invariably, etc.

LXXXVIII.
To a Young Lady in Illness.

Feb. 8, 1621.

FIRE on all sides, my dearest child! the fire of fever consuming your body, and the fever of fire destroying your house! But I hope that your heart is so filled with the fire of heavenly love as to be able to say amid all these troubles, "The Lord gave health and home, the Lord hath taken them away, the Lord's Holy Name be praised."

True, you say, but nevertheless we are grievously impoverished and discomfited. Doubtless, my dear child, but "blessed are the poor, for theirs is the kingdom of Heaven." Dwell upon the troubles and the patience of Job; meditate upon him, prince as he was, sitting on a dunghill. He endured patiently, and God gave him more abundantly than before of all temporal blessings, together with tenfold of such as are eternal.

You are the child of Christ Crucified; what wonder then if you have to carry His Cross? "I was dumb, and opened not my mouth, for it was Thy doing," David says. We reach eternal life through many a stormy wave and wind. Cast all your care upon God, and He will nourish you, and stretch forth His Right Hand to shield you. I pray Him to do so, and also that, in proportion to the trials He sends you, He may abundantly strengthen you with His Holy Grace.

LXXXIX.

To a Superior of the Visitation.

ANNECY, *April 2, 1621.*

. . . . As to your question, it is impossible to give any full answer—impossible to me, but also impossible to the Angels and Cherubim, for God is above all intelligence; and were there any intelligence equal to understand, or to say what God really is, it must, of necessity, be God itself, for it must be Infinite. . . . .

God is an Infinite Spirit, the cause and motive power of all creation, which exists and lives solely in and by Him. He is Invisible, nor has earthly eye seen Him, save in the Saviour's Humanity, Which He united to Divinity. God is Omnipresent, Omnipotent, Boundless, holding and containing all things, but Himself held and contained by nothing.

In short, my daughter, even as the soul inhabits the body, though invisible, so God is invisibly in the world; as the soul maintains life in the body while it abides therein, so God quickens all creation; and were God not in the world it must cease to be. As in a certain sense the soul, while it inhabits the body, yet has an independent existence, for it sees, hears, and understands things in which the body has no share, so while God is in the world He is without and beyond the world, beyond all that we can imagine; finally, God is the Sovereign Being, the principle and cause of all that is good and free from sin.

Oh, my daughter, this is a mighty abyss of thought; the Spirit Which gives life and creation, Which preserves all creation, without Which nothing can exist, while He has no need of anything, having been Infinite from all eternity; Infinitely Blessed, without beginning or end—Eternal. To Him only be all honour and glory. Amen.

I have not said this as meaning to tell you what God is, but rather to prove to you that I neither know it nor can tell you; that I can but confess myself to be a very nothing before Him Whom I adore devoutly, together with the Humanity of our Saviour Which He has united to Himself, so that therein we may approach Him by means of our thought and feeling in Heaven;—with our heart and body in the Blessed Sacrament of the Eucharist on earth. Amen.

XC.

To the Portress of a Convent of the Visitation.

MY VERY DEAR DAUGHTER, *Aug. 2, 1621.*

I am very much pleased to hear that you are fixed in the service of the Lord, in the house of His Holy Mother, and in an occupation which I hold to be most edifying. "I had rather be a doorkeeper in the house of my God than to dwell in the tents of ungodliness."[1]

Hitherto you have been happy in being able to serve God in the person of a mistress whose Master He is, and with whom you have had many spiritual

[1] Ps. lxxxiv. 11.

advantages; but now you are happier still in serving that same Lord in the persons of those who have given up everything for His Service.

It is a great honour, my dear daughter, to be in charge of a house where the Brides of Christ dwell; for she who keeps the door of a monastery keeps guard over the peace, tranquillity, and devotion of the house, and, moreover, she may have opportunities of edifying those who approach it.

There is nothing unimportant that concerns the service of God, but I hold your charge as portress to be one of great importance, and most useful to such as exercise it with thoughtfulness and humility. I thank you for letting me share in your satisfaction. Yours, etc.

XCI.

To a Lady. On Confession.

Aug. 21, 1621.

... INDEED, my dear daughter, this great fear which has so cruelly tormented you ought now to be at an end, inasmuch as you have every assurance which can be had in this world that your sins have been fully put away in the sacred Sacrament of penitence. No, you must on no account harass yourself with doubts as to whether the circumstances of your faults were told with sufficient explicitness. All theologians agree that it is not requisite to mention all the details and circumstances of a sin. Thus he who says, "I have killed a man," is not required to say that he drew his sword, or that he has caused infinite sorrow to his relations, or that he gave grievous scandal to those who saw the deed. All this is implied; it is enough if the penitent says whether he committed the deed in sudden rage or deliberately, whether his victim was a layman or an ecclesiastic; after which he must leave the priest who hears him to form his own opinion of the act.

Again, he who confesses to having set fire to a house is not obliged to say in detail what was in it; he need only say whether there were any living persons or not. So, my dear daughter, be at rest; your confessions have been perfectly good; now turn your thoughts to your spiritual progress, and do not dwell upon past sins, save to humble yourself meekly before God, and bless Him for His Mercy which has pardoned them through His Holy Sacraments.

The *Introduction to the Devout Life* will be useful to you, my daughter; but your mistake is that you want to be all it sets before you at once. Nevertheless, this very Introduction will show you that it is not the work of a day to shape your life to its teaching, but rather the work of a life, and that there is no reason to be surprised at your many failings and shortcomings in the work. My dear child, a devoted life is not a thing to be attained in a hurry; we must work hard at it, no doubt, but the chief thing in the matter is trust in God, and you must toil on quietly, though watchfully. . . . . Do not grow weary, my daughter; strive to place your quick, active mind in the attitude of a little child. Go on in lowliness, and God will lift you up. Write to me whenever you please.

Ever with a most fatherly affection, yours, etc.

XCII.

To a Lady.

Sept. 20, 1621.

IT was a real comfort to me to have tidings of your soul's state, my dearest child, for in truth I have a very special interest therein. The difficulty which you experience in prayer will not lessen its value in God's Sight, for He prizes a service offered Him amid contradictions, whether internal or external, more highly than one which is all sweetness and delight; even as our Lord Himself reconciled us to God through His own labours, His bloodshedding, His Death.

Neither should you be surprised not to see any great progress either in your temporal or spiritual progress. All trees, my dear child, do not bear fruit at the same season. Some of the best are longest in coming to maturity. I have heard it said that the palm tree grows a hundred years before it bears fruit. God has hidden within the secrets of His Providence when and how He vouchsafes to answer your prayers, and it may be that He will answer you most graciously by so doing rather according to His views than yours. Be at peace, my child, within His Fatherly Arms, and in His Loving Care. You are His, and His only. I have a most thankful remembrance of that day when, after your confession, prostrate before His Mercy Seat, you dedicated yourself and your whole life for ever and in all things to His most Holy Will. So be it, my dearest child. I am, irrevocably, your very humble, etc.

P.S.—Oh, dear child, by what various ways this Eternal Providence delights to comfort them that are His! Truly it is a great grace when He keeps back our reward and happiness until the life to come. This is only a last word. May God be our all for ever. Amen.

XCIII.

To a Novice. On her Profession.

ANNECY, *Jan* 27, 1622.

WELL, my dearest child, so at last you are in spirit laid upon the altar, ready to be sacrificed and consumed as a burnt-offering to the Living God! Surely this day is one to be counted among those "which the Lord hath made." May it be one of those hours which God hath blessed from all Eternity; may it have its beginning in the humility of the Cross, and its end in a glorious immortality! How many wishes I shall make on that happy day for my dear child's soul; how many aspirations and auguries of blessedness; how many invocations to the Blessed Virgin, the Saints, and Angels, that they may take part in the consecration of that dear child! In all this I include my beloved child, Sister N. . . . . I am greatly comforted to think that the words spoken to you,[1] "Thou art dead, and thy life is hid with Christ in God," will be most true to you, for, dearest child, on the truth of these words must hang the truth of those which follow : " When Christ, Who is our life, shall appear, then shall ye also appear with Him in glory."[2]

Dearest child, I salute your soul and that of Sister N., and am, for ever, yours in God, etc.

XCIV.

To a Lady.

ANNECY, *Feb.* 8, 1621.

.... As to the fear of death and hell, which

---

[1] In the profession of a nun of the Visitation the celebrant says to her, " My Sister, thou art dead to thyself and to the world ; henceforth live only to God." The other nuns chant, " Blessed are the dead which die in the Lord ; " and the newly-professed Sister lies down and is covered with a pall. A nun reads a lesson from the Book of Job, and the " De profundis " is chanted. After a prayer, the celebrant sprinkles the pall with holy water, saying, "Awake, thou that sleepest, and arise from the dead, and Christ shall give thee light."[a] The nun having risen, he gives her a taper, saying, "The path of the just is as a shining light, that shineth more and more unto the perfect day."[b] Then the nun chants the words, "The Lord is my Light and my Salvation, whom then shall I fear? the Lord is the Strength of my life, of whom then shall I be afraid?"[c] And after another prayer the celebrant gives her a crucifix, saying the words quoted by Francis de Sales, " Ye are dead, and your life is hid with Christ in God. When Christ, Who is our life, shall appear, then shall ye also appear with Him in Glory."[d] He adds, " God forbid that you should glory, save in the Cross of our Lord Jesus Christ."[e]

[2] Col. iii. 3, 4.

---

[a] Eph. v. 14.   [b] Prov. iv. 18.   [c] Ps. xxvii. 1.
[d] Col. iii. 3, 4.   [e] Gal. vi. 14.

troubles your soul, it is really a temptation of the enemy, but one which the Beloved of your soul will mercifully use to your advancement in purity and humility. If, with entire submission and resignation to His Providence, you put aside all self-seeking, even in spiritual things, and leave yourself absolutely in His Hands, He will either deliver you from this fear, or He will enable you so to bear it that you will eternally bless Him for it.

My dearest child, boastful thoughts, even such as are arrogant and self-sufficient, cannot harm a soul which repulses them as they arise, and which says daily with David, "So foolish was I and ignorant, even as it were a beast before Thee, nevertheless I am always by Thee."[1] As though he would say, "Helpless and worse than nothing as I am in Thy Sight, O Sole Good, I am full of trust in Thee, and my nothingness hopes all things from Thee."

My dearest child, be at rest, notwithstanding all that troubles you. You are intellectually convinced that God is too Good to reject one who is no wilful hypocrite, whatever temptations or suggestions may arise. I will commend your needs to our All-Wise, All-Powerful God; do you bring your sighs to His Ear, and tell Him all your intentions. "I am Thine, save me." He will do so, dear child. His Holy Name be blessed.

[All the letters, so far, are dated, and have been given in order up to the last year of S. Francis de Sales' life. There are other letters which bear no

[1] Ps. lxxiii. 21, 22.

date, and which follow here; the chief of these are on subjects connected with the spiritual life, and the precise date at which they were written is not of special importance.]

XCV.

To the Abbé .... On Friendship.
WITH HIS OWN LIKENESS.

MY DEAREST BROTHER,

You ask if my heart will not cleave to yours always and for ever? And I answer, dear brother, it is the maxim of three great lovers, all three saints, all three doctors of the Church, all three stedfast friends, all three great masters in moral theology,—namely, S. Ambrose, S. Jerome, and S. Augustine, " Amicitia quæ desinere potuit nunquam vera fuit."[1] There, my dear brother! there is a sacred oracle to tell you that our friendship is eternal and invariable, inasmuch as it is true and holy,[2] founded on truth, not vanity; on the mutual communication of spiritual gifts, not on worldly interests; and thus to love, and to be capable of ceasing to love you, are two incompatible things.

The friendships of this world are worldly;—the world passes away, and so do its friendships, but ours is of God, in God, for God. "Ipsa autem idem ipse est, et annis ejus non deficient. Mundus perit, et concupiscentia ejus; Christus non perit, nec dilectio ejus." This is an unfailing consequence.

---
[1] "A friendship which can diminish was never truly one."
[2] "Sainte et non feinte."

I send you the likeness of the earthly man ; I cannot refuse anything you ask. I am told that I have never been well painted, but I think it matters very little. "In imagine pertransit homo, sed et frustra conturbatur." I have borrowed this picture for you, I have none of my own. Alas ! if the likeness of my Creator were but graven on my mind, you might delight in that! O Jesu! tuo lumine, tuo redemptos sanguine sana, refove, perfice, tibi conformes effice. Amen.

XCVI.

To Madame de Chantal.

MY DEAREST MOTHER,

As regards receiving women (into the Order), there is great danger of erring on the side of human prudence—of trusting too much to nature, too little to God's Grace. I find it difficult to prevent too much weight being given to delicacy of health and bodily infirmity. You would have none that are blind, or lame, or feeble, come to the feast. In a word, it is hard work to fight against human respect, and give heed only to lowliness and simple charity.

I have written kindly, as you wished, to Sister N., and that most sincerely, for I have a real affection for the poor child. I do not believe any one has a more hearty, tender, sincere love of souls than I have, and perhaps I overflow somewhat in expression thereof at times. You know that this is the truth ; God has made me thus. But, nevertheless, I like independent, vigorous souls, who are free from feminine littleness : an excessive softness bewilders the heart, disturbs it, distracts it from loving communion with God, and hinders perfect resignation and death to self. All that is not God should be as nought to us.

It seems to me that I love nothing save God, and all souls for God. May it be in and for Him alone. Dear Mother, there is no end to this subject. Be happy, filled with God, and His Holy Love. Good night.

XCVII.
To Madame de Chantal.

I WOULD have you be extremely small and lowly in your own eyes, as soft and yielding as a dove, loving lowliness and cultivating it faithfully. Make good use of every opportunity for so doing. Do not be quick of speech; rather let your words be slow, humble, gentle, and let your modest thoughtful silence be eloquent.

Bear with your neighbour, and be ever ready to make excuses for him. Do not philosophise over the contradictions which beset you ; do not dwell upon them, but strive to see God in all things without exception, and acquiesce in His Will with absolute submission.

Do everything for God, uniting yourself to Him by a mere upward glance, or by the overflowing of your heart towards Him.

Never be in a hurry : do everything quietly and

in a calm spirit. Do not lose your inward peace for anything whatsoever, even if your whole world seems upset. What does anything belonging to this life matter, when compared with a peaceful heart?

Commend all to God, and then lie still and be at rest in His Bosom.

Whatever happens, abide stedfast in a determination to cling simply to God, trusting to His Eternal Love for you; and if you find that you have wandered forth from this shelter, recall your heart quietly and simply.

Maintain a holy simplicity of mind, and do not smother yourself with a host of cares, wishes, attachments, or longings, under any pretext.

Our Lord loves you, and would have you wholly His. Seek no other arms to bear you, no other breast whereon to rest. Let Him be the boundary of your horizon; fix your mind on Him alone.

Let your will be so closely bound to His, that nothing can come between—forget all else. God would have your undivided heart.

Be of good cheer, and prostrate yourself before Him, seeking nothing save your Dear Lord's Love.

Refuse nothing, however painful; put on Christ Crucified, love Him in His Sufferings, and often turn to these in ejaculatory prayer.

Do this, my dear daughter and mother, and may Jesus Christ fulfil all His Holy Will in us, for us, and by us. Amen.

XCVIII.

To a Superior of the Visitation.
On Supposed Visions and Revelations.

I HAVE not been able to answer your questions sooner, my dear daughter. So far as I have seen, I have no reason to think other than well of this girl, and she deserves to be loved and cared for; but as to her visions, revelations, and predictions, I hold them in the greatest suspicion, as useless, senseless, and unworthy of any attention. Their very frequency would be suspicious, and moreover they touch upon personal subjects, concerning which God very rarely vouchsafes us any manifestation, such as assurance of eternal salvation, confirmation in grace, the measure of individual holiness, and a hundred similar things which are of no possible use. It reminds me of S. Gregory, when a lady-in-waiting of the Empress asked him some such questions concerning the future, and he replied, "My daughter, you ask to be told that which is equally difficult and useless." Nor is it any answer to say that hereafter we shall know why such revelations were made,—this is a mere evasion.

Further; when God intends to make use of special revelations for His creatures' benefit, He generally prepares the way for them, either by undoubted miracles or by a very extraordinary saintliness in those who receive them. Accordingly, when the evil one wants to deceive any one with false revelations, he often begins by prompting idle presages and a sham holiness.

. . . . The evil one is very crafty in all this, and depend upon it, all these marvels must be treated with suspicion ; nevertheless, as I said, you must deal very kindly with this poor girl, who, I take it, is no further blameable in the matter, than inasmuch as she takes a vain delight in her foolish imaginations. Only, my dear Sister, you must treat all her revelations and visions with utter contempt, just as if she were narrating the dreams and fancies of feverish delirium. Do not either refute or argue about them, but when she begins to talk about such things, change the subject, and talk to her of solid virtue and the real perfection of the religious life, especially of the simplicity of true faith, in which the Saints lived, without any visions or special revelations, content to believe fervently in the revelation of Holy Scripture, and in the Church's apostolic doctrine.

Remind her sometimes of our Lord's announcement that "many will say unto the Lord, Lord, have we not prophesied in Thy Name, and in Thy Name have cast out devils, and in Thy Name done many wonderful works? And then will I profess unto them, I never knew you, depart from Me, ye that work iniquity."[1] But generally I should call her thoughts to His blessed words, "Learn of Me, for I am meek and lowly in heart."[2] In short, testify an absolute indifference to all her revelations.

. . . . As to the vocation of Mademoiselle N. I

[1] Matt. vii. 22, 23.   [2] Matt. xi. 29.

think it is a true vocation, although mixed up with sundry infirmities and intellectual hindrances, and it would be better if she had turned to God solely for His Sake, and in order to be wholly His. But God does not draw all His servants to Himself after precisely the same fashion ; indeed, there are but few who come to Him with a sole and undivided intention of serving Him. Of all those women whose conversion is related in the Gospel, only Magdalene came out of pure love ;—the woman taken in adultery was brought to Christ through her public shame ; the Samaritan through personal conviction of sin ; the Canaanitish woman came to Him seeking temporal relief. So the first hermit, Paul, withdrew from the world when only fifteen to avoid persecution ; S. Ignatius Loyola sought the Lord by reason of his tribulations, and so on of a hundred others.

We must not expect every one to make a perfect beginning ; it matters little how we begin, if we are firmly resolved to go on earnestly, and persevere to the end.

XCIX.

WE ought not to wish for extraordinary things ; as for instance, that God should do for us as for S. Catharine of Sienna, whose heart was replaced by His Heart. Rather we should wish that our poor hearts may henceforth be wholly obedient to that of our Dear Lord, a way of imitating S. Catharine which will make us gentle, humble, and charitable.

And inasmuch as there is nothing nearer to the Saviour's Heart than gentleness, humility, and charity, we must diligently cultivate these graces,— love to our neighbour, humility towards God. True sanctity consists in a capacity for the enjoyment of God, not in foolish imaginations and raptures, which only foster self-conceit, and drive out obedience and humility. It is a mere abuse to aim at extasy. Let us practise true hearty meekness and submission, self-renunciation, love of abjection, kindness to others, and we shall have attained the best and safest kind of extasy granted to God's servants.

When you see a person go into raptures and extasies in prayer, who at the same time knows no extasy in his life—I mean whose life is not lifted up and raised to God by renunciation of worldly desires, and the natural inclination and will; who is devoid of interior gentleness, simplicity, and humility, above all of continual charity—you may be sure that all his raptures are very questionable and dangerous; they are raptures which may excite the wonder of others, but which will never sanctify those who experience them. What gain is there to a soul in being rapt and ravished in prayer, if his ordinary life and conversation are wrapped up in low earthly things? Surely to live above oneself in prayer, and yet to be very low in life and action; to be angelic in meditation, and earthly in conversation, is to swear both by God and Baal; nor can there be any reasonable doubt that all such raptures and extasies are mere deceits and delusions of Satan.

Blessed indeed are they who live a supernatural extatic life, raised altogether above themselves, although they have never been carried away with any raptures in prayer. There is many a saint in Paradise who never tasted any rapture or extasy in contemplation : many who never knew any greater privilege in prayer than that of devotion and fervour! But there was never yet a saint whose life was devoid of those active raptures which consist in victory over self and natural disposition.

C.
To a Superior of the Visitation.

INDEED, my dearest daughter, I see great cause in your letter to bless God on your soul's behalf, for I can see that you possess a practical holy indifference, although you do not feel it. I think nothing of all you tell me about your little outbursts. Such little surprises of temper are inevitable in this mortal life, and even the great Apostle is forced to exclaim, "O wretched man that I am! I delight in the law of God after the inward man, but I see another law in my members, warring against the law of my mind,"—the two opposing forces, nature and grace; "Who shall deliver me from the body of this death?"[1] My daughter, self-love only dies with our bodily death; so long as we are in exile here we must always be liable to its overt attacks or its hidden workings : enough if we do not consent deliberately or intentionally to the one or the other.

[1] Rom. vii. 22-24.

And the grace of holy indifference is so great that our "old man," the sentient, earthly part of our nature, is incapable of bringing it to perfection. Even our Lord Himself, inasmuch as He took upon Him Adam's nature, while free from sin and all which appertains thereto, was not indifferent, but asked that the cup might pass from Him. Perfect indifference was only to be attained by His Higher Nature, in which He was God. So do not be disturbed about yourself. When we break the law of holy indifference in ordinary matters, or by sudden sallies of self-love or earthly passions, we ought to prostrate our hearts as soon as possible before God, crying out in all humility and trust, "Have mercy upon me, O Lord, for I am weak!"[1] And then we should rise up in peace and composure, mend our broken nets, and go on with our work. When our lute is out of tune, we need neither break its strings nor cast it aside ; we must rather listen attentively till we ascertain where the fault lies, and then make that particular string tighter or more slack, according to the need.

Be at rest, my dear daughter, and write to me in all confidence when it is any comfort to you; I shall always answer you faithfully and with sincere pleasure.

CI.

To a Superior of the Visitation.

. . . . You are going on well enough, dear daughter,

[1] Ps. vi., 2.

and your only danger is that you gaze too anxiously at your own steps through fear of falling. You ponder too much upon your sallies of self-love, which doubtless are frequent, but which will never be dangerous so long as you put them from you quietly, without being annoyed by their importunity, or astonished by their multitude. Go on in all simplicity; do not be so anxious to win a quiet mind, and it will be all the quieter.

What makes you so anxious? God is very Good; He sees you exactly as you are. Your inclinations cannot harm you, however bad they be, if they only serve to exercise your better will in resolutely uniting itself to God. Raise your eyes, my dear daughter, and fix them high through perfect trust in the Goodness of God. Do not be eager and cumbered even for Him; remember that He told Martha that He did not will her to be cumbered even about well-doing.

Do not examine so closely into the progress of your soul. Do not crave so much to be perfect, but let your spiritual life be formed by your duties, and by the actions which are called forth by circumstances. Do not take overmuch thought for to-morrow. God, Who has led you safely on so far, will lead you on to the end. Be altogether at rest in the loving holy confidence which you ought to have in His Heavenly Providence.

Pray very earnestly to our Dear Lord for me, who, for my part, cease not to wish you all the sweetness of His Holy Love, and therein that of promoting your neighbour's happiness, which He desires so greatly. I think of you as in an exalted place, whence you look down upon the world, and up to Heaven, whither you aspire. Indeed, dear daughter, I am wholly yours, and I believe that you do well to live entirely in the Arms of Divine Providence, without Which all is vanity and helplessness. May God ever be in your heart. Amen.

CII.
To a newly appointed Superior.

THE service you are about to render to our Lord and His Dear Mother is apostolic; you are going to gather together certain souls in a congregation, with a view to leading them in a united band to the spiritual war we have to make on God's behalf against the world, the flesh, and the devil; or rather you are going to collect a new swarm of bees, who will gather the sweet honey of Divine Love within their hive. Be all very courageous, through full confidence in His Goodness Who calls you to this holy task. Who ever trusted in God, and was put to confusion?

Your mistrust of self is good, so long as it is the groundwork of confidence in God; but if it ever should lead you to being discouraged, disturbed, vexed, or melancholy, then I intreat you reject it as the greatest possible temptation, and do not allow your mind to argue or dally with the anxiety or depression to which you are disposed. It is a simple and certain truth that God permits those who seek to serve Him to encounter many difficulties, but also that He never leaves them to sink under the burthen so long as they trust in Him. The great thing you must heed is, never to let your mind argue in favour of the temptation to be discouraged, under any pretext whatever, not even under the plausible pretext of humility. Humility, my dear daughter, would fain refuse responsible positions, but it does not persist in refusing them; and if placed in any such by those who have rightful authority, humility does not dwell upon its own unworthiness, but goes on believing all things, hoping all things, bearing all things in charity, always being perfectly simple-hearted. Holy humility is a close follower of obedience, and while not daring to think itself capable of anything, it believes obedience capable of everything. Just as true simplicity would shun responsibilities through humility, so true humility fulfils them simply. Your body is weak, but the wedding garment of charity will cover all that. Weak people draw all who know them to give what support they may, and are objects of great affection when they carry their Cross meekly and lovingly.

We ought to be alike foremost in seeking and taking remedies, and patient and brave in bearing our ills. He who can maintain meekness amid pain and weariness, and peace amid worry and overwhelming cares, is well nigh perfect; and although there are but few even among Religious who have attained to so blessed a height, still at all times some such have been found, and we ought all to aim at it. Almost every one finds certain virtues easy to practise and others more difficult; and every one contends in favour of that which is easy to himself, exaggerating the difficulties of that which is not so easy to him. Among the ten Virgins of Holy Writ, only five possessed the blessed oil of wisdom and holy joy. Perfect evenness of temper, true gentleness and sweetness of heart, are more rare than perfect chastity, but they are so much the more to be cultivated. I commend them to you, my dearest daughter, because upon these, like the oil of a lamp, depends the flame of good example. Nothing is so edifying as a loving good temper.

Mete out a very even measure among your spiritual daughters, and do not let yourself be led by natural gifts to bestow affection or kindness unfairly. How many people whose external manner is disagreeable are most acceptable in God's Sight! Beauty, a pleasant manner, gracious words, often make persons very attractive, who nevertheless are living wholly to themselves; true charity looks for real goodness and moral beauty, and pours itself out upon all without preferences.

Go on then, my dear daughter, in the work to which God has called you: He will be on your right hand, so that no difficulty need move you; He will lead you along His own path with His own Hand. Be of good courage, and let your courage be not merely great, but stedfast and enduring. In order to win such, ask it continually of Him Who Alone can give it; He will give it, if you correspond to His Grace in all simplicity of heart.

May the love, the peace, and the consolation of His Holy Spirit be ever in your soul, Amen. I give you God's Holy Blessing with a most fatherly affection. May you be blessed as you go and as you come; serving God, and serving your neighbours; humbling yourself to the depths of your own nothingness, rising to the heights of His Grace. May God be ever your all, my dearest daughter. Amen.

CIII.
To a Superior of the Visitation.

MY DAUGHTER,

Beware of answering those good Sisters or their foundress otherwise than with the most invariable humility, gentleness, and sincere simplicity. "Dearly beloved, avenge not yourselves;" they are S. Paul's words, inspired by the Holy Spirit.[1] Human frailties are to be found sometimes even among God's own special servants, but if we are governed by true Love, we shall bear peacefully with them.

If those good souls despise our institution because they think it to be below their own, they lose sight of charity, which never despises those that are weaker or smaller than itself. True, they are more numerous than you, but do the Seraphim despise the lower Angels? and in Heaven, where our pattern of perfection is to be sought, do the greater Saints despise the lesser? After all, the truth is that he who loves most will be most loved, and he who has loved best will receive the greatest glory. Love God devotedly, and love all His creatures for His Sake, especially those who despise you, and

[1] In the Vulgate, "Non vosmetipsos *defendentes*, charissimi." Rom. xii. 19.

De Sales' Sp. L.]

then do not be perturbed. The evil one exerts himself because he sees that our little institution promotes God's Service and Glory, and he hates it the more that it is the least and last of all, for he is an arrogant spirit, and hates whatever is lowly, because it tends to foster humility, and he, ever proud, haughty, and arrogant, fell from his first estate because he would not accept the spirit of humility. Do you labour on in humility and abjection, and let others say or do what they will. "Except the Lord build the house, their labour is but lost that build it."[1] But if He build it, their labour is but lost who would pull it down. He knows when and with what souls He will fill your monastery. Be at rest. I am, etc.

CIV.

To a Superior of the Visitation.

MY DEAR DAUGHTER,

As to that good person, she deceives herself greatly if she imagines that she can become perfect through prayer, without heeding obedience, which is the favourite virtue of the Bridegroom, in which, by which, and for which He vouchsafed to die. History and experience tell us that both Religious and other men have come to be Saints without the help of mental prayer, but never without obedience.

You are quite right, my daughter; there must be neither reserve nor condition, for if you were to admit Sisters subject to any such, the congregation

[1] Ps. cxxvii. 1.

would soon be filled with the subtlest and most dangerous of all self-love. One Sister would make a condition that she should communicate every day; another, that she might hear three masses; another, that she should have four hours daily for meditation; another, that her work should always be among the sick; and in this way, every one would follow her own taste or presumption rather than Christ Crucified. Those who join our congregation must understand that its object is to be a school and guide towards perfection, and that we aim at helping our spiritual daughters to advance therein by the most effectual means;—moreover, those are not such as are self-chosen. "He who governs himself," says S. Bernard, "has a great fool for his governor."

We should love prayer, but we should love it because we love God. Now he who loves prayer for God's Sake, desires no more time for it than God wills him to have; and what that is is signified to each by obedience. If, therefore, this child (whom I love by reason of all the good which you tell me of her) wishes to grow perfect after her own fashion, she must be given up to her own guidance; but I do not think she will wish it. If she is really devout, and has a true spirit of prayer, she will submit to holy obedience.

The true servant of God takes no thought for the morrow; she fulfils that which He requires of her to-day in a faithful spirit; and in like wise she will fulfil to-morrow's duty; and each as it follows, without let or hindrance. This is how we must unite our wills, not to the means of serving God, but to His Will and pleasure. "Take no thought for the morrow, saying, What shall we eat, or what shall we drink, or wherewithal shall we be clothed, for your Heavenly Father knoweth that ye have need of all these things; but seek ye first the Kingdom of God and His righteousness, and all these things shall be added unto you." This is applicable to our spiritual as well as to our natural life.

Let this daughter, then, win a childlike heart, a will soft as wax, and a mind divested of wishes and inclinations, save the wish to love God. She should be wholly indifferent as to the means by which she is led to love Him. Go on patiently, and in a holy mind amid the cares of your charge, my very dear and beloved daughter. I pray God that He may ever be the life of your soul. Amen.

CV.

To a Religious of the Visitation.
On the Earthly and Spiritual Mind.

IT is most fitting, my dearest child, that I should write a few words to you, and I do so with sincere pleasure. Would to God that I had the power to comfort you! To live after the spirit, my beloved child, is to think, speak, and act according to spiritual graces, and not according to the senses and feelings which appertain to the flesh. We must make use of these, but we must subdue them, and not be led by them; while, on the other hand, we must obey those spiritual graces, and subject all else to them. What are these spiritual graces? Faith, which teaches us truths far beyond the power of the senses; Hope, which teaches us to aspire to an invisible gain; Charity, which teaches us to love God above all things, and our neighbour as ourself, with a love which is not sensual, natural, or self-interested, but pure, solid, and unchangeable, which has its foundation in God.

You see, my child, our earthly mind, with its carnal tendencies, often hinders us from a sufficiently real dependence upon God. We imagine that, worthless as we are, He will not heed us, even as men in their worldly wisdom despise that which is feeble and useless. But, on the contrary, the spirit of faith takes fresh courage amid difficulties, from the certainty that God loves, bears with, and succours the weakest, provided they trust in Him.

The earthly mind seeks to take its share in all that goes on; and it is so full of self-love that it thinks nothing can prosper without its aid. But the spiritual mind cleaves to God, realising that whatever is not God is as nought; and though it takes a charitable and loving share in such matters as come in the way of duty, it willingly abstains from all else, in simple abnegation and humility.

To live after the spirit is to love spiritually; to live after the flesh is to have a carnal affection; for love is the soul's life, just as the soul is the life of the body. One Sister is very gentle and agreeable, and she is most acceptable to me; she loves me, and she seeks to please me; and I reciprocate her love. Who does not see that this is a mere carnal, sensual affection, just as the very brute beasts love those who are kind and useful to them? Another Sister is rough, quick, and uncourteous, but she is very devout, and anxious to grow gentler and more amiable ; therefore, not for any pleasure or profit I find in her, but for God's Sake only, I esteem her, serve her, caress her. This is a spiritual affection, in which the flesh has no part.

"I am mistrustful of myself, and therefore I would fain live according to my inclination." Who cannot see that this is not living after the spirit ? No indeed, my dearest child ; when I was quite young, and had very little of the spiritual in me, I did the like. But although naturally of a timid, anxious mind, I strove to overcome my natural passions, and little by little to perform whatever belongs to the office laid upon me by obedience to God : This is to live after the spirit. My dear child, we live after the spirit when we do the actions, speak the words, and think the thoughts which God's Holy Spirit requires of us. When I speak of thoughts, I mean voluntary thoughts. I am sad, and therefore I do not choose to talk : a waggoner, or a parrot, would do the same. I am sad ; but since charity requires it of me, I will exert myself to talk. This is what the spiritual mind does.

I am despised, and I grow angry; so does the peacock or the monkey.

I am despised, and I give God thanks ; that is what the Apostles did.

So, then, to live after the spirit is to do what faith, hope, and charity teach, in things temporal as well as things spiritual.

Do you, my dearest child, live wholly after the

spirit, abide in restful peace, be certain that God will help you, and come what may, abide within the Arms of His Fatherly Love and Mercy.

May God ever be All in All to you. You know that I am wholly yours in Him.

Your father, and all your natural relations, are well: may it be the same with all appertaining to you through spiritual bonds. Amen.

CVI.
To a Religious of the Visitation.

I HAVE received your letter, my dearest daughter, in which you lay your failings and troubles before me with so much sincerity, and I would that I could fulfil your hopes that I might remedy them; but I have not leisure to do so, nor do I think you really need it, for in truth, my dearest child, the greater part of what you tell me requires no other remedy than the natural course of time and the practice of the Rule under which you live. There are in the same way certain bodily disorders which are only to be cured by a well-ordered plan of life. Self-love, self-esteem, and a false spirit of liberty, are roots which can never be entirely eradicated from the human heart; but we may hinder the ripening of their fruits,—that is, sin. All through this mortal life we are unable altogether to hinder their impulses and outbreaks as they spring forth, although we can moderate and restrain them by cultivating the opposite virtues, and above all by the Love of God. We must have patience, so as by degrees to amend and cut off bad habits, conquer repugnances, and overcome tempers and inclinations as they arise, for indeed, my dear child, this life is a perpetual warfare, and no one can say, I am free from attacks. Rest remains for us in Heaven, and the palm of victory. On earth we must always fight on between hope and fear; but in the main hope will be the strongest, by reason of His Omnipotence Who succours us. Do not be weary then of labouring ceaselessly to correct yourself and attain to perfection. There are three kinds of charity,— Love of God, love for yourself, and love of your neighbour. Now your Rule puts you in the way of growing in all these. Cast your whole mind and heart and care upon God many times a day, saying to Him, with David, "I am Thine, O save me." Do not distract your mind with dwelling much upon what kind of prayer God enables you to make; rather follow simply and humbly where His Grace leads you. Keep your eyes open to your own ill-regulated inclinations, in order to uproot them. Never be surprised to find yourself poor and miserable, and overwhelmed with evil tempers. Deal with your heart as having an earnest desire for its perfection; be indefatigable in recalling it gently and patiently when it has stumbled. Above all, do whatever lies in your power to strengthen the higher part of your mind, not dallying with feelings and consolations, but cleaving stedfastly to such resolutions and efforts as may be put before you by faith, your Rule, your Superior, and by reason.

Do not be over-tender with yourself: over-indulgent mothers spoil their children. Do not be given either to tears or complaints; do not be surprised because you have so many troubles and difficulties, and find such difficulty in making them known. No, my child, do not be surprised,—God allows them in order to teach you true humility, to make you abject and vile in your own eyes. Be kindly to your neighbour, and, in spite of your impulses and even outbreaks of anger, say in the Gracious Words of the Saviour, "I love these neighbours, Holy Father, because Thou lovest them. Thou hast given them to be my brothers and sisters; Thou wouldst have me love them, and I do love them." Above all, love the dear Sisters to whom God's Own Hand has bound you; bear with them, cleave to them, and cherish them in your heart, my dear child. Be sure that I take a most special interest in your progress,—God has willed it so.

CVII.

To a Religious of the Visitation.

I HAVE received all your packets, my dear child. Raise your heart to Heaven; remember that not one of those mortals who has there put on immortality reached it save through continual trials and afflictions. Amid all your troubles say constantly to yourself, "This is the way to Heaven; I see the haven; I know that no tempest can hinder my entrance therein." May God comfort and bless you a thousand times. I am, more entirely than I can say, yours, my dearest child, etc.

CVIII.

To a Widowed Religious,
WHO WAS EXPECTING TO HEAR OF HER CHILD'S DEATH.

My Dearest Mother,

You must await the result of this illness as meekly as you can, with a full resolution to conform to God's Will in your loss, if indeed we may call a temporary absence loss, when it is to be replaced by an eternal presence.

How blessed is the heart which can love and accept God's Will in every event! Oh, if once our hearts were thoroughly fixed on that holy and happy eternity, we should be ready to say to all we love best, "Go, dear friends, go to that Eternal Father at the moment in which He calls you; we shall follow soon." And forasmuch as time is given us but for that end, and the world is intended to people Heaven; when we go thither we shall have accomplished the purpose for which we were created.

Oh! Mother, let us leave our children to the Mercy of that God Who gave His Son for very mercy's sake. Let us offer our children's lives to Him, since He gave up His Son's Life for us. We must, indeed, keep our eyes fixed on His Heavenly Providence, and acquiesce in all He sends with a humble heart. We must be firm and stedfast before the Cross, and even on the Cross, if it is God's Pleasure to nail us there. " Blessed are the crucified, for they shall be glorified." Of a truth, my dear Mother, our portion in this world is the Cross; in the next world it will be Eternal Glory.

Dear Mother, I wish you most earnestly all perfection, and I have every hope and belief in our Sovereign Lord and His Holy Mother that "your life will be hid with Christ in God." May He bless you, and stamp the Eternal Sign of His Pure Love upon your heart. Let us strive in all humility to be like the Saints, and to spread abroad the precious incense of charity. May God kindle His Holy Love within us, so that all else may be as nought to us. May our Dear Lord be the abiding Rest of both our souls and bodies. My daily lesson is not to do my own will; rather to do that which I do not will. Be at peace within His Arms for ever.

CIX.
To a Religious.

INDEED, my dear daughter, I do not think it any way strange that you should wish for my letters, for (not to say that it is God's Will, which is the key-note of our correspondence), I gain so much comfort from your communications, as to be easily able to imagine that you find some small measure thereof from mine, and we may look on the one side and the other for a spiritual benefit, and mutual consolation to our souls.

I have nothing to say, daughter, as to your tearless heart; no indeed, my child, the poor heart is not to blame; this does not arise from any want of resolution or warm desire to love God, but from the want of external emotion, which does not depend upon the heart, rather upon other causes over which we have no control. Just as in this world we can neither make it rain nor cease raining when we will, so neither can we weep when we would fain do so out of devotion, nor restrain our tears when some sudden gust of feeling calls them forth. For the most part this is no fault of ours, but so ordered by God's Providence, which wills us to travel by a dry and desert road, enduring toil and hardness.

Keep your bouquet in hand,[1] but if any other sweet and gracious odour presents itself, do not fail to enjoy it thankfully; the only object of the bouquet is to supply you through the day with spiritual delight and comfort. Be steady as to the one thing, that your heart be wholly given to God —there is nothing more profitable.

On no account wish for persecution in order to test your faithfulness; it is far better to wait for such as God may send, than to wish for anything of the kind. Meanwhile your fidelity is tested in manifold other ways,—humility, gentleness, charity, in tending your poor invalid with a hearty, loving care. God gives you leisure to lay in a store of patience and vigour, and in due time the occasions for using them will come. My dear daughter, lay aside the garments of your bondage by continually renouncing your earthly affections, and believe that

---

[1] This is an allusion to the "Vie Dévote," where Philothée is recommended at the close of her meditation to gather a spiritual bouquet, and to smell it often through the day.

the King does give you royal robes to win you to His Holy Love. Hail Jesus! My dear daughter, that must be the watchword by which we live and die, and in which I am ever yours, etc.

CX.

To a Religious.

SERVE God with stedfast courage, and to the utmost of your power, in the exercises pertaining to your vocation. Love all your neighbours, but especially those to whom God has given the strongest claims upon your affection. Set yourself stedfastly to those duties which have the least attractive exterior; it matters not whether God's Holy Will be fulfilled in great or small matters. Long ceaselessly after perfect union of your will with that of our Lord. Be patient with yourself and your own failings; never be in a hurry, and do not yield to longings after that which is impossible to you. My dear Sister, go on steadily and quietly;—if our Dear Lord means you to run, He will "strengthen your heart;" but meanwhile abide by His precept, "Learn of Me, for I am meek and lowly of heart."

CXI.

To a Religious.

MY DEAREST DAUGHTER,

My answer will be brief, for I know all that you wanted to say as well as if I had heard you speak.

In truth it is the same as it has been in past years, and I can but answer you as before, that you must be patient with yourself, while humbling yourself very deeply before God, without fretting or being any way discouraged.

Then next, you should renew all your former resolutions of amendment, and although you have found that in spite of all these you have gone on amid the entanglement of your faults, you must none the less heartily endeavour to amend, leaning solely on God's Help. All your life long you will be full of faults;—there will always be plenty to correct in yourself, and therefore you must not grow weary of the undertaking. Thirdly, labour to attain true gentleness of heart towards others, remembering that your neighbour is the work of God's Hand, and hopes through His Goodness to share that Paradise to which you look :—surely we might bear patiently with those whom our Dear Lord bears with, and that too with real compassion for their spiritual infirmities.

Accept gratefully the little visit which His Divine Goodness has granted you ; we must strive to be faithful in little things if we would be faithful in those which are greater.

Be altogether at peace, and let your heart feed upon the sweetness of Heavenly Love, without which our hearts are lifeless, and our life devoid of happiness. Beware of giving way ever so little to sadness, the enemy of all true devotion. What ought to sadden her who serves our Dear Lord, Who is our endless joy? Nought save sin should have the power to grieve and sadden us, and even that sorrow, if sin be duly resisted, will end in joy and consolation. I am for ever, my dear child, yours, etc.

CXII.
To a Religious.

OF a truth, is not God very good to you, my dear daughter? But to whom is He not good, He, the Saviour and Lover of Souls? Those who have tasted of His Sweetness cannot drink deeply enough thereof; and those who come near His Heart will ever pour out their own in praising and blessing Him! Continue in the holy silence of which you tell me;—truly it is well to spare our words for God and for His Glory. God has upheld you with His loving Hand through your affliction. "How is it," S. Gregory said, to a Bishop who was in affliction, "how is it that our hearts, which aspire to Heaven, should yet be so moved by all the events of this life?" In truth the mere sight of our Dear Crucified Jesus has power to still all our agonies, which are but as flowers compared to the thorns with which He was pierced. And, moreover, we have a glorious prospect in eternity, which cannot be touched by these things, which have their end in time.

Go on, my child, uniting yourself more and more closely to that Saviour; plunge your heart into the depths of His Love, and say always with sincerity, "May I die, and may He live." Ours will be a blessed death, if we die in Him. "I live," the Apostle said,—but then he retracted his words, and said, "Yet not I, but Christ liveth in me."[1]

May you be blessed, my dear daughter, with that blessing which His Goodness has prepared for all those hearts which give themselves up to His Holy Love. Be of good cheer. God is very Good —if all else be against us, what does it matter? Be cheerful and happy in this thought. The years go by, and Eternity draws near. May we so spend these years in His Love, as to spend Eternity in His Glory. Amen.

CXIII.

To a Religious.

ANOTHER time you must open your heart fully, and without any sort of fear. It would be much more useful to you to confess what you have to say face to face, than in writing.

Those inclinations of which you speak are precious opportunities given you by God for exercising your faith by carefully repressing them. Let your prayers take the shape of the opposite affections, and directly that you find yourself falling, repair the fault by some act of gentleness, humility, or charity towards those people who excited it; it may be reluctance to obey, to submit yourself, to do them good, or to love them. As you know the side on which your enemies press you the hardest, you must keep special watch over that side of the

[1] Gal. ii. 20.

fortress. Make your pride stoop, and force yourself to act contrary to your habits and inclinations, commending the effort to our Lord, and striving everywhere, and in everything, to soften your disposition, scarcely heeding anything save the achievement of this victory. I, for my part, will pray our Dear Lord that He would grant it you, and give you a triumphant entrance into Paradise. Be sure, my dear daughter, that He will do so, if you persevere in seeking His Holy Love, striving to live humbly before Him, kindly towards your neighbour, and patiently towards yourself. I am ever heartily yours, etc.

CXIV.

To the Abbesse Angélique Arnaud, of Port Royal.

I SEE plainly what swarming ant-heaps of inclinations self-love fosters in your heart, my dearest daughter, and I know very well that the state of your subtle mind, so sensitive and fertile, contributes to increase this. But, after all, my dear daughter, these are but inclinations; and, as you are conscious of their importunity, and are sorry for it, it would seem that your will does not consent to them —at all events, not with a deliberate consent. No, my dear daughter, your soul has accepted the earnest desire with which God has filled it, to be His only; so do not be ready to fancy that you are consenting to these opposing influences. Your heart may be shaken by the action of passions within, but I think it rarely sins by deliberately consenting to them. "O miserable man that I am," the great Apostle exclaimed, "who will deliver me from the body of this death?" He felt himself encompassed by a whole army of tempers, natural likings and dislikings, which warred against him, seeking his spiritual destruction : fearing them, he expresses his hatred ; hating them, he suffers pain ; and that pain draws forth this exclamation, to which he makes answer himself; " I thank God through Christ Jesus our Lord."[1] God's Grace will deliver him, not from fear, not from terror and alarm, not from the strife, but from defeat—he will not be conquered.

My daughter, to be alive in this world, and not to feel the movement of such passions within us, are two incompatible things.

Our glorious S. Bernard calls it a heresy to say that here below we can persevere in one condition, quoting what the Holy Spirit spoke by the mouth of Job, "He fleeth as a shadow, and continueth not."[2] I say this in answer to your complaints of the levity and inconstancy of your soul. I believe truly that it is perpetually tossed about with its own passionate feelings, and that consequently it often totters ; but I believe as truly, that God's Grace, and the resolution with which it inspires you, will continue to guard your mind, to maintain the standard of the Cross, and to enable you in firm faith, hope, and charity, to cry out aloud, " Hail Jesus !"

Indeed, my daughter, these tendencies to pride, vanity, and self-love, mingle with everything ; they

---

[1] Rom. vii. 24, 25.   [2] Job xiv. 2.

slip in visibly or invisibly, and take part in all we do; but all the same, they are not the mainspring of our actions. One day, some such thoughts harassed S. Bernard while he was preaching. "Get thee hence, Satan," he exclaimed; "I did not begin to please thee, nor will I make an end for thy pleasure!"

There is one thing I would say, my dear daughter, in reply to what you tell me about fostering your pride by affectation in conversation, and in letters. Sometimes, in conversation, this glides in so imperceptibly that one scarcely finds it out; but directly you do become aware of it, you should change your manner. In letters, affectation is rather more—I should say a great deal more—insupportable, because one can see better what one is about; and if you are conscious of any notable piece of affectation, you must punish the hand which wrote it, by writing a fresh letter in a different tone.

Altogether, my dear daughter, I have no doubt but that among all these numerous ups and downs of your mind, some venial faults make their way in, but being mere fleeting frailties, they do not deprive you of all the benefit of your good resolutions, though perhaps they may deprive you of the pleasant sense of being free from such infirmities.

Now, be fair; do not either accuse or excuse your poor soul without deliberate consideration; lest, if you excuse it unduly, you make it presumptuous; and if you accuse it without just cause, you spoil its courage, and turn it into a mere coward. "He that walketh uprightly walketh surely."[1]

[1] Prov. x. 9.

I must add on this scrap of paper one more important word of advice. Do not lay any further austerity than that which your Rule imposes upon your weak body; preserve your bodily strength the better to serve God in those spiritual exercises which we are sometimes forced to give up when we have been indiscreet in taxing the outward frame, because it must co-operate with the soul in their performance.

Write to me when you please, without ceremony, and do not let respect hinder the affection which God has called forth between us, in which I am always your very humble brother and servant, etc.

CXV.
To the Superior of a Carmelite Convent.

MY DEAREST DAUGHTER,

It ought to be a great comfort to you to feel that God Himself has made you a Superior, inasmuch as you have come to that charge, not because you sought it, but by the ordinary course of events. His Providence, Which has thus placed you, is bound to uphold you with His Hand, so that you may rightly fulfil your calling. Believe me, dear daughter, you must go on bravely, trusting to the guidance of that Good Lord, and not doubting the promise, that God Who has begun in you an excellent work, will finish it, according to His own Loving Wisdom, if only you are faithful and humble.

But "it is required in stewards that a man be

found faithful."[1] Now, I promise you that you will be faithful if you are humble. "But shall I be humble?" Yes; if you desire it. "But I do desire it." Then you are what you desire. "But I feel that I am not so really!" So much the better; that tends to becoming more so. Do not go into such refinements; go on in straightforwardness; and since God has given you charge over these souls, give Him the charge of yours, and ask Him to bear both you and your burden. There is room for you in His capacious Heart. Rest upon Him, and do not be astonished when you fall into faults and errors, but humble yourself before God, remembering that "His strength is made perfect in weakness."[2]

In a word, my dear daughter, your humility must be bold and brave through your confidence in Him Who has committed this trust to you; and in order to cut short all the arguments with which human prudence is wont to ply us, under the name of humility, bear in mind that our Lord taught us to ask for our bread, not yearly, or monthly, or weekly, but daily. Try to do well to-day, without thinking about to-morrow; then the next day the same; and do not dwell upon what you will have to do all through your time of office. Rather let it glide away, day by day, without giving way to anxious care, certain that your Heavenly Father, Who guides you to-day, will guide you to-morrow, and next day, in proportion to your conscious weakness and absolute trust in Him. I think, dear daughter, that I am very bold in speaking thus to you, as

[1] 1 Cor. iv. 2.   [2] 2 Cor. xii. 9.

though you did not know all this better than I do: but never mind; such words make more impression when they come from a friendly heart. I am, etc.

CXVI.
To a Religious.

.... Now, to say somewhat concerning my dear child's own heart. What feats of valour it would accomplish in face of a mighty enemy, judging by its overwhelming trouble before one scatter-brained, naughty little girl! But do not be distressed, my dear child; no annoyance is so hard to bear as one made up of a number of continual little worries. Our Dear Lord permits us to be hindered by these little matters, in order that we may humble ourselves, and realise that if we have overcome greater temptations, it was not through our own strength, but through His Grace and Goodness.

I see plainly that these trifling annoyances give plenty of opportunity for the exercise of a willing abjection; for what will be said of a Sister who has not been able to teach or improve this little girl? And then, too, what will the other Sisters say when they see one upset by the least vexation; complaining, scolding! There is no remedy, my daughter. There was one of old would fain have bought wisdom with gold—my child is not so ambitious— she would rather have the cause removed than face her difficulty. You must have recourse to humility, and for the short time which this trial lasts try to bear it as in God's Presence, and try to love the poor unhappy little creature who causes it for love of Him Who died for her. Never correct her when you are angry. Try to accept the trouble she gives you willingly. Believe me, ever yours, etc.

CXVII.
To a Religious.

. . . . THERE is no harm in saying a *Pater* for your headache, but, indeed, my child, I should not have boldness to pray to our Dear Lord by the pains of His Holy Head to take away a headache in mine! Of a truth, He bore it all that we might be spared. S. Catherine of Sienna was offered two crowns by her Saviour, one golden, the other of thorns. "Give me the painful crown in this world," she cried, "the other will be for Heaven." I would rather pray, through the merits of our Lord's Crown, that I might have a crown of patience to soothe my headache.

CXVIII.
To a Religious.

. . . . I KNOW that you are often called upon to practise the love of contempt, rebuffs, and your own abjection. Do it heartily; it is a main feature of humility to perceive, to accept, and even rejoice in such occasions when they come before us (for we are not to go out of our way to seek them), and to be humble, submissive, calm, and patient under them. This is a very important matter, for you see, my child, that humility which makes least show is the truest. Meanwhile, as to exterior things, I would have you correct yourself of the habit of speaking haughtily and sharply, which is most unbecoming to one professing religion.

Never mind these impatient angry feelings, so long as you crush them as they arise, striving to recover calmness and peace of mind. While you do this it will be practice in holiness, not any hindrance to you, even if the strife lasted all through the day. Be of good cheer, my daughter; I see plainly that the Lord will draw you to Himself as His Own.

CXIX.

To a Young Lady.

MADEMOISELLE,

I received your letter some little time ago, and rejoice in it as a proof of your confidence in my affection, of which, indeed, you have no cause to doubt. I am only sorry that I am so little able to answer your questions concerning your prayers: but I know that you are in a place and in the company of those who can give all you want; still, I cannot altogether refuse to say what little I may.

The anxiety you speak of as disturbing your meditation, and the eagerness you indulge in seeking somewhat whereon to fix and satisfy your mind, is alone sufficient to hinder you in finding what you want. We pass over the thing we are seeking a hundred times when we seek it too eagerly. Nothing can come of such useless hurry and restlessness, save weariness of spirit; and hence the coldness and languor of your soul. I do not know what remedies you should employ; but I think that if you can conquer this eagerness you will have gained a great step, for it is one of the worst traitors we have to deal with in devotion and true holiness. It pretends to kindle us, while, in fact, it chills our life, and it makes us run merely that we may stumble. Eagerness and hurry must be perpetually guarded against, above all in prayer.

To help you in doing this, remember that the graces and gifts of prayer are not streams of earthly water, but come from Heaven; and all our unassisted efforts are incapable of winning them, although we ought to make ready in all humility and meekness to receive them. It is our part to keep our hearts open to Heaven's Grace, ready for the outpouring of celestial dew. Never forget, when you begin to pray, that you are entering God's Presence, for two main reasons: first, to pay Him the honour and homage due to Him; which may be rendered without the utterance of a word on either side. It lies mainly in a silent acknowledgment that He is our God, and we His worthless creatures; and in placing ourselves before Him in an attitude of humble waiting upon His Will. How many courtiers are there who appear continually before the King, without expecting to speak to him or to be spoken to by him, all their object being that he may see them, and that they may testify the devotion with which they seek to serve him.

And, in like manner, it is a very good and holy and pure object with which to present ourselves before God, when we do so merely to set forth our gratitude and our will to render Him a devoted service.

The second reason which takes us into God's Presence is, that we may talk with Him, and hear Him speaking within our hearts by His Gracious Inspirations. This is usually a most intense enjoyment; it is a great privilege to speak familiarly with our Dear Lord, and when He speaks to us He sheds an abundance of His precious balm and sweetness upon the soul.

Now, my dear child, there must be one or other of these graces in your prayer. If we are able to speak to our Lord, let us do so,—let us praise, pray, and hearken; if our utterance is hindered, let us, nevertheless, remain bowed down before Him; He will behold us, He will accept our patient waiting, and look graciously upon our silence; it may be He will amaze us by leading us by the hand and bringing us into His realm of prayer; but if He never did this, let us rest satisfied to be among His followers, confessing that it is a greater grace and privilege than we deserve that He should suffer us even to remain in His Presence.

So doing we shall not be restless and eager to speak with Him, knowing that to be silent before Him may be as useful, nay more so, to our souls, although it is less to our liking. When, therefore, you come before the Lord, speak to Him if you can;—if you cannot, remain quietly in His Sight, and do not disturb yourself because you can do no more. This is my advice;—I do not know if it will help you, but I am content to think that you are within reach of many much better counsellors than I am. As to your fear lest you should lose the desire to become a Carmelite, during the long period of waiting imposed on you by your father, say to God, " Lord, all my desire is before Thee," and leave the rest to Him. He will guide your father's heart and turn it to His own Glory and your good. Meanwhile continue to cherish your good desire, and keep it alive beneath the embers of humility and resignation to God's Will.

You ask my prayers,—be sure they shall not be wanting to you ; I will not forget you, especially at Holy Mass, and I trust to your charity likewise to remember me in your prayers.

CXX.
To a Young Lady.

MADEMOISELLE,

You must resign yourself entirely under our Dear Lord's Hand, and be sure that when you have done what little you can to carry out your good intentions, He will accept that little favourably. In a word, be very brave in striving to become a Religious, since God gives you so earnest a desire thereto; but if after all your efforts you cannot succeed, be sure that you cannot please our Lord better than by sacrificing your will to His, and awaiting His Good Pleasure in calm trust and humility. And His Will and Pleasure will be clearly recognised in your disappointment if, after all rightful efforts, you cannot attain your wish. Our Dear Lord sometimes tests our stedfastness and love by depriving us of things which we esteem necessary, and which may be highly profitable to our souls. If He sees that, while ardent in pursuit of our desire, we are nevertheless humble, calm, and resigned to forego the object of our aspirations, He will give us greater blessings in the room of that which He withholds. Everywhere and in everything God accepts those who can say heartily and unreservedly, "Thy Will be done."

CXXI.
To a Widow.
Concerning her Child's Education.

.... As to your dear little girl, if it is God's Will that she should enter upon the religious life, she will come to it sooner or later, notwithstanding the present opposition of her grandmother. God will, if He sees fit, make use even of the world and its influences to draw her to taste the sweetness of religion. I can assure you, my dear daughter, that not unfrequently when young children are brought up with a view to the religious life without any choice of their own, they cast it off as a bondage, like a horse which has been put too early into harness. A religious vocation is too sacred and special a grace to be given by human training or labour. God often makes education tend to develop a vocation, but He will effect His own purpose without the help of education, if it be His Will,

You will do more by offering your child to God, than by striving to educate her to a religious vocation. . . . .

CXXII.
To one of the Bishop's Married Sisters.[1]

MY DEAR SISTER,

I only write just to say "good evening" to you, and to wish you and my brother countless blessings; above all, that you may ever be transfigured into the likeness of our Lord. Oh, how beautiful is His Countenance! how past telling the marvellous sweetness of His Eyes! and how blessed a thing it is to go up with Him to the mountain of glory! There it is, my dear sister child, that we should fix our longings and desires, and not on this world, where all is vain beauty and attractive vanity! But thanks be to our Saviour, we have gone up to Mount Tabor, by means of our firm resolves to love and serve Him, and we must confirm these with a holy hope. Let us go ever upwards, dearest sister, unwearyingly upwards towards the heavenly vision; little by little let us quit all low and earthly clingings, and aspire only to the happiness Christ has set before us.

I intreat you, dear child, to pray much for me, that our Lord may keep me henceforth in the paths of His Will, and that I may serve Him sincerely and stedfastly. Indeed, dearest child, I would wish to die or to love God—death or love;—for a

---
[1] Apparently written on the Transfiguration.

life without that Love is far worse than death. Ah, my dearest child, how happy we may be, if we love His Sovereign Goodness above all things, remembering all His favours and blessings.

Let us give ourselves up wholly to Him, amid all the weariness of earthly things. How else can we prove our stedfastness amid all trials? Alas! my dearest sister-child, solitude has its conflicts, and the world its difficulties;—in each and everywhere we must be firm, remembering that God's Help is ever ready for all who trust in Him, and who seek His Fatherly guidance.

Beware of letting your care degenerate into anxiety and unrest; tossed as you are amid the winds and waves of sundry troubles, keep your eyes fixed on our Lord, and say, "Oh, my God, I look to Thee Alone, be Thou my Guide, my Pilot;" and then be comforted. When the shore is gained, who will heed the toil and the storm? And we shall steer safely through every storm, so long as our heart is right, our intention fervent, our courage stedfast, our mind and our trust fixed on God. If at times we are somewhat stunned by the tempest, never fear; let us take breath, and go on afresh. I am sure that you are adhering to our good resolutions;—do not be disconcerted by the fits of vexation and uneasiness which are sometimes produced by the multiplicity of your domestic worries. No indeed, dearest child, all these are but opportunities of strengthening yourself in the loving, forbearing graces which our Dear Lord sets before us. Believe me, true holiness is not formed amid external freedom from care, any more than good fish come out of the stagnant waters of a marsh. Hail Jesus! Ever yours, etc.

CXXIII.

To the Same.

April 30.

MAY our Saviour take out your heart, as He did to the holy Saint Catherine of Sienna, whose festival we keep to-day, and give you His Own Heart, in which you may live wholly to Him. What a blessing, dearest sister, if some day, on coming from Holy Communion, I were to find my weak, wretched heart gone, and the Precious Heart of my God in its place! But, dear child, although we may not seek after such extraordinary things, at all events we may desire that henceforth our poor hearts may live wholly in obedience to His precepts. In this way we can imitate S. Catherine, and so doing we shall be meek, humble, and charitable, for there is nothing nearer to His Heart than meekness, humility, and charity.

You will be very happy, my dearest sister-child, if, amid all these frivolous distractions, you can live an inward life for God, Who Alone is worthy to be served and followed with earnestness. In so doing you will set a good example to all around, and you will ensure a holy peace and calm to yourself.

Pray let others speculate as they please concerning your motives for communicating often. It is quite sufficient for your conscience that you and I know such diligent reviewing and repairing of your soul's breaches to be most needful for its welfare. If you wish to give explanations to any one, say that you need to partake so frequently of that Sacred Food because you are very weak, and without that strength your spiritual force would soon perish.

Give heed, dearest sister, to clasp that Dear Lord closely to your bosom. Let Him be the bouquet which rests upon your heart, so that every one who comes near you may perceive the perfume, and recognise the incense of Heaven. Try to keep an even mind, in spite of the troubles around. Refer all your difficulties to God's hidden Providence, and believe firmly that He will lead you gently on, guiding you, all your affairs, and your whole life. When Arabian shepherds are overtaken by a thunderstorm they hide with their flocks beneath the laurel bushes; and so, when persecution or contradiction seem to overwhelm us, we must take shelter beneath the Holy Cross, with a firm confidence that everything will work together for good to those that love God.

And now, dearest child-sister, keep your heart well in hand, beware of over-eagerness, put all your confidence in our Dear Lord. Be certain that Heaven and earth will pass away rather than He fail you, so long as you are His obedient child, or while you seek to obey Him. Examine yourself two or three times during the course of the day, as to whether your heart is disturbed by anything, and if you find that it is not at rest, strive at once to put it right.

Adieu, my dearest child. May God ever be in the midst of your heart. Amen.

[753.] CXXIV.
To a Cousin.

MY DEAR COUSIN,

You do well truly to realise how good God is to you, and to appreciate His Fatherly solicitude for you, now that you have no time for meditation, and yet find Him so frequently present within your heart, strengthening you with His Sacred Gifts. Be ever faithful to the Heavenly Bridegroom of your soul, and you will find out more and more the thousand-fold ways in which His Love for you takes shape.

Indeed, dear cousin, I am no ways surprised if, as God enables you to taste the sweetness of His Presence, you gradually grow more and more disgusted with the world. Doubtless, my child, nothing makes wormwood so bitter to us as having eaten honey; and when we have tasted heavenly delights it is scarcely possible that worldly pleasures should give us any satisfaction. Who can really weigh the Goodness, the Power, the Eternity of God, and then cling fondly to the miserable vanities of this life? Undoubtedly we must bear with and tolerate this world's vanities, but we must strive to fix our own affections on our Dear Lord's truth alone. I thank Him that through it He has led you to despise these earthly follies.

Alas! yes, dear cousin, poor Madame de Moiron is dead! We little thought how it would be last Lent. And we too shall die some day, we know not when. Ah, dear child, how happy we shall be if, when we come to die, our Gracious Lord is found dwelling in our heart. To that end we must strive ever to keep Him there, with many desires, resolutions, protestations, and holy exercises. A thousand times better is it to die with Our Dear Lord than to live without Him. Let us live cheerfully and bravely in Him and for Him, and not shrink from death. I do not say let us not fear it at all, but let us not be greatly disturbed at the thought. If we have a share in our Lord's Death, our own will be blessed. And to that end let us think often of His Death; let us cleave to His Cross and Passion. Yes, dearest child, when we watch our friends depart, let us weep gently for them, with a peaceful sorrow—free from impatience, and let us turn their departure into a quiet happy preparation for our own. . . .

CXXV.

To a Lady.

I RETURN your book corrected, my dear child; may it be as useful to you as I wish it to be. No doubt it is well to make and remake our resolutions concerning union with God, until we attain to it. But I would not have you led by your fervour to wish in this way for temptations or occasions of mortification. By God's Grace you are not without them already, and there is no need for you to seek more; strive rather to prepare your heart to receive all such trials, not as you might choose, but when and how God wills to send them.

There is no harm in a certain satisfaction and gratitude to Divine Grace, when we are successful in our undertakings, provided we keep tight hold of humility the while. As to those matters which concern your household rather than yourself, you must attend duly to them, with one condition :— that of waiting patiently for whatever issue it may please God to send. But as to your complaints that you are miserable and unfortunate, indeed, my dearest child, you must absolutely abstain from all such ; they are both unbecoming in a servant of God and they indicate too great depression of heart ; they are more signs of anger than of impatience.

Now, my dearest child, I would have you make a special practice of meekness and of acquiescence in God's Will, not merely as regards extraordinary matters, but chiefly in respect of these little daily vexations. Prepare yourself for them in the morning and in the afternoon, before and after supper, and at night, and make this your special point of attention for a time. But let it all be done with a quiet, cheerful spirit, and if you fail, humble yourself, and begin anew.

It is well to aspire generally towards the uttermost perfection of Christian life, but it is not well to speculate too much concerning details ; strive to amend and advance in the occurrences of daily life, leaving the fulfilment of your aspirations to God, and trusting absolutely to Him, as a little child who takes the food his father gives him day by day, trusting to him to go on supplying all that he may require as time goes on. You will see what I have said in your book about your temptations to envy.

Since you find so much benefit from Communion, be constant therein, with a fervent spirit and a pure conscience. Always be cheerful amid your temptations. Do not seek any other penance at present, but endeavour to attain a spirit of gentleness and true patience towards your neighbour, visit the sick, and be of good cheer. . . . I am, most heartily yours, etc.

CXXVI.
To a Lady. On the Death of her Sister.

WELL, my dearest child, they have just told me that your dear sister is gone, leaving us here below with our natural grief, the grief which must come upon those who are left behind in such separations. God knows, my dearest child, I have no mind to bid you not weep ;—no indeed, it is but right and reasonable that you should weep a little—only a little, dear child,—through the true love you bore her, even as our Dear Master wept a little over His friend Lazarus ; but not to excess, as they are wont to do who, fixing all their thoughts upon this miserable life, forget that we too are hastening towards that eternity where we hope to rejoin our blessed dead, never more to part. We cannot hinder our poor earthly hearts from feeling earthly sorrow in the separation from those who were the delight of our life, but nevertheless we must not forget our solemn resolution to unite our will wholly to that of God.

How blessed your dear sister is to have seen the hour of her departure come so gradually, and to have been able to make such fit preparation to meet it well. Let us adore God's Providence in this, and say, "Blessed art Thou, for all that Thou willest is good." Oh, my dear child, how lovingly our hearts ought to receive all these little sorrows— hearts which, forsooth, should be fixed and stayed on Heaven rather than earth! I shall pray for her soul, and that all who mourn her may be comforted. . . .

CXXVII.
To a Widowed Lady.

MY VERY DEAR MOTHER,

What shall I say to you? It can be but a word, for lack of time. Cultivate a perpetual peace of heart, both internal and external, and strive to be very calm amid the multitude of cares which press upon you. Beware of excitement, which is the bane of true devotion, and continue to keep your soul fixed on high, looking at this world with nought save contempt,—at time only in order to aspire to Eternity. Submit your will continually to that of God; as ready to adore Him amid tribulation as amid consolation. May God ever be in our hearts, my very dear mother. In Him I am most unreservedly and in true filial affection your most humble son, etc.

CXXVIII.
To a Friend.

If you would have nothing mar your life, do not seek reputation or this world's glory. Do not cleave to human friendships and consolations. Do not "love your life," but despise all that ministers to mere natural inclinations. Bear all bodily pain or sickness cheerfully, and in perfect submission to God's Will. Be indifferent to the opinion of men. Be much given to silence, and you will find inward peace—there is no other secret by which either you or I can gain that peace, save by bearing calmly with man's judgments. Do not be anxious as to what the world thinks of you; wait for God's Judgment, and your patience will bear witness against those who have judged you. Those who ride in the ring (at a tournament) think less of the bystanders than how best to ride so as to win the prize. Bethink you for Whom you work, and then those who trouble you now will have but little power to do so. Your most humble, etc.

[773.]
CXXIX.
To a Married Lady.

NEVER imagine, my dearest daughter, that distance can separate those souls which God has united together in His Love. The children of this world are widely separated, because their hearts are fixed hither and thither; but the children of God, whose heart is with their treasure, and whose treasure is God, are indissolubly united in a common bond, and so we must be comforted concerning any separation, but as soon as possible I shall return to my charge. Meanwhile we can meet continually at the foot of the Crucifix, if we remember our mutual promise. Indeed it is there only that all meetings are profitable.

But, my dear daughter, I will begin by telling you that you must in every way strengthen your mind against these idle fears which agitate and torment it so habitually. To this end, first of all try so to regulate your religious exercises as not to weary your own soul, or to inconvenience those among whom God has placed you by their length. Half a quarter of an hour, or less, is enough for your morning preparation; three-quarters of an hour, or an hour, for mass; and through the day you can raise your mind to God without occupying more than a moment of time; then there would follow your self-examination before supper, besides the ordinary blessings and thanksgivings at meals, which call your heart into union with God. In a word, I would have you do all I have taught Philothée, and no more,—the *Introduction* was written for you and such as you.

As to society, my dear daughter, be at rest concerning all that is said and done. If it is good, you have cause to thank God: if otherwise, your part is to turn your heart away from what is evil, without affecting surprise or indignation at what you cannot hinder; sometimes even interference does but make matters worse. But you can preserve your own innocence amid the poison which surrounds you, and thus you will be unharmed.

I cannot understand how you can indulge in such unreasonable sadness. A child of God, so long since sheltered in the Bosom of His Love, and devoted to His Service, you ought to be able to find comfort, and to reject all these gloomy distressing suggestions of the enemy, which he brings forth with a view to harass and weary you.

Give good heed to show all becoming humility and gentleness to your dear husband, and to all around you. This is the virtue of virtues, taught us by our Lord Himself. If you fail therein, do not be disturbed, but in all simple confidence rise up again, and go on perseveringly in your efforts.

I send you a little plan for keeping up union with our Lord all through the day. This is all I have to say at present, my dear daughter, but pray do not stand upon ceremony with me,—I have neither time nor inclination to do so with you. Write freely to me when you will, I shall always be glad to hear of what concerns your soul, and am, yours, etc.

CXXX.

To a Married Lady.

My Dear Sister and Child,

.... I am very glad that you are free from scruples, and that frequent communion is so helpful to you; by all means go on with it. But since your husband objects to your going to N. . . . as a confessor, do not persist in doing so. You do not require any very especial help, and almost any confessor would be useful to you. You know how to act, be therefore quite at ease in this matter, only, dear child, be very gentle and obedient to your husband. You are quite right not to be fretted by evil thoughts, so long as your will and intentions are good. God looks at these. . . .

Be most particularly watchful in striving after gentleness and meekness at home, and in your own household. I do not mean that I would have you weak and lax, but gentle and mild. You must study this as you go out and come in, morning, noon, and night. Make it your chief aim and care for a time, and leave other things alone the while.

CXXXI.

To a Lady under Depression.

WHAT can I say to you, my dearest child, as to the return of your troubles, save that when the enemy assaults us anew, we must take up our arms afresh, and fight more earnestly than before? I do not see anything very important in that note. But, for God's Sake, beware of letting yourself grow mistrustful; His Heavenly Goodness does not let you fall into these mistakes because He forsakes you, but rather to humble you, and teach you to cling the tighter to His Guiding Hand. I highly approve of your stedfastness in your spiritual exercises, in spite of all inward dryness and languor. Our only object is to serve God, because we love Him; and if He chooses us to serve Him amid dryness and weariness rather than in sweetness, we ought to accept it willingly, believing that though the one may be more acceptable to our taste, the other is more profitable to our soul.

As to your temporal concerns, since you have tried to put them into order, without success, you must now be patient and resigned, willingly accepting your cross.

Be at peace, my dearest child; often tell our Dear Lord that you desire to be whatever He wills you to be, and to suffer what He wills you to suffer.

Struggle diligently against your impatience, and strive to be amiable and gentle, in season and out of season, towards every one, however much they may vex and annoy you, and be sure God will bless your efforts.

Good night, dear child; may God Alone be your portion. In Him, I am, most heartily yours, etc.

CXXXII.

To a Lady. On Spiritual Coldness.

MY DEAR CHILD,

You should not be disturbed at your own coldness, so long as it does not lead you to neglect your minor religious duties. Tell me, dear child, was not our Blessed Jesus born amidst the winter's cold? And why may not He dwell in a heart which owns its own chilliness? I imagine that the coldness of which you complain involves no slackening of your good resolutions, but merely a sort of lassitude and heaviness of spirit, which makes you go wearily along your way, without, however, seeking to wander from it until you reach the haven. Is it not so, my child?

I shall come, if possible, to your *fête*, and will give you holy Confirmation. . . . I will then tell you some of the precious truths which the Saviour impressed so earnestly upon His disciples' hearts. Meanwhile live wholly to God, and for the Love He bears you bear with yourself in all your infirmities. To be a faithful child of God does not mean always to be enjoying sweetness and consolation, always free from struggles and reluctance to do what is right. At this rate neither S. Paula, S. Angela, nor S. Catherine of Sienna were His children! But to be His child is to be charitable towards one's neighbour, to have an unconquerable resolution in our heart of hearts to do His Holy Will, an absolute and single humility and confidence in Him, however often one may fall; to be patient with oneself and one's weakness, and to bear gently with the imperfections of others. You know, dear child, how my heart cleaves to you; in truth it is beyond what you can tell. May God ever be our All in All. In Him I am, ever yours, etc.

CXXXIII.
To a Lady.
On the Restraint of Natural Quickness.

. . . . You tell me that you have meditated but little, because you cannot control the quickness and activity of your mind. But you must learn to control it, and gradually to quiet its rapid movements, so that it may set to work in all things gently and calmly. Do not imagine that such quietness and gentleness hinder a prompt and vigorous action; on the contrary, they rather tend to promote and confirm it.

You must try this in some such way as the following :—For instance, you must eat while in this life; well then, sit down quietly, and take the food needful to the restoration of your body composedly. When you go to bed, undress quietly; when you get up, do it calmly, without hurry and scuffle, without putting those who wait upon you to any undue inconvenience; and so in all ordinary matters strive to overcome your natural temperament, and little by little, bring it into subjection to a holy moderation and composure. To one of a naturally slow, indolent temperament, I should say, "Make haste, time is precious;" but to you I say, "Do not be in a hurry; peace, calm, and rest of mind are precious, and the time you spend in quietness will be time well spent."

As to the subject of a former temptation, I say most emphatically you must submit wholly to God's Will and Providence, and accept it as His Good Pleasure that you are in the position in which you find yourself. One must make up one's mind to remain in the ship where we are, for the voyage between this life and the next, and moreover to do so willingly and cheerfully, because, even though sometimes we may have been placed therein by the hand of man rather than God, once there it is God's

Will, and as such to be accepted meekly and gladly.

. . . . How better can we prove our love to Him Who bore so much for us than amid what is disagreeable, repugnant, contrary to our will? We must let the thorns of difficulty pierce our brow, and the spear of contradiction penetrate our heart; we must drink the gall and swallow the vinegar; we must eat wormwood and bitter herbs, since it is His Will. In short, dear child, as once you admitted and encouraged temptation, so now you must heartily and sincerely foster this spirit of submission. If any real difficulty arises through the fault of N. . . . do nothing till you have faced the matter under the light of Eternity, in a calm spirit, and with the guidance of some worthy minister of God, if the question be urgent, or my own, as your spiritual Father, if time admits of that. When the enemy sees that you are conquering your temptation by submission to God's Will he will raise up every kind of hindrance, be sure.

As to other matters, let a holy simplicity and humility be your rule. Let your dress be simple, but consistent with what your position requires, so that you may rather attract than repulse other young ladies; let your words be simple, courteous, and gentle; your general intercourse with others neither constrained and reserved, nor lax and over-easy; in a word, let your whole conduct be influenced by the modesty and gentleness which ought to be the characteristics of one of God's own children. Ever yours, etc.

CXXXIV.
To a Lady.
Concerning her Child's Frequent Communion.

MADAME MA TRES CHÈRE SŒUR,

I am thankful for the confidence you put in me, while I am grieved not to be able to write to you as I should wish; but our Lord in His Love for you supplies what is lacking through the many means of help you have at hand.

I should advise that in prayer you should persevere yet awhile in a small beginning, preparing your mind by learning to arrange points of meditation, without exercising the imagination more than is necessary. I know very well that when we are so favoured as to find God, (in meditation,) it is good to pause in contemplation, and fix our minds on Him; but, my dear daughter, I do not think it is desirable for beginners to expect always to find Him thus, without preparation; we novices have more need to ponder over the marvels of the Crucifix one by one, than to indulge in a general and admiring contemplation. But if, after having given the mind to such humble preparation, it still does not please God to give us any sweetness or consolation, then we ought patiently to go on eating our dry bread, content to do our duty without any present reward.

I am glad to hear that you go to the good Père Gentil for confession. I know him well by reputation, and what a good and active servant of our

Lord he is. You will do well to continue going to him for confession, and to follow his kind advice, according to your needs.

I would not recommend you to urge your daughter to such frequent communion, unless she thoroughly enters into what it is. Holy Communion is a different matter from other ways of approaching the Blessed Sacrament;[1] and there is a great (spiritual) difference between frequent and rare communion. If the dear little soul is able to realise that in order to receive Holy Communion frequently great purity and fervour are required, and if she aims at these, and strives earnestly to attain them, then I should advise allowing her to come frequently, that is to say, every fortnight. But if she has only warm feelings at the time of Communion, and is not earnest in striving against the little faults incidental to childhood, I think it would be better for her to go to confession once a week, and to communicate once a month. My dear daughter, I believe Holy Communion to be the great means whereby to attain perfection, but then it must be received with the desire and effort to cleanse our hearts of whatever could displease Him Whom we desire to receive.

Persevere in striving to conquer yourself in the trifling daily vexations of which you complain; make this your principal study;—be sure it is what God specially requires of you at present. Do not amuse yourself with other matters, or try to sow other people's gardens, but cultivate your own diligently. Do not wish that you were not what

[1] "Les autres participations."

you are, but rather wish to be perfect as you are;—occupy your thoughts in attaining such perfection, and strive to carry every cross, be it great or small, that is sent you, patiently. Believe me there is no greater truth in the spiritual life, and none less understood than the saying, "Every one's desires are according to his own likings, but few according to duty and our Lord's likings."[1] What is the use of building castles in Spain, when we must live in France?[2] It is an old story, and you have often heard it; but tell me, my dear daughter, whether you follow it.

Let your religious duties be well regulated, and let them all have reference to the Will of your Head. Set at defiance the childish onslaughts with which the enemy tries to induce you to return to the world; treat them with contempt, as a mere impertinence;—they deserve no answer save our Lord's own words, "Get thee behind Me, Satan, tempt not the Lord thy God." My dear daughter, we are treading in the footsteps of the Saints; let us go on boldly, whatever difficulties we may meet.

I think I have answered all that you asked of me, and I have no greater pleasure than to help you faithfully. I should have been glad to see you, but it was not to be done. Perhaps God will so order things that we may meet, and if it be to His Glory I would fain have it so. May He ever reign in our hearts. I am, etc.

---

[1] "Chacun aime selon son goût; peu de gens aiment selon leur devoir et le goût de notre Seigneur."

[2] "Chateaux en Espagne"—the French equivalent for "castles in the air."

CXXXV.
To a Lady.

I SEE that you are always craving after a greater perfection, and I approve of this craving, for I am sure it does not keep you back;—on the contrary, it kindles and urges you to victory.

You tell me that you are a prey to a thousand imperfections. No doubt it is true, my dear sister, but are you not incessantly striving to uproot them? Unquestionably, so long as we are cumbered by our mortal and corruptible bodies, we shall be deficient in many things.

Am I repeating myself? We must be patient with all the world—above all with ourselves, for we are more troublesome to ourselves than any one else can be, feeling as we must the difference between the old Adam and the new man, between the outward and the interior life.

You say that you can do nothing in meditation without the help of a book. Well, what does it matter? What does it signify whether you use a book at intervals, or not? When I said you were only to spend half an hour in meditation, it was because I feared that at first you might overstrain your imagination, but now there is no danger in your taking an hour for the purpose.

There is no harm in pursuing any good and lawful occupations on the days you have communicated. Do you suppose that in the Primitive Church, when the faithful communicated daily, they folded their hands and did nothing? When S. Paul was celebrating daily, he was also gaining his bread by the labour of his hands. There are but two things from which we are bound to abstain on the days of our Communion, sin and mere voluptuous indulgence; but as to whatever is necessary or lawful, or a matter of charity, no such things are forbidden; on the contrary, they are enjoined, subject to a wise and holy moderation. Certainly I would not have you abstain from ordinary society, or rightly ordered festivities.

You ask whether those who aim at perfection ought to mix with the world? My dear lady, perfection does not lie in abstaining from the world so much as in not delighting in and making common cause with it. There is danger in what we see of the world, lest we should love it, but there is not much of this danger to those who are determined and resolute. Perfect charity involves a perfect life, for charity is the very life of the soul. The primitive Christians were in the world in the body, not in spirit, and they were very near perfection. I would have you without any pretence whatsoever;—simplicity and openness are great graces.

But you say that you are vexed by the false judgments men make concerning you, and you ask what to do? My dear daughter, the Saints tell us to rejoice if the world despises us, inasmuch as we are really contemptible; and if the world esteems us highly, they bid us despise its judgment, for the world judges blindly. Do not heed what the world thinks, do not trouble about it; be indifferent alike to its praise and its blame, and let it say what it will. I would not have you do amiss in order that men may think ill of you, wrong is wrong, and you may lead your neighbour to fall;—on the contrary, I would have you fix your eyes on our Dear Lord, and go on your way regardless of what the world says or thinks. You may shun giving others a good impression of yourself, but you must not try to give a bad impression; above all, by any intentional faults. In a word, be indifferent to the world's opinion, one way or the other. It is all very well to say that you are not that which the world assumes you to be—it is a mere charlatan, and generally overstates both our good and our evil deeds.

What is this that you tell me, about envying others because I prefer them to you, and you know that it is so? How do you know it, my dear sister? How do I show my preference? No indeed, you are dear to me, very dear; and I know that you do not prefer others to me, although you well might do so. But to speak in all confidence, our Sisters in the country need more help than you do in town, where there is abundance of every kind of spiritual advantage, while they have none. Is it not reasonable that I should try to help them more than you?

CXXXVI.

To a Young Nobleman.

(There are only two fragments of this letter extant.)

WELL! I will grant that you have the greatest possible aversion to all that is good! but, nevertheless, I affirm that you can alter this natural inclination; and if you will do as I tell you, you need have no very great difficulty in becoming what you ought to be, or in acquiring such goodness as is becoming to one in your position. Now, sir, I would beg you often to call to mind what God in His Goodness has intended to effect in your soul, and what He would have of you when He endowed you with property, influence, and power. Princes and nobles usually possess, from their birth, many things which other people strive wearily to obtain. Nothing is lacking to them which they cannot acquire; they have but to will a thing, and it is accomplished. But in order to conform this will to that of God, men in such a position should seek after a perfect will, which desires nothing save His Good Pleasure. And God requires of a prince that he should rule over his people by means of fear and love, himself fearing and loving God with a filial fear, and a most pure, holy, and hearty love. Often, the indulgence of princes is real cruelty, and their justice is true mercy; the happiness or misery of their people often depends upon their example. Well were it if all princes would say with Trajan, "I must be such a prince over my subjects as I should wish my prince to be were I a subject." And in like manner, as every nobleman and gentleman is a monarch on a small scale over his own household, he ought to bear in mind the Apostle's words: "Masters, give unto your servants that which is just and equal, knowing that ye also have a Master in Heaven." [1]

[1] Col. iv. 1.

They must not be as lions in their own homes, angering and oppressing their dependants; their piety should be generous, their courage full of kindliness and mercy. This is the first lesson they must learn, so as to give due submission to God and the King, and to use their power over others to the ends of justice and charity. . . .

Fragment II.

My brother, what should hinder you from the paths of holiness? A poor man may indeed become saintly, but a powerful lord, such as you are, not only may, but ought to be holy, and to work for good upon all who behold the tenor of his life.

CXXXVII.
To a Lady, recently come under his Direction.

Madame,

Your letter of January 20 was a source of great satisfaction to me, because amid all the troubles which you set before me, I thought I could see that you had made progress in the spiritual life. I must answer you more briefly than I should wish, for I have less leisure and more hindrances than I expected.

You say that you are grieved because you do not seem to open your heart sufficiently to me. To this I reply that, although I cannot know what you do in my absence, and I am no prophet, still I think it would be impossible to know your disposition and inclinations better than I do, considering the short time I have known you. I think there are few folds of your heart into which I have not penetrated; and if you continue to open the door of your mind, I can see everything plainly. It is a great advantage to you that it should be so, if you wish me to help you on the way of salvation.

You complain that sundry imperfections and faults come across the longings you feel after perfection and a pure love of God. And I answer that it is not possible to be altogether quit of self while we live in this world. We must carry our own load steadily, until it pleases God to carry us to Heaven; and while we carry this burden, 'tis truly but a worthless one! So we must have patience, and not fancy that we can cure the bad habits formed through years of spiritual carelessness in a day.

There have been those whom God has cured suddenly, taking away every trace of past evil; such as Magdalene, who was converted from a sink of corruption into a fountain of pure water, never to fail again. But then, too, God left the stamp of past evil dispositions upon many of His chosen servants, after they were converted, and that for their greater good. For instance, S. Peter fell sundry times after he was called of Christ, and even denied his Master. King Solomon says that "the handmaid who is heir to her mistress" is a troublesome thing;[1] and there would be a danger lest the soul, which has long been the slave of its own passions, should become vain and proud were it

---

[1] Prov. xxx. 23.

suddenly to be perfectly free from them. We must rather win this victory little by little, step by step; it has cost saints many a long year's struggle. You must, if you please, be patient with everybody, and first of all with yourself.

Next, you tell me that you can do nothing in prayer. But what would you do, save that which you can achieve, namely, ever and again lay your nothingness and misery before God? Beggars generally think they can make no more touching appeal to the charitable than the exhibition of their sores and griefs. Sometimes, however, you do not even do this, you say, but you are cold and impassive as a statue. Well, even that is something. In royal palaces we often find statues which serve no purpose save to gratify the prince's eye. Be content to stand thus in God's Presence, and leave Him to quicken the statue into life when He sees fit. Trees cannot bear fruit unless the sun's warmth fertilizes them ; and some bear it sooner than others, according to their kind. Let us count ourselves happy if we may but stand before God, and wait patiently to bear fruit sooner or later ; every day, or at rare intervals, according to His Holy Will, to which we must submit absolutely.

That is, indeed, a wonderful saying which you quote : " Let God treat me as He will, it is all one to me, if I may but serve Him."[1] But be sure that you feed diligently upon it in your heart ; let it melt in your mouth, do not swallow it whole. S. Theresa (whom you love so much, of which I

---

[1] "Que Dieu me mette en telle sauce qu'il voudra, ce m'est tout un, pourvu que je le serve."

am very glad) says somewhere that we are very apt to use such words as these mechanically, and without really apprehending their meanings. We fancy that we say them sincerely, and mean them, although practically it is proved not to be so. Well, then, you say that it is all one to you how it may please God to treat you. Now you know very well how He has treated you—in what condition and circumstances He places you—but tell me, is it all one to you? Nor are you ignorant of the daily debt which He requires you to pay, but nevertheless that is not "all one" to you? Alas, how craftily self-love insinuates itself into our hearts, however earnest they seem to be!

The real remedy is to find out what God wills, and having found that, to try and do it cheerfully, or at all events heartily. Further still, we must love that Will, and the duty it lays upon us, were that duty herding swine, or any other of the most distasteful kind; for "let God treat us as He wills, it should be all one to us." This is the point of perfection at which we should all aim, and he who comes nearest to it will win the prize. But I intreat you, do not be downcast; mould your will by degrees to that of God, and follow where it leads you. Learn to be deeply moved when conscience whispers, "It is God's Will;" and little by little this repugnance of which you complain will grow less, until it finally disappears. Especially you must strive to conquer the outward exhibition of your inward repugnance, or at least you must diminish it. Some persons, when angry or displeased, know how to restrain their feelings, while others break out into sharp words, which indicate pride and vexation. Now all such demonstrations must be corrected and conquered by degrees.

As to your wish to see all belonging to you advancing in God's service and towards Christian perfection, nothing can be better, and I willingly grant your request that I would join my poor prayers to yours for that end. But, madame, I must honestly tell you that I am afraid these wishes are not always absolutely pure, or free from a certain self-seeking and self-love. For instance, sometimes we dwell upon such wishes which are not absolutely necessary, to the exclusion of an earnest desire for more indispensable things; our own growth in humility, resignation, gentleness, and so forth. Or perhaps these ardent wishes for the progress of others lead us into over-anxiety or restlessness; and we do not remember that we must submit in these, as in all else, to God's Holy Will. This is what I fear in such wishes, and I intreat you to be watchful lest you should fall into any of these errors; as also to seek the furtherance of your desires very quietly and patiently, without making those who are their object uncomfortable, even without betraying that object; for, believe me, if you do so you will hinder, not promote, your end. Let your example and your words quietly sow the seeds of all that is good, and that can further your object among those you love; and without appearing to teach or dictate, strive here and there to make a good impression upon their minds. By this means you will gain more than in any other way, above all, with the help of prayer.

CXXXVIII.
To a Lady, expecting her Confinement.

MADAME,

Your letter of May 16 gives me cause to thank God for keeping alive in your heart the longing after Christian perfection, which I can trace so plainly in the pious simplicity with which you describe your temptations, and your struggles against them. I see that our Dear Lord is helping you, inasmuch as day by day, step by step, you gain greater freedom from your former faults and failings. I doubt not that you will soon be altogether victorious, since you are so vigorous in resistance, and so full of hope and trust in our Good Lord's Grace. . . .

I am glad to hear that you are more cheerful than you were. Assuredly, madame, your happiness will increase daily, as the sweetness of our Saviour's Love spreads itself more within your soul. I feel sure that your cheerfulness and content will specially make themselves felt in your social intercourse, and chiefly in your own family, where your first duty lies, and where your religion should be most exercised. If you really love religion, live so as to lead all around you to love and reverence it too; they will do so if they see its favourable results set forth in you.

In truth you have great means of doing good! You have every opportunity of making your house a very paradise of goodness, with a husband who is so well disposed to help you. You may indeed be most happy, if you take pains to suit your religious exercises to the convenience of your household, and to your husband's wishes. I know few married women who have better opportunities of being religious than you, madame, and consequently, you are bound to make great progress in holiness. . . .

I heard that you were expecting your confinement, and I thank God, Who wills to add to the number of His children and yours. The trees of the earth bring forth fruit for the service of men; but it is given to women to bear children for God's Service; and therefore Holy Scripture reckons child-bearing as a blessing. Do you make a double use of your prospects;—first, by offering your unborn child continually to God, as S. Augustine was offered by his mother; and next, by offering the inevitable discomfort and suffering of your condition to our Lord, blessing Him for that through your pain He wills to bring into the world one who, thanks to His Grace, will praise Him with you through all eternity. May God be glorified in all our troubles and joys.

CXXXIX.

To a Lady.

. . . . You tell me that you have slackened your religious exercises since you went into the country; well, if so, string your bow afresh, and begin with greater pains; but another time do not let the green fields produce this effect upon you. Why should they? God is in the country as much as in town.

CXL.

To a Lady.

FOR the last month, my dear sister, I have been ill with fever, and unable to answer your letters. . . . I am not sure that I know what you mean, but I will try to answer what I think you wish to ask. You see, it often happens that just when we fancy we have quite overcome our old foes, they attack us anew from some unexpected quarter. Even the wise King Solomon, after all the marvels of his youth, was taken by surprise, and overcome by his enemy. From this we must learn two plain lessons ;—first, always to mistrust ourselves, to tread our path in holy fear, ever seeking God's Help with humble devotion; and next, that though our enemies may be repulsed they are not exterminated. They sometimes leave us alone awhile, in order to return more vigorously to the charge ; but nevertheless, dear sister, you must not be disheartened, but quietly and bravely set to work to heal the breaches made within your soul, humbling yourself before the Lord, noways amazed to find yourself so weak. Indeed, the thing to astonish us would be the absence of such weakness and such onslaughts. All such little troubles, dearest sister, serve to remind us of our own weakness, and send us more earnestly to our real Protector. S. Peter walked boldly upon the waves until the wind rose and he was about to sink. Then he cried out, "Lord, save me!" And Christ stretched forth His Hand, saying, "O man of little faith, wherefore didst thou doubt?" It is chiefly amid the waves and storms of passion and temptation that we seek our Saviour's Help—and He only permits us to be alarmed in order to incite us the more to invoke His aid. In a word, then, do not be troubled because you have been troubled; do not be annoyed because of your past annoyance, or anxious because you have allowed these vexing thoughts to disturb you. Recall your heart, put it gently into your Saviour's Hands, imploring Him to heal it, while for your part you do what you can by the help of renewed resolutions, by the use of suitable books, and other appropriate means; by so doing your loss will be turned into gain, and you will be all the stronger for your moral sickness. My dearest child, if your condition makes lengthened mental prayer a difficulty to you, be content that your meditations be brief and hearty. Make up for this by continual aspirations of your heart to God; often read a few lines of some suitable spiritual book; let your thoughts when out of doors turn upon holy things; offer all your languor and oppression to our Crucified Lord; and then, by and by, after your confinement, resume your former habits quietly.

CXLI.

To a Young Lady.

MY VERY DEAR CHILD IN JESUS CHRIST,

I have received your letter, in which you try to lay the state of your mind open to me. I am gratified by your confidence in my affection, which is as true and stedfast as you can wish: God be thanked in and for all things. But I must say a word or two concerning the subject of your letter.

First of all, I beg you to understand clearly that the notion that you can only receive God's Help through me is simply a temptation of the evil one, whose aim it is to make us dwell on the thought of distant help, so that we may while so doing neglect to make use of that which is at hand. It is a mere moral disease when those who are suffering from bodily sickness set their heart on the assistance of some physician who cannot be had, to the exclusion of those who are at hand. We must never persist in wanting what is impossible, or reckon upon what is difficult and uncertain. Nor is it enough that we believe God to be able to succour us by any instrument; we must go further and believe that He does not choose to make use of those whom He puts at a distance, and that He means to make use of such as He brings near. While I was near you I would not have rejected your wish, but now it is altogether unreasonable.

Next, I think you have hit off the real source of your difficulty, when you say that it lies in a multitude of longings which can never be fulfilled. Practically, this is a similar temptation to the other, or, to speak more correctly, that is an offshoot from this, which is the root. Now, a great variety of food tries any digestion, but it is fatally mischievous to one that is weak. When the soul has broken free from worldly and evil affections, it comes across spiritual and pious attractions, and like one a-hungered, it seizes upon them with such greedy haste as to be altogether overwhelmed. You must seek the remedy for this at our Dear Lord's Hands, and from the spiritual guides who are near you; they, being able to put their finger upon the evil, will know best what remedy to apply. Still I will tell you briefly what occurs to me about it.

I think that if you do not begin trying to put some of these longings into practice, they will continue to multiply, and will at last so entangle your mind as to produce hopeless confusion. Well, then, we must come to results, but where to begin?

We must begin with visible external results, which are most in our power. For instance, you doubtless wish to tend the sick, and to render them mean and disagreeable service for love of Christ. These are a sort of groundwork of such longings as yours, without which others would be suspicious. Well, practise such results of your longings as these — neither object nor opportunity can be lacking—it is entirely within your power to do this, and consequently you ought to do it. It is useless to imagine that you would do those good works which are beyond your reach or impossible, if you neglect such as are attainable. So henceforth be diligent in the practice of common lowly works of charity, humility, and the like, and you will soon find the benefit of so doing. Magdalene needed to wash the Saviour's Feet, and to wipe them with her hair before she dared speak heart to heart with Him; she anointed His Head with oil before she was filled with the balm of Heavenly contemplation.

It is well to aim high, but we must regulate our aims and desires according to what is seasonable and possible. Gardeners prune away the leaves of certain plants, in order to let all the sap and juices go to the formation of fruit, rather than to mere exuberant foliage. And in like manner, it is well to hinder the mere multiplying of wishes, lest the soul should rest in them, and neglect to produce those results, of which the smallest, when practical and real, is worth all imaginable vague impossibilities. God requires a faithful fulfilment of the merest trifle given us to do, rather than the most ardent aspirations for things to which we are not called.

After all, if these remedies do not help you, be patient; wait till the sun arise, and it will disperse the mists. Be of good cheer, "this sickness is not unto death, but for the Glory of God." . . . I wished to say something to you, rather as a proof how sincerely I wish your well-doing, than because I feel able to help you. But do not doubt that I will commend you to the Father of Light; I do so gladly, hoping that you will do the like by me, as indeed I greatly need it, being, as I am, embarked in the most stormy part of the Church's ocean. . . . Finally, I intreat you to persevere in the resolution you made in the midst of your letter: "I protest before God, and before you, that I desire Him only, and would serve Him alone. Amen."

This is right and just, for He on His part asks you for nothing, save—yourself!

I am, truly and heartily, my dearest child in Jesus Christ, your very affectionate, etc.

[794.]   CXLII.

To a Lady of high Rank, who was being involved in Law Proceedings.

I DO not dwell upon the more than fatherly love which I have in my heart for you, my dearest child, for I think that God, Who called it forth, will tell you of that, and if He does not, it is not in my power to do so. But why should I say all this? Because, dear child, I have not written to you so often lately as perhaps you may have wished, and sometimes people measure affection more by sheets of paper than by the rarer but more useful proofs of the heart's inward feelings. . . .

Now, without further preface, I am going to say plainly and without disguise what my soul bids me say to you. How long, my dearest child, are you going to strive after other victories in the world, and over the things of the world, than those which our Saviour sought for, and at which He bids you aim? What did He do, Lord of all the world as He was? My child, He was the true Lord of all things, but did He ever strive even for "where to lay His Head"? He was wronged on every side; did He ever go to law? Did He ever bring any of His enemies before the judgment seat? Never, of a truth! nor would He even summon the traitors who crucified Him before God's tribunal, but rather He pleaded for their pardon; "Father, forgive them." And He has given us as a precept, "If any one will take away thy coat, let him have thy cloak also."

I am not superstitious, nor do I condemn those who go to law, provided it be with truth, judgment, and justice; but I say, I exclaim, I cry out, and if need be, I would write with my own blood, that he who would be perfect and wholly the child of Jesus Christ Crucified, had need follow our Lord's teaching in this respect. Let the world rave, let worldly prudence tear her hair, let all the wise men of our day invent as many subterfuges, and excuses, and pretexts as they will; before all the maxims of prudence, there rise up the words, "If any man will take thy coat, let him have thy cloak also."

But, you will say, this is to be understood in a certain sense. True, my dearest child, but thanks be to God, we can take it in that certain sense, for we aim at perfection, and we seek to follow as closely as we can him who said in his apostolic fervour, "Having food and raiment, let us be therewith content;"[1] and who exclaimed to the Corinthians, "Now, therefore, there is utterly a fault among you, because ye go to law one with another."[2] Now listen, my child, to what this man went on to say, one who, though he lived, it was "not I, but

[1] 1 Tim. vi. 8.   [2] 1 Cor. vi. 7.

Christ liveth in me." "Why," he asks of his spiritual children, "why do ye not rather take wrong? why do ye not rather suffer yourselves to be defrauded?" Observe, my child, that he does not speak thus to a spiritual daughter who has specially high aspirations after a life of perfection, but to all the Corinthians. Take notice that he bids them "take wrong;" he accuses them of sin in going to law with those who deceive and defraud them. Why sin? Because, in so doing, they give cause for scandal to the unbelieving world, which would say: "See how these Christians follow out their doctrine! Their Master said: Let him that would take thy coat have thy cloak also; but they risk eternal gain for that which is temporal; they sacrifice the brotherly love they ought to maintain for mere profit." S. Augustine bids us notice that the Lord did not say, If any man take thy ring let him have thy brooch—both superfluities—but He speaks of coat and cloak, which are necessaries. Oh, my dearest child, this is the true wisdom of God, His Prudence, which is a holy adorable simplicity —or, to use an Apostle's language, "the foolishness of the Cross."

But you will reply in the tone of human prudence, To what would you bring us? Are men to trample us under foot, insult us, make mere puppets of us, tear away our very garments, and are we to keep silence? Yes, indeed—all this—I would have it so; yet, not I, but Jesus Christ speaking by me. Listen to His Apostle, who exclaims, "Even unto this present hour we both hunger and thirst, and are naked and buffeted, and have no certain dwelling-place ; being reviled, we bless ; being persecuted, we suffer it ; being defamed, we intreat ; we are made as the filth of the world, and are the offscouring of all things unto this day."[1] The inhabitants of Babylon do not understand this doctrine, but those who dwell upon Mount Calvary follow it.

I can fancy, dear child, that I hear you say, "Oh, Father, you have become very severe all of a sudden." It is not suddenly at all events, for ever since God gave me grace to know anything of the Cross, this conviction took hold of my soul, and has never varied. If I have not lived consistently with it, that has been my own weakness, not lack of conviction ; the world's clamour may have made me do the external wrong which I loathed in my heart, and it humbles me while I whisper these words into your ear, dear child. I never gave back ill for ill save *à contre cœur.* I have not examined my conscience specifically, but so far as I can tell, generally speaking, I think this is true, and I am all the more inexcusable.

My child, I am writing hurriedly ; this letter has been twice resumed, and love is not always prudent or discreet ; it is apt to hurry on. There are so many honourable, wise, kind, good people about you, cannot some of them bring Madame de C. . . . and Madame de L. . . . to reason, so that you may arrange matters ? Are they tigresses who cannot hear reason ? Have you not M. N. . . . whose wisdom in all things is so sure? Would not M. de . . . . charitably help you in such a Christian work of peacemaking ? Or the good

[1] 1 Cor. iv. 11-13.

Père .... would he not rejoice to serve God in this matter, which really affects the welfare of your soul, and at all events must hinder your spiritual progress? What a string of artifices, secularities, dishonesties, perhaps lies ! what endless little quiet bits of injustice, almost imperceptible calumnies, occur in such a maze of legal proceedings! One would think you were going to be married, or to live in the world and wished to keep up your position, that you require this and that ! What will be the result of all this swarm of worldly thoughts and considerations? Leave the things of this world to worldly men ; what do you want with them ? Two thousand crowns or less is ample provision for one who serves a Crucified Saviour ! A hundred and fifty crowns is an all-sufficient income for one who believes in Apostolic poverty ! "But if I am not an inclosed nun, if I only reside associated with some monastery, I shall not be able to keep up any position, or have any attendants." Well, did you ever hear that Our Lady had any ? What does it matter whether people know that you are of a good worldly house if you belong to God's House? "Oh, but I should like to found some good work, or at least to help on some religious house. I am but feeble in body, and that would ensure me a better reception." Indeed, my dearest child, I knew that your piety was but a scaffolding to self-love, it is so pitifully earthly. No, forsooth, we will none of the Cross, unless it be of gold, well chased and enamelled. It is a very lordly, though most devout and admirable spiritual piece of abjection to be looked upon in a congregation as its foundress, or at least as its benefactress. Why, Lucifer himself might have remained in Heaven at this rate! But to live upon alms, as our Lord lived, to accept charity when we are sick, being as we are high born and proud, this is very difficult and hard to bear! True, it is hard to man, but not to the Son of God, and He will work in you. "But is it not well to keep one's own property and use it as one will for God's Service?" The words "as one will" explain the secret of our difference. "Well then, as *you* will, dear Father, for I am your dutiful child." Ah, then, my will is that you should be satisfied with whatever M. and Madame de . . . . decide on, and that you give up the rest for the Love of God, and your neighbours' edification, and the peace of mind of your sisters. In this way you will really devote it to the good of mankind, and to the promotion of God's Glory. Oh, my dearest child, what blessings, what graces, what spiritual riches will pour in upon your soul if you do thus. You will abound and overflow; God will bless the little you have, and abundantly satisfy you. Indeed it is not hard to Him to do as much with five barley loaves as Solomon could do with all his train of purveyors.

Be at peace. Ever your most devoted father, etc.

[796.] CXLIII.

To a Young Lady. On Meekness.

MAY God's Blessing be on you, my dear child; I send these few words according to my promise.

You should make a special point of asking God every morning to give you, before all else, that true spirit of meekness which He would have His children possess. You must also make a firm resolution to practise yourself in this virtue, especially in your intercourse with those two persons to whom you chiefly owe it. You must make it your main object to conquer yourself in this matter; call it to mind a hundred times during the day, commending your efforts to God. It seems to me that no more than this is needed in order to subject your soul entirely to His Will, and then you will become more gentle day by day, trusting wholly in His Goodness. You will be very happy, my dearest child, if you can do this, for God will dwell in your heart, and where He reigns all is peace. But if you should fail, and commit some of your old faults, do not be disheartened, but rise up and go on again, as though you had not fallen. This life is short, it is given to us for no other end than the attainment of a better life, and you will make a good use of it if you are meek and gentle towards those with whom God has bound you. Pray for my soul, that God may draw it to Himself. I am, etc.

[797]   CXLIV.

To a Lady.

MY DEAREST CHILD,

I had noticed the little disturbance which has troubled you during the last few days, and the struggles in your heart between the desire to give up your own way and the contrary inclination to follow your individual liking.

Well, dear child, you will soon see that the worst thing you have done is to have been so troubled at your own folly; for if you had not been so perturbed by your first failure, but had gently recollected yourself and kept yourself in hand, you would not have fallen the second time. But the best thing to do now is to take courage, and confirm all your good resolutions, especially the resolution not to be anxious, or at all events to put away anxiety as soon as you discover its existence.

Your expression, "I am torn to pieces," was not quite what it should have been. Dear child, we must strive to be indulgent to our neighbours, and humble ourselves, not over-ready to think that they are too well off, and ourselves not sufficiently blessed. Alas! we shall always find something to do, some enemies to resist! Do not be surprised at this, but when you are harassed by such evil inclinations, turn your inward gaze to the Crucified Saviour. "Lord, Thou Who art all sweetness, soften the asperity of my heart through Thine Own Meekness." Try to divert your mind for a time from the cause of irritation, and then prepare to conquer yourself. God will help you. Ever yours, etc.

[798.]   CXLV.
To the Same.

I HAVE received your two letters, my dear child, and I see plainly that all your trouble has been caused merely by mental disturbance arising from two unsatisfied longings. One was a desire to serve God, in the special occasion which presented itself; the other was a wish to know whether you had been faithful to your duty. Now you were eager and excited about both these matters, and so you became restless and disturbed, and hence all the trouble. Well, I have no doubt that you were faithful to your duty; your mind always leans to the side of severity,—and you were consequently not satisfied with what you did; and then being very anxious to fulfil a duty, and not able to satisfy yourself that you had so done, you became a prey to discouragement and melancholy. But now, my dear child, you must forget it all, and be cheerful, humbling yourself sincerely before our Lord, and remembering that your sex and position hinder you from dealing with external evils, save by setting a good example, or sometimes by using simple, humble, charitable remonstrances, or possibly through those set over the delinquents. Remember this another time. Then, as a general rule, bear in mind that if we cannot feel sure whether we have done our duty in any particular matter, and are afraid lest we may have offended God, we must humble ourselves, ask His Forgiveness, and pray for greater light another time. Then we must put it all away, and go on as usual; for an inquisitive, eager search as to whether we have acted rightly most assuredly comes from the spirit of self-love, which makes us want to know whether we are brave in the very thing concerning which God's Love would have us say, "Mere weak coward that I am, I humbly throw myself upon God's Mercy, I ask His Pardon, I will strive to be more faithful, I will go on and seek to come nearer to Him."

I am content that you should not sleep as much as you would like, unless you really need the rest; but to prevent injury to your health, you must take rather more exercise instead of sleep. In this way you may cut off an hour's sleep in the morning, not at night, and you will be all the better for it. As to other austerities, do not impose anything extra upon yourself; your constitution and your position will not admit of it. Nor do I approve any great retreat (from the world) at present. I would rather that you exercised your patience amid these contradictions without being discouraged, but taking great pains to bear them well. May God ever be our sole aim and object, my dear child. In Him, I am, wholly yours, etc.

[793.] CXLVI.

To a Lady, expecting her Confinement.

ABOVE all things, my dear daughter, strive to attain a calm mind, not because it is the source of content, but because it is the result of true Love of God, and resignation of our own will. We have daily occasions for exercising this.

Go where we may there are sure to be plenty of contradictions awaiting us; even if they do not arise through others, we bring them upon ourselves. Oh, my dear child, how holy and acceptable to God we should be, if we did but know how to use rightly the many opportunities for self-mortification which our natural position affords us! They are practically more frequent than those which surround Religious; the thing is that we do not make such good use of them as Religious do.

You must take care of yourself under your present circumstances; do not be distressed if you are unable to carry out your wonted religious practices. If kneeling tries you, sit down; if you cannot keep up your attention for half an hour, limit your prayer to a quarter of an hour, or even less. Place yourself in the Presence of God, and offer all your pain to Him. Do not be afraid of expressing what you suffer, but pour out your complaints to God with the loving spirit of a child to its mother. So long as that loving spirit exists there is no danger in complaining, or seeking relief, or healing, or in striving to get alleviation by means of change. Only do it all with love and resignation to God's Holy Will.

Do not be troubled because you cannot make your acts of faith, etc., as you wish. They are not lost in God's Sight, although they are made wearily and painfully, almost, as it may seem, against the grain. You can only offer to God that which you have, and at this time of trial you cannot help being weary and oppressed. Just now "your Beloved is as a bundle of myrrh"[1] to you; but give good heed that you press it closely to your breast. "My Beloved is mine, and I am His."[2] He shall ever rest within my heart; but Isaiah calls Him "a Man of Sorrows."[3] He looks favourably upon suffering, and upon those that bear it. Do not torment yourself with trying to do much, rather seek to bear what is laid upon you in a loving spirit. God will look upon you with a Gracious Eye, and will bring you to that Life where we shall be wholly His, wherein nothing can separate us from His Love; we shall live to and for Him only, He will be our God for ever and ever. I will not fail to ask it of Him, or in Him to be, sincerely yours, etc.

[802.]   CXLVII.

To a Young Lady.
On the Right Use of High Aspirations.

MADEMOISELLE,

My brother brought me your letter, and I thank God that He has given some light to your mind; you must not be surprised if you do not yet see altogether clearly. Spiritual maladies, like those of the body, are generally followed by some relapse, which are not unprofitable, especially inasmuch as they remind us of the past, and make us watchful not to fall again through over great

---

[1] Cant. i. 13.   [2] Cant. ii. 16.   [3] Isa. liii. 3.

freedom and laxity, before our strength is re-established.

And now that you have nearly escaped from all the terrible trials through which you have been led, I think, my dear child, that you should rest awhile, and pause to reflect upon the vanity of our earthly mind, and see how prone it is to get itself entangled and distorted. I am sure that you see plainly how the interior troubles which have beset you were caused by a multitude of over-eager thoughts and aspirations after an imaginary perfection. I mean that your imagination formed an ideal of absolute perfection to which your will aspired; but overwhelmed by its great difficulty, or more truly its impossible nature, the will remained paralysed. Then it overflowed in useless wishes, which were like useless drones, devouring the honey, while your really good desires were neglected and starved.

Now then, take breath and reflect; look back upon the dangers from which you have escaped, and so turn aside from such as may be before you. Be suspicious of all such aspirations as are generally acknowledged to be unpractical, all visions of a Christian perfection so ideal that it cannot be exercised, a perfection altogether theoretical, never reduced to practice.

Remember that no grace so tends to perfection as that of patience, and we need it, not only with others, but with ourselves. Those who aim at a pure Love of God require more patience with themselves than with other people. If we would attain perfection, we must bear with our imperfection; that is, bear with it patiently, not cherish or encourage it. True humility is fostered by such endurance.

We must honestly confess that we are poor creatures, who can do but little that is good, but God, Who is Infinitely Good, looks favourably on our poor attempts, and accepts the preparation of our hearts.

Now what is this preparation of heart? According to Holy Scripture, "God is Greater than our heart," and our heart is greater than the world. When it goes apart, and makes ready to serve God, by serving our neighbour, by self-mortification, and similar good works, it "prepares" itself for a high degree of perfection. But all this preparation bears no proportion to God's Goodness, which is infinitely "greater than our heart," although it is beyond the measure of the world and of our ordinary strength. A mind which has pondered upon God's Greatness, His Infinite Power and Goodness, cannot but strive to make great preparation for Him. It prepares a body, mortified without rebellion; diligence in prayer, without distraction; gentleness in ordinary life, free from any bitterness; humility, free from all outbreaks of vanity. All this is good; it is an admirable preparation. Not but what it falls short of a fitting service rendered to God, but, even so, the question is who really renders such a service? When we come to practise we stop short, and find that we cannot carry out our theories of perfection. We can mortify the flesh, but not to the absolute exclusion of all rebellious passions; we shall often still be liable to distractions, and so must we then be troubled, restless, disappointed, despairing? Certainly not. Must we entertain a host of desires? No! Our gratitude may be very simply expressed. We may wish that we had the Seraphim's fervour, therewith fitly to serve and worship God; but we must not waste time in mere longings, as though in this world we could attain real perfection, and then grow irritable because we do not succeed.

Not but what we must aim at perfection, while we must not expect to attain it in this mortal life, or we shall torment ourselves unprofitably. Those who would tread safely must set themselves stedfastly to travel along the road which is appointed for them, nor must they fix their minds on the end of the journey, in such wise as to make them neglect to make a good beginning.

One word which I would have you remember: sometimes we amuse ourselves in playing at being good Angels, till we forget to be good men and women. Our imperfection must cleave to us till we rest in our grave; we cannot walk without touching the ground. We must not lie down or grovel upon it, but neither must we fancy that we can fly; we are yet but as unfledged birds. Physical death comes nearer day by day, and even so we must strive to destroy our imperfection day by day; "I die daily." It will be a precious imperfection if it makes us acknowledge our weakness, and strengthens our humility, our self-depreciation, our patience, and diligence. Through it all God looks upon "the preparation of the heart."

I do not know whether what I write will fit in with your needs, but it came into my heart to say all this because I think part of your late trouble has arisen from your making a great preparation, and then, finding the results very small, and your power insufficient to carry out your aspirations and plans, you have been seized by impatience, perturbation, restlessness, irritability; the result of which is mistrust, languor, depression, and disgust. Now if this is true, be wiser in future. Let us be content to travel by land if the sea turns us sick. Keep with Mary Magdalene, close to our Saviour's Feet; be content with lowly virtues, suitable to your own insignificance. "Little things for little folks."[1] I mean such graces as are easier to exercise while going down than while mounting up; they suit our weak limbs better; patience, forbearance, dutifulness, humility, meekness, affability, toleration of our own imperfections, and the like. I do not say but what we must try to rise up in prayer, but slowly and by degrees.

Study to attain a holy simplicity; look straight before you, and do not dwell upon all those dangers which you tell me you foresee. You take them for armies, and they are but willow trees, but all the same you may easily stumble while you are gazing upon them. Keep ever before you a firm intention of serving God always and with your whole heart, and then "take no thought for the morrow;" only strive to do your very best to-day. When "to-morrow" arrives, it will have become "to-day," and then it will be time enough to take thought for it. In all such matters we must have absolute trust and confidence in God,—we must gather our

---

[1] "A petit mercier, petit panier."

provision of manna for the day that is passing, no more;—never doubting but that God will send it again to-morrow, and the next day, and as long as we need it.

[805.] CXLVIII.
To a Lady.

MY DEAR DAUGHTER,

Keep your soul in an attitude of heartfelt trust in God, and the more you are encompassed with troubles and infirmities, hope the more stedfastly in Him.

Be very humble: it is the virtue of virtues, but let it be a generous, restful humility. Be very faithful in serving our Master, but let your service be childlike and loving, free from all that is harsh and repulsive. Strive to maintain a holy gladness, which may shine forth in your words and actions, and be attractive to those around you, leading them to glorify God—our only aim. And since you cannot practise any bodily mortification or hardness, as indeed it is quite unfit for you to think of so doing, according to what we settled before, keep your heart ready for your Saviour, and strive as far as possible that all you do may be done with a will to please Him, and let what of suffering comes to you in this life be accepted in a like spirit. So doing God will dwell wholly in you, and some day He will give you grace to dwell for ever with Him, for which I devoutly pray, and am ever, most heartily yours, etc.

[1809.]

CXLIX.

To a Young Lady.
On her Entrance into the Fashionable World.

My Dearest Child,

You will often find yourself among the children of this world, whose wont it is to ridicule whatever they see, or fancy they see, in you different from their own bad ways. Now do not take pleasure in arguing with such people;—be cheerful and bright, laugh at their ridicule, treat their contempt with contempt, divert their remonstrances, treat their mocking with playfulness, pay as little attention to it all as you can, and go on cheerily in God's Service, and often commend all such poor souls to God's Mercy in your prayers. They deserve pity when they treat things which should command reverence and respect with levity.

You are surrounded with all that makes this life pleasant; give good heed that your heart does not cleave to such things. Solomon, the wisest of men, began his downward course by taking delight in the magnificence and grandeur with which he was surrounded, although it was all in keeping with his position. It is well always to remember that we are really no better than others because of all we possess, and in truth it is all less than nothing in the Sight of God and His Angels.

Remember, dearest child, to try and do God's Will in that which is hardest to you. It is but a small thing to please Him after our own liking;

true childlike dutifulness requires us to please Him when we do not like it, recollecting the words of His Own Beloved Son, "I came not to do Mine own Will, but the Will of Him that sent Me." You were not made a Christian that you might work your own will, but that of Him Who has adopted you as His child and heir.

Well, and so you are going, and I too am going away, and without any hope of ever seeing you again in this world. Let us pray that God will give us both grace so to fight through our pilgrimage that when we reach the Heavenly Country we may rejoice that we had met here, and had talked together about the mysteries of Eternity. The only real cause for rejoicing in earthly ties is when they tend to His Eternal Glory, and our everlasting salvation.

Strive to retain a hearty, holy brightness, which strengthens your own heart, and edifies others. Go on in peace, my dearest child, and may God ever be your Protector. May He ever uphold you with His Hand, and lead you in the path of His Holy Will. So be it, dearest child. I promise daily to renew my prayers for your soul, which will be beloved eternally by me. To God be all praise, thanksgiving, and blessing. Amen.

[810.]   CL.

To a Young Lady, living in the World.

IN answer to your last letter, my child, I say that fervent expressions of love in prayer are good, if they leave good results behind them, and do not tend to occupy you with yourself, rather than with God and His Holy Will. Strive to love and seek after that which can never be sufficiently loved and sought.

May God give you grace, my child, really to despise that evil world which is ready to crucify us, if we reject it. But mental renunciations of vanity and worldly pleasures are easily made,— the reality when practised is a very different thing. You are now in a position thoroughly to practise this virtue, inasmuch as your privations are accompanied by contempt; and though it is you who do and suffer, it is still more God, in, for, and with you.

I am not satisfied, as I told you the other day, with these worldly repartees, and this vivacity, which so often leads you on. My child, let it be your special study to mortify this tendency; make the sign of the Cross often upon your mouth, that it may only be opened as God would have it.

It is true that readiness of wit often fosters vanity, and we are even more apt to turn up our noses mentally than literally! You may *faire les doux yeux* in words as well as in glances. It is never well to walk on tiptoe, either in mind or body; if you fall so doing, it will be heavily. Well now, my child, take pains to prune your superfluities gradually, and keep a lowly heart, laying it often in silence at the foot of the Cross. Go on telling me all about that little heart frankly and often; I love it very truly for His Sake, Who died that we might live.

[818.] CLI.

To a Married Lady.

. . . . WHAT do you lack? Even in those troubles, when your confidence in God was feeble, did He ever forsake you? I know you will answer that He did not. Then why should you not take courage in other trials? So far God has never forsaken you; why should He do so now, when you are more His child than before? Do not dread possible worldly trials; perhaps they will never come, and if they do, God will strengthen you. . . .

It matters little what we are during this brief life, if only we be eternal partakers of God's Eternal Glory. My daughter, we are journeying towards eternity—one foot is already well nigh there:—if that be granted us, what do these passing trials matter? Is it possible that we can believe that these temporary tribulations are to work out "an exceeding weight of glory"[1] for us, and yet we will not bear them patiently? Be sure that all which is not eternal is but vanity. The Apostle said, "God forbid that I should glory, save in the Cross of our Lord Jesus Christ."[2]

Fix Him in your heart, and all temporal crosses will seem but as rose-leaves to you. Those who have been pierced with the thorns of their Dear Lord's Crown will be very indifferent to all other thorns. . . .

[1] 2 Cor. iv. 17.   [2] Gal. vi. 14.

[832.]

CLH.
To a Lady.

INDEED, my dearest child, nothing can give us a more profound restfulness in this world than a stedfast gaze, fixed upon our Dear Lord in all His afflictions, from the cradle to the grave. What endless contempt, calumny, poverty, need, abjection, pain and sufferings, and every conceivable form of bitter trial, were heaped upon Him!—trials, in comparison of which we must feel afraid to call the little contradictions and annoyances which trouble us by the name of trials. We shall be half afraid to talk of seeking patience under such trifling woes, which a very small portion of humility ought to make bearable.

I think I am thoroughly acquainted with the condition of your soul, and I seem to be looking at it now with all its little gusts of agitation, anxiety, and sadness; emotions which harass it because you have not as yet laid the foundations of the Cross and of abjection deeply enough within your will. My dearest child, a heart which knows how duly to love and prize Jesus Christ Crucified will love His Death and His Pain, the scourge and the spitting, the mockery and shame, the hunger and thirst, which He bore; and if any passing share in all this is granted to such a heart, it will rejoice, and accept the portion lovingly. Well, then, try every day (not in meditation, but apart,—perhaps when you are out walking) to fix your thoughts upon our Dear Lord amid the pains which our Redemption cost Him, and bethink you how great the blessing of sharing in those pains must be; examine where and when you may receive this blessing; I mean the contradictions which cross your wishes, especially those wishes which seem to you altogether good and lawful, and then—your heart full of love for the Cross and Passion of our Lord—cry out with S. Andrew, "O good Cross, O dear Cross of my Saviour, when shall I be stretched upon thine arms!"

Indeed, my dear child, we are much too sensitive and too ready to apply the word *poverty* to a condition in which we are not suffering either from cold or hunger, or ignominy, but only from some little discomfort, or it may be some hindrance or restriction as to our tastes. When we meet again, remind me to speak more at length to you concerning this fastidious delicacy to which you lean too much. If you would win true rest and peace, this must above all else be cured;—we must strive to give you that deep realisation of eternity which, once grasped, makes the trifles of this brief life a matter of almost total indifference. . . . . Farewell, ever yours, etc.

[828.]   CLIII.

To a Gentleman. On Depression of Spirits.

DEAR SIR,

I am very anxious to know how you have borne this severe and painful illness, from which I hope

you are recovering, and which would have been a
still greater care to me, if I had not been assured
that you are in no danger, and that you are beginning to regain strength.

What seems of most importance now is, that I
hear you are tried by very great depression of
spirits, in addition to your bodily suffering. I fear
this will tend to delay your recovery, and keep you
from regaining a healthy tone.

Now, dear sir, the exceeding and true affection
which I bear you makes me feel deeply about this
trial, and I intreat you to tell me what cause you
have for encouraging this most harmful melancholy.
I have some idea that you are still troubled with
the fear of sudden death, and of God's judgment;
and in very truth I know what a wondrous trial
that fear is. Having undergone it myself for six
weeks, I can most thoroughly sympathise with
others under the affliction.

But I would fain speak to you from my innermost
heart, and assure you that no one who sincerely
wishes to serve our Lord and to avoid sin, need or
indeed ought to torment himself with the fear of
death or of judgment. Undoubtedly both are to
be feared, but not with that merely natural fear
which through its terror chills and depresses the
mind;—rather with a supernatural fear, which is
so blended with trust in God's Goodness as to
strengthen and comfort the soul.

Neither ought we to admit of doubts as to
whether we dare trust ourselves to God, because of
the difficulty we feel in avoiding sin, or because we
have misgivings as to our power of resisting temp-

tation and occasions of sin. No, indeed,—mistrust of our own strength does not imply a failure in resolution, but rather consciousness of our own weakness. It is better to be doubtful as to our capacity for resisting temptation than to be bold and presumptuous; provided that what we do not look for in our own strength we do look for from God's Grace. Many a man who went forth in conscious strength, intending to work great things for God, has failed when it came to the point; and many too who have greatly mistrusted themselves, and feared lest they should altogether fail, have unexpectedly done great things, because that very sense of their own weakness has thrown them so entirely upon God's Grace and Help, and so has led them to watch and pray and humble themselves, lest they enter into temptation.

Further, supposing that we feel convinced that were temptation to come upon us at this moment, we have neither strength nor courage to resist it;—yet, if we wish to resist, and hope that should such temptation come, God would help us, craving such help at His Hands,—then we need not be alarmed. It is not essential that we should always possess conscious strength and courage; enough if we trust that they will be supplied in the time of need. Samson was not conscious of his great strength save on special occasions; we are told that when he required it to encounter wild beasts or human enemies, "the Spirit of the Lord came upon him." So God, Who does nothing without a purpose, does not give us strength and courage except when we need them; consequently we have good ground for believing that whenever we do need them, His Help will be supplied, if we do but seek it.

I would have you continually use the words of David, "Why art thou so vexed, O my soul, and why art thou so disquieted within me? O put thy trust in God."[1] "Leave me not, neither forsake me, O God of my salvation!" If you desire to belong solely to God, why should you fear your own weakness, which you know cannot be trusted? You do trust in God:—who ever trusted in the Lord and was put to confusion? No indeed, it cannot be. I intreat you, my dear friend, to put aside all the arguments which arise in your mind, and to which you need make but one answer, namely, that you wish to be stedfast, come what may, and you hope by God's Help so to be. Be content with this, and do not be ceaselessly trying to find out whether your courage is likely to fail:—such examinations are deceitful; some men are very brave before they come within sight of the enemy, yet tremble when he appears;—and others who have been fearful, gather courage when face to face with danger. Do not be afraid of being afraid! But I have said enough. Any way, God knows that I would do or bear anything possible to see you set free from these troubles. Ever yours, etc.

[1] Ps. xlii. 14, 15.

[831.] CLIV.

To a Lady, who was calumniated; and concerning an Annual Review of Conscience.

MY DEAREST SISTER,

I have not seen M. . . . . but all the same, I heard that you have been distressed by certain caricatures and satires which have appeared. I wish I could always bear your troubles for you, or at all events help you to bear them. But inasmuch as the distance between our respective homes makes it impossible for me to help you, save by prayer, I do indeed pray that our Lord would be the Guardian of your heart, and drive all excessive sadness forth from it. Indeed, my dear sister, most of our troubles are more in imagination than reality. Do you suppose the world believes these satires? Very likely some people are amused by them, and others may give them some weight; but be sure that while your soul is at rest and leaning on your Saviour's Arms, all such attacks will melt away like smoke before the wind, and the higher the wind the faster they will vanish. We cannot counteract calumny so effectually as by disregarding it, treating contempt with contempt, and proving by our calmness that we are out of its reach; especially in such a case as these satires. Calumnies which can bring forward no authors of their existence, prove themselves to be illegitimate. I should like to quote to you what S. Gregory once said to a Bishop who was the victim of calumny.

"If your heart was anchored in Heaven," he says, "the storms of this world could in no wise reach it: nothing which belongs to this life can harm him who has renounced it." Cast yourself at the Feet of our Crucified Lord, and bethink you of all the insults He endured;—intreat Him, by the meekness with which He bore them, to give you strength to bear these passing annoyances, which have fallen to your lot as His sworn follower. "Blessed are the poor in spirit, for theirs is the Kingdom of Heaven. Blessed are ye when men shall revile you, and persecute you, and shall say all manner of evil against you falsely, for My Sake."[1]

Now as to what you ask me. You are quite right in looking upon the annual review of one's soul as intended to supply the defects of one's ordinary confessions, and to excite us to deeper humility; still more to lead us to renew, not our good *intentions*, but such good *resolutions* as we require to correct those habits, inclinations, and other matters which most frequently cause us to sin.

It is certainly more desirable that this review should be made before the same Priest who has received your general confession, in order that, taking the circumstances of both into due consideration, he may guide you as to what resolutions you most require to make. But when, as in your case, this cannot be, it is well to go to any other wise and good confessor who may be at hand.

As to your second difficulty, I answer that it is not necessary in this review to note the specific

---
[1] Matt. v. 3, 11.

number or the trifling details of your faults. It will suffice to say generally what your chief failings, and the cause of your wanderings, have been; not so much how many times you have fallen, but whether you are very prone to fall. For instance, you need not examine how many times you have given way to anger—perhaps that would be hard to say,--but you should simply acknowledge whether you are subject to bad temper, how long it lasts, whether it is violent and sharp, and what are the occasions which the most frequently excite it; as for instance, amusements, pride, haughtiness, obstinacy, depression—(I am only giving you an illustration of my meaning.) In this way you will be able to make your little review without taxing your time or your memory very severely.

As to your third question, I would say that some falls, even into mortal sin, so long as they are not deliberate or caused by indifference, do not necessarily prove that you have made no progress in a devout life. You lose your devotion when guilty of mortal sin, but you regain it through the first sincere repentance to which you attain, that is, when the soul has not been long steeped in sin. It is for this reason that such annual reviews are so very useful to weakly souls: their first good resolutions have done somewhat; the second and third time they will be strengthened and confirmed; and at last, by dint of frequent renewal, they will become stedfast. Only do not be disheartened, but face your own frailty with holy humility; confess it, ask that it may be forgiven, and seek God's Help for the future. Ever yours.

[1856.]   CLV.

To a Widow. On her Husband's Death.

MY DEAR MADAM,

I cannot tell you how deeply I feel for your sorrow. I loved your dear husband with a most special affection, for many reasons, but chiefly for his goodness and piety. One feels that in these times, when there is such a dearth of holy souls among the highest classes of society, such a loss is very great to the world at large. But, dear lady, we must accept the conditions of our present life —a brief, mortal life; and death, which has the mastery over it, has no set rules: he seizes one or another, so to say, without choice or plan—good and evil, old and young. Happy they who ever live so expecting death that they look through it to the eternal life which knows no ending!

The dear one we have lost was of these; and that alone may comfort us—for in a little while, more or less, we shall follow him, and the ties and companionships begun here will be knit again, never more to be loosed. So let us be patient, and wait bravely till the hour of our departure comes; let us go on loving those we have loved so dearly here, no less where they now are; and let us do that which they would have wished, and do still wish, for very love of them.

Most unquestionably, my dear friend, the foremost wish of your husband would be that you should not give way overmuch to your grief at his loss, but that you should strive to moderate it for the sake of that great love you bear him. Be sure that in his present blessed state, where he awaits you confidently, he asks that you may receive a holy consolation, and that you may calm your grief and use your eyes for a better purpose than tears, your mind for more worthy tasks than mere sorrow. He has left you some precious pledges of your union—use your eyes for their benefit, and your mind for the raising and developing theirs. Do this for love of that cherished husband. Believe that it was his parting wish,—that he still requires it of you. All indulged grief may be natural to your earthly heart, which is still in this world, but it is altogether contrary to his heart, which is safely stored in the next world.

True love ever seeks to please its object, and therefore, for love of your husband, I bid you be comforted; lift up your heart, and take courage. Strive, if you can, to cast yourself before the Lord, accepting His Will, and dwelling upon the thought of your dear one, who desires above all things to see you stedfast in firm Christian resolutions. So give yourself up wholly to the Heavenly guidance of the Saviour of your soul, Who will lead and comfort you, and will finally reunite you to your treasure, no longer as mere husband and wife, but as co-heritors of the Kingdom of Heaven, and as eternal and faithful lovers.

I have written hastily, almost without a moment's leisure, but my long-standing friendship for you and your husband would not let me be silent. May God ever be with you. Amen.

[1839.] CLVI.

To a Lady. On the Death of her Sister.

WELL, my dear child, this is how one by one we are crossing the river Jordan, and entering into the Promised Land, to which God calls us one after another. Oh, Dear Jesus, there is not much in this world that we should wish to detain those we love very long here! I knew your good sister, not only by sight, but through certain spiritual intercourse which I had with her during my visit. It is about a year since I sent her the habit of the Third Order of Carmelites at her request; and at her reception she made a general confession to a very able man, who either wrote or spoke to me about it. Well, dear child, is it not a proof of God's Loving Care for her that He has taken her only a year after to Himself? Glory be to the Father, and to the Son, and to the Holy Ghost. Yes, my dearest child, weep a little over your dead, even as our Lord wept over His beloved Lazarus. But let your tears be rather tears of holy tenderness than of bitter sorrow; such tears as Joseph wept for very love, rather than Esau's, which were called forth by excessive and bitter grief. These are times when, above all others, we need to accept our Dear Lord's Good Pleasure lovingly.

Ah, dear child, when shall we too reach that Home which waits us? Alas, we are on the eve of our own departure, and yet we mourn over those who are already gone! It is a bright hope for that dear soul that she had borne so many trials;

having been crowned with thorns, we may believe that now she will receive the Crown of Life. Let her go, then; let your dear sister go, and enter upon her Eternal Rest in the Bosom of God's Mercy. . . . I will tell you in all confidence, that although no man living ever loved more tenderly and deeper than I do, or felt parting from those I love more keenly, yet I hold this short, vain life to be so very worthless that I never come back with more fervent love to God than after He has smitten me with such losses. Dear child, let us fix our thoughts in Heaven, and we shall rise above earthly sorrows. Your sister's "soul pleased the Lord, therefore He hasted to take her away." We cannot but hope that He did so to her great gain. Let us wait patiently till He calls us too. Dear child, look upon this world as merely the plank which serves us to pass into the better world. I am, ever yours in Him Who became wholly ours when He died on the Tree of the Cross.

[841.] CLVII.

To a Friend, who had lost his Brother.

MY DEAR BROTHER,—

For I would be such in the stead of him whom our Dear Lord has taken to be with Himself,—I hear that you continue to grieve sorely over this separation, which is indeed a most trying one to you. But this must not go on; for either you weep for him or for yourself. Now if you weep for him, why should you weep because he is in Paradise, where tears are wiped away for ever? And if you weep for yourself, does it not become at least selfishness?

I speak thus plainly because it seems as though you cared more for yourself than for his infinite happiness. Would you keep your brother away from Him "in Whom we live and move and have our being," so long as we accept His Holy Will and pleasure? Come and see us, and let us "turn your sorrow into joy;" dwelling upon that blessedness which our dear brother now enjoys, never to lose. With such thoughts you too will be glad once more, the which I most heartily desire, and commend myself to your prayers. Ever most truly yours, etc.

CLVIII.

[*The following letter was written partly by Madame de Chantal in the form of queries on subjects connected with her spiritual life, leaving blank spaces in which S. Francis de Sales wrote his replies.*]

IN THE NAME OF JESUS AND MARY.

I. I will ask my dear lord[1] whether he approves of my renewing my vows and my general self-abandonment to God, every year, before him, begging him to point out whatever he thinks will touch me most closely, and enable me to make this self-renunciation more unreserved and more perfect, so that I may learn truly to say, "I live, yet not I, but Christ liveth in me." To this end I will ask my dear lord not to spare me, nor to allow me to make any reservation in things great or small; as also to appoint such exercises and daily prac-

[1] "Mon très cher seigneur."

tices as may be necessary, in order that my self-renunciation may be real and true.

Answer. I answer in our Lord's Name and that of Our Lady, that it would be well, my dear daughter, for you to make the proposed renewal of your vows year by year, and that you should also renew your resolution to give yourself up absolutely into God's Hands. To this end I will not spare you, but you shall retrench all superfluous words concerning the love, however lawful, of all creatures, whether relations, country, home, even of your father; and so far as may be you shall control all prolonged thought concerning these matters, save when duty obliges you to attend to them, so that you may the better obey the words, "Hearken, O daughter, and consider, incline thine ear, forget also thine own people and thy father's house." Before dinner and supper, and at night, examine yourself whether, judging by what you are actually doing, you can say honestly, "I live, yet not I, but Christ liveth in me."

II. When my soul has taken up this position, is it not bound, as far as possible, to forget all things in order to seek a continual remembrance of God, and to place an entire, undivided trust in Him?

Answer. Yes; you must strive to forget all that is not of and for God, and to remain in perfect trust beneath His Guidance.

III. Ought not the soul (especially in prayer) to strive to check all discursive movement, and instead of dwelling upon what it has done, or does, or may do, look to God Alone, thus purging itself from self, beholding God only, given up to His Will, and abiding at rest therein, without exercising either its own will or understanding? Even in good actions, or in faults, it seems to me that one should strive to remain passive, since the Lord puts such feelings as are needful into one's heart, and gives one such light as one requires; and this is better far than wandering about in quest of one's own imaginations. You will reply, Why then do I not so abide? But alas, that is my trouble. Whether I will or no, I do wander forth, and experience has taught me how much harm ensues; but I am not mistress of my own mind, which persists in travelling hither and thither without my consent. It is on this account that I would ask my dearest lord to help me through holy obedience to fix this wretched wanderer, for I think perhaps it would submit to an absolute command.

Answer. Since our Lord has for long past drawn you to this kind of prayer, teaching you how great the advantage is thereof, and the evil arising from a contrary habit, be stedfast; and as quietly as you can, restrain your mind thereto, and to perfect simplicity in God's Presence and forgetfulness of self. As you wish that I should make use of the claims of obedience, I say, "Why would you strive to take Martha's part in prayer, when God gives you to know that He wills you to take that of Mary?" I desire you then simply to abide in His Presence, without striving to do anything, or ask anything, save that to which He may move you. Do not look within upon yourself, but abide patiently before Him.

IV. Once more, my dear father, I would ask if the soul, when thus resting upon God, ought not to leave the disposition of all things, internal and external, to Him, waiting upon His Will, without any choice or effort, or any voluntary hindrance? Oh, my God, how can I win this grace, save through the prayers of this Thy servant?

Answer. God be gracious to you, my dear daughter. The child which rests in its mother's arms needs only to cling to her, and leave all else.

V. Will not our Lord order all things specially for the needs of a soul thus given up to Him?

Answer. Such souls are as the apple of His Eye.

VI. Ought one not to receive everything, even to the veriest trifle, as from His Hand, and seek His Guidance in everything?

Answer. In this respect God would have you to be as a little child; only be careful not to be fanciful or unreal.

VII. Would it not be profitable to wait patiently and without effort on God's Will in the numberless little matters which cross and trouble us? Greater things one sees from afar. I mean, for instance, the deprivation of comfort which seems desirable or necessary, hindrance in doing some good action or some mortification, while useless or dangerous things are forced upon us.

Answer. So long as you do not consent to what is wrong, you should study to attain a holy indifference in all else.

VIII. How to become dutiful and prompt in obedience to one's Rules. There are so many opportunities (in obedience to Rule) for little mortifications. The summons comes while one is in the middle of some occupation: one's accounts, etc. etc. It is so hard to leave off, one wants but another minute to finish what one is doing, to write one word more, just to warm oneself, or what not.

Answer. Yes, it is well to make everything give way to your Rules, and unless there is some signal reason to the contrary, obey them in preference to all these trifling inclinations.

IX. Is it well to let oneself be absolutely governed in all that concerns the body, merely accepting whatever is given or done to one, good or ill; accepting what is too much, according to one's own judgment, without murmur or remark; submitting to any appointed infliction or indulgence as to sleep, rest, warmth, exemption from what is painful, or from mortifications, merely saying what one feels able to bear, but not persisting? This is a very difficult subject to me.

Answer. You should say honestly what you can bear, but not so as to restrain those who are set over you; and after that you should be perfectly pliable. That is what I specially wish to see in you.

X. Ought I to be very yielding to the wishes of the Sisters, and of others, as soon as I know them, when I might easily set them aside, or consider them? This is rather a difficulty, it leaves one so little time to oneself. So often one longs for a few minutes alone, or of time for one's own wants, and then some Sister comes who would fain occupy that quarter of an hour, or a visitor comes, etc.

Answer. You must secure such time as is necessary for yourself, and you will be the better able to attend to the wants of your Sisters.

XI. I think I could practise more self-denial. If my dear lord approves it, let him enjoin what he sees fit, and, God helping me, I will obey.

Answer. Do so, and you " shall live." Amen.

XII. I ask you, for the love of God, help in humbling myself. I want to learn never to say anything which can tend to my own praise or glorification.

Answer. No doubt, it is a good thing to speak as little of ourselves as possible, for whether we excuse or accuse ourselves, whether we praise or blame ourselves, such words are apt to foster vanity. So that, unless charity requires us to speak of ourselves, it is better to be silent. You will find teaching concerning all this in the *Traité de l'Amour de Dieu.* May the Grace of God be with us always. Amen.

[852.] CLIX.

To a Friend. On the New Year.
(PROBABLY PRESIDENT FAVRE.)

MY DEAR BROTHER,

I close the year with giving myself the pleasure of wishing you all good for that which is coming. These mortal years pass away, dear brother; their months melt into weeks, weeks into days, days into hours, hours into moments; and after all, these moments are all that we can really call our own! Even these we only possess as they pass away, setting forth how swiftly we too are passing away; a fact which might be willingly accepted if we consider how full of sorrow this life is, and how when it is ended it will be merged in that blessed Eternity which God in His Merciful Goodness has prepared for us, and to which our hearts continually tend, not through our own natural instincts, but through His gracious drawing.

Dear brother, I never dwell upon the thought of Eternity without great delight, and this because I cannot do so without feeling that my soul would not be able to reach after so mighty a thought, were there not some true affinity between them. There must be some correspondence between the soul and that to which it tends; and when my longings fix themselves upon Eternity, my satisfaction becomes exceeding, because I know that we never long intensely save for that which God wills us to attain. Therefore my longing is a proof that I may attain that Eternal life; what more need I save to hope for it? And that hope is confirmed to me through my knowledge of the Infinite Goodness of Him Who would not have created a soul capable of meditating upon and longing after Eternity, without giving it the means whereby to attain thereto. So, dear brother, we find ourselves at the foot of the Crucifix, which is the ladder by means of which we pass over these temporal seasons to the Eternal years. Well then, I wish for your dear self that the coming year may be followed by others here, and that they may all be well spent in winning Eternity. May you live long in holiness and happiness among those who love you in this brief life: and then live for ever in that unchangeable blessedness to which we look. This is what my heart asks for you, pouring itself out with the confidence which rises from our deep affection, and makes me ever yours, etc.

Made in the USA
Lexington, KY
13 April 2014